S0-BOL-393

The President's Partner

Recent Titles in
Contributions in Women's Studies

THE PRESIDENT'S PARTNER

The First Lady in the Twentieth Century

MYRA G. GUTIN

CONTRIBUTIONS IN WOMEN'S STUDIES, NUMBER 105

GREENWOOD PRESS
New York • Westport, Connecticut • London

Library of Congress Cataloging-in-Publication Data

Gutin, Myra G.
   The president's partner : the first lady in the twentieth century
/ Myra G. Gutin.
      p. cm.—(Contributions in women's studies, ISSN 0147–104X ;
no. 105)
   Bibliography: p.
   Includes index.
   ISBN 0–313–25335–8 (lib. bdg. : alk. paper)
   1. Presidents—United States—Wives—History—20th century.
I. Title. II. Series.
E176.2.G88   1989
973.9′092′2—dc19   89–1926

British Library Cataloguing in Publication Data is available.

Copyright © 1989 by Myra G. Gutin

All rights reserved. No portion of this book may be
reproduced, by any process or technique, without the
express written consent of the publisher.

Library of Congress Catalog Card Number: 89–1926
ISBN: 0–313–25335–8
ISSN: 0147–104X

First published in 1989

Greenwood Press, Inc.
88 Post Road West, Westport, Connecticut   06881

Printed in the United States of America

The paper used in this book complies with the
Permanent Paper Standard issued by the National
Information Standards Organization (Z39.48–1984).

P

In order to keep this title in print and available to the academic community, this edition
was produced using digital reprint technology in a relatively short print run. This would
not have been attainable using traditional methods. Although the cover has been changed
from its original appearance, the text remains the same and all materials and methods
used still conform to the highest book-making standards.

This book is dedicated to four men who made me realize the extraordinary potential of women:

Vito N. Silvestri—scholar, teacher, friend, and the world's greatest cheerleader;

Howard H. Martin—scholar, teacher, friend, and motivator par excellance;

Stanley Greenberg—my father, my friend, and the one who told me to "go for it";

and especially

David Gutin—my husband, my best friend, and the man who has made me feel extraordinary.

CONTENTS

ACKNOWLEDGMENTS

I began to research the communication activities of First Ladies in 1977. Needless to say, many people aided me in my original effort and even more have helped with this book.

Mrs. Lyndon B. Johnson and Mrs. Gerald R. Ford, two of the subjects of this study, were generous with their time and provided invaluable insights into the public communication efforts of the First Lady. Liz Carpenter (former staff director and press secretary to Mrs. Lyndon B. Johnson), Edith (Kit) Dobelle (former U.S. Chief of Protocol), Mary Finch Hoyt (former East Wing Coordinator and press secretary to Mrs. Jimmy Carter), Margaret B. Klapthor (Emeritus Curator of Political History, the Smithsonian Institution), Helen Thomas (Chief White House Correspondent, United Press International), and Sheila Rabb Weidenfeld (former press secretary to Mrs. Gerald Ford) were also generous with their time, and helped me to understand the First Lady as an institution and how the press covers her activities.

One of the great "natural resources" of this country is the presidential library system. I was priviledged to visit or correspond with the research staffs of all the presidential libraries involved, and I gratefully acknowledge their assistance. A number of people went well beyond the requirements of their positions to help me, and I would like to express my thanks to Lessa Tobin (Archivist, Gerald R. Ford Library), a good friend, critic, and source of much information about presidential libraries; Dale C. Mayer (Archivist, Herbert Hoover Library); David Alsobrook (Chief Archivist, Jimmy Carter Library), and Nancy K. Smith (former Archivist, Lyndon B. Johnson Library). I would also like to acknowledge the assistance of the research staff of the Library of Congress, where I have spent more hours than I care to remember.

Dr. Lewis L. Gould, Chairman of the Department of History, University of Texas, shared his perspectives and ideas about First Ladies with me. My colleagues in the Department of Communication at Rider College, Lawrenceville, New Jersey, have been both sympathetic and encouraging. I would also like to extend my thanks to Rider College for providing grant support so that I could travel to complete my research.

I am indebted to my editor at Greenwood Press, Mildred (Mim) Vasan, who combined patience with encouragement, and understood my oft repeated refrain, "I'll send it soon."

Further plaudits must be extended to Ellen Kolodner, Kari Fisher, Jennett Medders, Dorothy Smith, and Joanne Moore. Without their aid, this volume would not have been finished.

My family and friends have been a continuing source of strength. It is not easy to deal with a working mother, but my children, Laura, Sarah, and Andrew Gutin, were understanding and made me laugh when I most needed to. Lillian and Stanley Greenberg and Rose and Henry Gutin were always helpful and willing to aid me in any way possible.

Eleven years have passed since I naively decided that it would be interesting to study a group of First Ladies; it has been a long but enriching journey, and I thank my family and friends for sharing it with me.

The President's Partner

1
INTRODUCTION

Eleanor Roosevelt enjoyed speaking to inmates at correctional institutions and sharing her experiences after her frequent trips. "One day when she was so occupied President Roosevelt had been trying to reach her and finally phoned her secretary, who informed him that Mrs. Roosevelt was in prison. 'Just where she belongs!' F.D.R. exclaimed with delight and hung up."[1]

Bess Truman is credited with calming her excitable husband. Frequently the President utilized scatalogical language, and the First Lady, fearful that reporters would write negative stories, counseled a more careful word choice. On one occasion, a well-known Democratic woman went rushing to the White House to plead with Bess to have Harry clean up his language. "It seemed that he'd called somebody's statements 'a bunch of horse manure.' Unruffled, Bess Truman is said to have smilingly replied, 'You have no idea how long it took to tone it down to that' "[2]

In 1964 Lady Bird Johnson and her entourage were returning to Washington by car following the dedication of an old-age home in Cleveland. The group stopped for dinner at a Howard Johnson's restaurant, and when they had finished their meal, reporters asked the group's waitress how it had felt to serve Mrs. Johnson.

"Well, I was pretty nervous," the waitress said. "Have you ever met a First Lady before?" The waitress looked stunned, "First Lady?" she asked, "First Lady!" "Yes," said a reporter, "That was Mrs. Lyndon B. Johnson, the First Lady of the Land." "Oh my God," said the waitress. "Thank goodness I didn't know it. I would have fainted dead away. I thought it was Mrs. Howard Johnson—that was bad enough!"[3]

These three anecdotes comprise just a fraction of the lore of First Ladies. Most people have a favorite First Lady or respect one more than another.

However, few people and relatively few scholars have looked beyond the glitter and pomp of the White House to critically analyze the office of First Lady.

The term First Lady is relatively new. *The Dictionary of American History* notes that it was first applied to Lucy Webb Hayes upon her husband's inauguration in 1877, but it did not come into general use until 1911. At that time, Charles F. Nirdlinger's play about Dolly Madison, *The First Lady of the Land,* was produced, and the new designation for the president's wife was popularized.[4]

The First Lady occupies a unique position. She is not an elected official, she draws no salary, and there is no written description of her duties. Indeed, she has no status in official Washington. *The Congressional Directory* (first published in 1834), a guide listing the names of all of the people working in official Washington, did not mention the First Lady until the edition of March 1965.[5] The first acknowledgment of a member of the First Lady's staff actually preceded that of the First Lady by twelve years, when Mary Jane McCaffree was listed as Acting Secretary to the Wife of the President in 1953.[6] Today the First Lady finds herself performing the functions of White House hostess, occasional presidential surrogate, campaigner, and advocate for certain positions or causes. She is often viewed as a visible symbol of her husband's administration. There is nothing a First Lady must do, but much she is expected to accomplish.

Those who study First Ladies realize that there is a major problem inherent within the topic. There is no standard methodology for studying these women. In the past (and even currently), books about First Ladies were either "kiss-and-tell" treatises or general biographical studies. More ambitious writers attempted to examine the lives of all the First Ladies chronologically. As Lewis L. Gould has observed, to study all the First Ladies is to study all of American history.[7] The resulting works were often too lacking in detail or perspective to be of much use. Moreover, change has not occurred chronologically in the First Lady's role. In an article entitled "First Ladies," Gould suggests a new approach and looks at presidential wives as political celebrities.[8]

It is the contention of this book that communication may offer the best vantage point from which to scrutinize the First Lady of the United States. By analyzing the communication activities of the President's wife—the speeches, radio and television broadcasts, interviews, press conferences, and magazine and newspaper articles written by the First Lady—one is able to best understand and appreciate the changes that have taken place over sixty years. There is no dearth of material about the First Lady, but none of it evaluates the First Ladies' perceptions of their responsibilities as communicators or the impact of their actions.

A systematic evaluation of the twelve First Ladies since suffrage shows that these presidential wives have assumed one of three distinct stances as public communicators. Florence Harding, Grace Coolidge, Bess Truman, and Mamie Eisenhower perceived their role in strictly ceremonial terms. These social hostesses and ceremonial presences had extremely limited contact with the public, and devoted little if any thought to communicating their ideas to the country.

The emerging spokeswomen, Lou Hoover, Jacqueline Kennedy, and Pat Nixon, engaged in more extensive communication activities, and used these activities and the press to discuss their respective projects. They seemed to be more aware of the need to share their ideas and projects with a national audience.

The political surrogates and independent advocates, Eleanor Roosevelt, Lady Bird Johnson, Betty Ford, and Rosalynn Carter, used all the available communication outlets to support projects or positions forcefully. Not only were these women cognizant of the power of the White House, but they actively and frequently exploited this podium. During her eight-year tenure as First Lady, Nancy Reagan's role evolved from one of ceremonial presence to that of political surrogate and independent advocate.

This study commences in 1920, a turning point for women in American public life. The passage of the Nineteenth Amendment granting women the vote, sweeping changes in social behavior, the birth of radio, and the expansion of other communications media invest this year with great significance.

On August 26, 1920, the states ratified suffrage, and millions of female voters were finally enfranchised. Suffragists were satisfied with their victory and confident that the female vote would function as a great equalizer. Unfortunately, these goals were not immediately achieved; "only about one-fourth of the eligible women cast ballots in the Harding-Cox" race.[9] A number of factors had militated against women's participation in the presidential election. A Harding victory was almost a foregone conclusion; the suffrage amendment was not ratified until late in August 1920, just over two months before the general election; and "women saw little relationship between their votes and the conduct of public policy . . . and felt no urgency to go to the polls."[10] Suffragists' hopes for a more responsible electorate and ultimately responsive government were crushed by the lack of female voter participation.

The 1920s were a decade of profound changes in social behavior, and were labeled the age of flaming youth. The flapper, the young woman "with her short, straight skirt, her lean torso and her cropped hair, the rouge on her cheeks and the cigarette in her mouth, . . . was the epitome of youth, adventure and healthy sex."[11] The young people of the 1920s were indifferent to the concerns and achievements of their elders, especially gains in women's rights.

The 1920s were also an age of tremendous growth in communication. By the end of World War I, radio, which had been used by the Navy for wartime operations, was ready for commercial use. On November 2, 1920, KDKA made its maiden broadcast from the roof of the Westinghouse factory in Pittsburgh. So great was radio's influence and growth that by the end of the decade one of every three American homes had a radio, and the new device had changed the way most Americans got their news.[12]

There were changes in newspapers and magazines. The number of daily newspapers dropped from 2,500 to 2,001 during the period of 1914 through 1926.[13] *Reader's Digest*, the first of the "pre-digested reading" group of magazines, was founded in 1921.[14] On March 3, 1923, *Time*, the "Weekly News Magazine" came into existence. This new publication presented hard news in an anecdotal form, a style that would be emulated by other magazines in the future.[15] The increasing popularity of the news media in the 1920s created a greater mass audience which was immediately available to public figures.

The extension of the franchise to women meant that they might have a role in politics and public life. The President's wife especially might now see herself able to assume a more significant role. She might embrace a cause or project or campaign for her husband or others of his party, or she might make her own opinions and commitments known by speaking out or meeting with the press. The First Lady's options were clearly expanded by the Nineteenth Amendment.

Prior to 1920 all First Ladies were principally hostesses, dispensing the hospitality of the White House to visitors. Sarah Polk, Helen Taft, and Edith Wilson were exceptions to this stereotype, giving advice and counsel to their husbands, but they were a distinct minority. Although the sweeping social changes of the 1920s did not immediately or profoundly affect the First Lady, the new freedom allowed breaks with tradition and permitted the First Lady a degree of flexibility in her role.

The country wanted to learn about the First Lady, and the new and expanded media made this possible. The First Lady became the topic of frequent articles in newspapers and magazines. Lou Hoover became the first First Lady to speak to audiences independently of her husband and to speak over the radio about matters of concern to her. Eleanor Roosevelt expanded the First Lady's media use, employing radio, press conferences, and a daily newspaper column to air her special concerns. Subsequent First Ladies did not always choose to share their ideas with the American public, but as stated earlier, they always had the opportunity and the means to do so if they desired.

The sixty-nine years between 1920 and 1989 saw the First Ladies assume communication stances as social hostesses and ceremonial presences, emerging spokeswomen, or political surrogates and independent advocates. The period covered by this study juxtaposes the public and private personae of twelve women on a historical period of great change and innovation. Ultimately, the First Lady's role as public communicator changed as well.

NOTES

1. Frances Spatz Leighton, *They Call Her Lady Bird* (New York: MacFadden-Bartell, 1964), p. 238.

2. J. B. West, *Upstairs at the White House* (New York: Warner, 1974), p. 72.

3. Liz Carpenter, *Ruffles and Flourishes* (New York: Pocket, 1971), p. 171.

4. Stanley R. Pillsbury, "The First Lady of the Land," in *Dictionary of American History Volume III*, eds. Harold W. Chase, Thomas C. Cochran, Jacob E. Cooke, Robert W. Daly, Wendell Garrett, and Robert P. Multhauf (New York: Scribner, 1976), p. 26.

5. *The Congressional Directory* (1965) (Washington, D.C.: United States Government Printing Office, 1965), p. 635.

6. *The Congressional Directory*, (1953), p. 352.

7. Conversation with Dr. Lewis L. Gould, Austin, Texas, August 1987.

8. Lewis L. Gould, "First Ladies," *The American Scholar,* 55 (Autumn, 1986), pp. 528–535.

9. Martin Gruberg, *Women in American Politics* (Oshkosh, Wis.: Academia, 1968), p. 9.

10. William H. Chafe, *The American Woman: Her Changing Social, Economic and Political Roles 1920–1970* (New York: Oxford, 1968), p. 32.

11. Lois W. Banner, *Women in Modern American History* (New York: Harcourt, 1974), p. 146.

12. Frederick Lewis Allen, *Only Yesterday: An Informal History of the 1920s* (New York: Harper, 1957), p. 166.

13. Allen, *Only Yesterday,* p. 188.

14. Richard N. Current, T. Harry Williams, and Frank Friedel, *American History: A Survey* 2d ed. (New York: Knopf, 1966), p. 730.

15. Robert T. Elson, *Time Inc.: The Intimate History of a Publishing Enterprise 1923–1941* (New York: Atheneum, 1968).

2
THE WHITE HOUSEKEEPERS:
SOCIAL HOSTESSES AND
CEREMONIAL PRESENCES

Florence Harding
Grace Coolidge
Bess Truman
Mamie Eisenhower

Is it accurate or fair to say that a First Lady is ever inactive as a public communicator? Any woman who occupies the White House is busy; even those who crave privacy have some responsibilities that simply cannot be ignored. The First Lady, whether in 1920 or 1988, was and is expected at the very least to be a visible presence and a gracious hostess.

Florence Harding, Grace Coolidge, Bess Truman, and Mamie Eisenhower were inactive public communicators. They gave no speeches, advocated no causes, and campaigned for no candidates. Their press relations, though generally cordial, were not productive. This group of women made no attempt to impress their respective views or images on the public consciousness.

Despite the enormous potential of the First Lady's position, these women either sought to be or were cast into the role of inactive communicators. Florence Harding enjoyed the ceremonial trappings that accompanied the First Lady's job, but she was not interested in addressing the public. Mrs. Harding attempted to focus her efforts on influencing her husband's decisions. Grace Coolidge might have been more active and engaged in more communication activities but was prevented from doing so by Calvin Coolidge. Bess Truman lived her life as she wanted, avoiding all but the most important public duties with the concurrence of her husband. Mamie Eisenhower was often physically unwell and, like Bess Truman, avoided all but the most significant events.

Florence Harding, Grace Coolidge, Bess Truman, and Mamie Eisenhower were figureheads who viewed their roles and responsibilities as strictly ceremonial in scope. All performed the expected First Lady role of entertaining, but did very little else.

FLORENCE KLING HARDING

Probably more misconceptions and myths exist about Warren and Florence Harding than about any other presidential couple. Most notable among these are the myths that Harding ran for President because Florence Harding wanted to be First Lady, that Harding took his political orders from his wife and Harry Daugherty, that the twenty-ninth President was lazy and unintelligent, and that the First Lady poisoned the President to save him from the embarrassment and humiliation of the coming Teapot Dome scandal.

In recent years historians have found that these time-honored myths simply are not true. Though he gave the appearance of reluctance, Warren Harding ran for the presidency because he wanted to. He was a capable and opportunistic politician who trusted his own judgment, and later died a natural if unexpected death.

Mrs. Harding is still an enigma, but her role as First Lady has been better delineated. Contrary to popular belief, she was not enthusiastic about her husband's presidential bid, she was not her husband's major political advisor, and she was not a murderess.

Florence Kling DeWolfe Harding was an ambitious, shrewd, and resourceful woman who made herself part of the Harding administration with or without her husband's consent.

Route to the White House

On August 15, 1860, a daughter, Florence Mabel, was born to Amos and Louisa Bouton Kling of Marion, Ohio.[1] Young Florence was sent to the best school in Marion, and when she demonstrated a flair for the piano, was sent to study at the Cincinnati Conservatory of Music. When her mother died she returned home to live with her father and give piano lessons.

When she was nineteen, Florence eloped against her father's wishes with Henry "Pete" DeWolfe, the idle and hard-drinking son of a wealthy and aristocratic Ohio family. DeWolfe married Florence because "he had to"; six months later, Eugene Marshall DeWolfe was born.[2] The responsibilities of fatherhood did little to steady the ne'er-do-well Pete, however, and he often would vanish for days or weeks at a time. Florence sought and was successful in obtaining a divorce from DeWolfe a few years later.

In 1890 Florence met Warren G. Harding, the handsome, affable young publisher of the *Marion Star*. At that time Florence was thirty, a divorcée with a child, and she was determined to marry Harding. There is little doubt that she was the aggressor in their courtship, but Harding had more to gain from their union than she. Florence was heir to a considerable fortune and possessed a social position to which Harding aspired. The couple was married a year later. A biographer writes of Harding, "He never loved her. . . . In time he would achieve a qualified affection for her."[3]

Shortly after their marriage Harding became ill and required a long rest. Florence decided to help run the *Star* in her husband's absence. " 'I went down there,' she told an interviewer, 'intending to help out for a few days and remained for fourteen years.' "[4]

While she did have a good understanding of business, Mrs. Harding's contributions to the paper were somewhat less seminal than previously thought. She did not edit or dictate its policy: Her contribution was to manage circulation and develop the home-delivery system.[5] At the conclusion of her tenure, the *Star* had grown from a weekly newspaper to a daily.

Warren Harding had started working for the Republican Party before he was old enough to vote, and had always maintained an interest in politics. Now that the *Star* was becoming more influential, he found himself in an ideal position to launch a political career. Tall and distinguished, he looked the part of a politician. An above-average to good speaker, he progressed to spokesman for local Republican functions. Florence encouraged Harding, feeling that these appearances enhanced their standing and prestige in the community.

Harding was elected to the State Senate in 1899 and was elected Lieutenant Governor of Ohio in 1904. After losing a bid for the gubernatorial nomination, Harding returned to Marion. With the help and advice of Harry Daugherty, a local businessman, Harding ran a successful campaign for U.S. Senator in 1914.

Harding was popular with both parties, and played poker regularly with colleagues from the Senate and from his own state. Mrs. Harding accompanied him to many of these informal parties. She mixed drinks for the men or chatted with other wives while keeping an eye on her "Wurr'n." Her husband enjoyed Washington far more than did Florence. She was uncomfortable with Washington society, sensing "that she was unequal to mingling in this urbane, uncertain world."[6]

Harding was chosen to deliver the keynote speech at the 1916 Republican National Convention. Daugherty records that he made a positive impression on the delegates and was mentioned as a potential presidential candidate in 1920.[7]

Initially Harding was reluctant to be considered as a possible candidate because he enjoyed serving in the Senate,[8] and he doubted his ability to lead.[9] Mrs. Harding also opposed her husband running for President because she feared for his health. Despite a robust appearance, he was not a well man.[10] Moreover, Mrs. Harding had been frightened by the predictions of a Washington clairvoyant, Madam Marcia, who told her that if Harding was elected president, he would not live out his term.[11]

Despite both Hardings's misgivings, Warren Harding accepted the Republican nomination for President. While she was pleased with her husband's achievement, Mrs. Harding's enthusiasm was somewhat subdued, and she told a reporter just after her husband's nomination, "I cannot see why anyone should want to be President. . . . I can see but one word written over the head of my husband if he is elected, and that word is tragedy."[12]

Much of Harding's campaign was conducted on the front porch of his home in Marion. Mrs. Harding had pictures circulated of herself and Harding on the porch. "I want the people to see these pictures so that they will know we are just plain folks like themselves," she said.[13]

Mrs. Harding proved to be a valuable campaign asset. Well liked by the press and the voters (especially women's groups), she welcomed delegations to Marion and later accompanied her husband on campaign speaking tours. Impeccably groomed and modest, she told the press; "you really shouldn't ask me to talk politics. My husband will do that."[14]

On at least one occasion, Mrs. Harding served as campaign strategist. Rumors concerning Harding's possible black ancestry were circulating, and his advisors planned to issue a denial of this charge. Mrs. Harding vetoed the idea of any statement on the topic. "No formal or official denial of the Negro allegation was ever to be made by Warren Harding," she declared.[15] The rumor caused the Harding campaign little concern after that.

Voter turnout was light in 1920, but a majority of Americans harkened to Harding's call for a return to normalcy. He received 60.3 percent of the popular vote, 16,133,314 votes to Cox's 9,140,884.[16]

It was said that the Hardings represented Main Street come to Washington. They brought a gay new social life to the capital; the President and First Lady appeared frequently at public events. The first year of the Harding administration seemed to pass peacefully.

During the second year of his tenure, the increasing strain and burdens of the presidency caused Harding to feel depressed and isolated. He and Florence quarreled frequently. Plagued by self-doubt, the President played golf and cards with his cronies, and occasionally left the White House to satisfy his prurient interests.

In September 1922, Florence Harding fell seriously ill with a kidney infection. The couple's relationship had deteriorated considerably, but Harding sat by his wife's bedside until she was declared out of danger. Florence's illness may have caused the President to confront his own mortality, because from that point he became more serious about his politics and his legacy as President.[17]

Originally, Harding had planned to visit Alaska in 1923 for a vacation. Now he saw his proposed trip as an attempt to win acceptance for U.S. membership in the World Court. He planned to make a series of speeches as he traveled west to Alaska.

Just as the President and First Lady were preparing to leave Washington, there arose subtle suggestions of scandal within the Harding administration. From the vantage point of the years, it seems almost impossible to believe that Warren Harding did not have any prior knowledge of the Teapot Dome scandal. Nonetheless, the evidence indicates that he knew nothing until it was almost too late for him to deal with the culprits in his administration.

During the trip to Alaska, Harding was frantic and preoccupied with the treachery of those he had trusted. On the way home he became ill with bronchial pneumonia. After a few days he seemed to rally, but he died suddenly on August 3, 1923.

Mrs. Harding refused to permit an autopsy. Rumors suggested that the First Lady had poisoned the President to spare him the embarrassment of the coming scandals.[18] The Presidents' doctors attributed death to a cerebral hemorrhage.

Shortly after the funeral in Marion, Mrs. Harding returned to the White House. With the aid of staff members, she began burning correspondence and files. When she finished her task a few weeks later, six to eight ten-foot-long boxes crammed with Harding's papers had been reduced to two.[19]

Florence Harding only survived her husband by fifteen months, and died of her old kidney ailment on November 21, 1924, at the age of sixty-four.

Major Communication Activities of the First Lady

Florence Harding made no attempt to communicate her ideas to the American public. She gave no speeches and made no statements on any substantive topic. Her activities were entirely ceremonial in nature, yet she had strong feelings about the symbolic importance of her role. Though often ill, Mrs. Harding was tireless in her contact with the American people, and became famous for being willing to receive anyone who took the time to visit her.[20]

Ceremonial Presence. Mrs. Harding participated in approximately 120 White House events from March 1921 through August 1923.[21] She traveled with the President whenever possible. She visited injured and ill soldiers and sailors at Walter Reed Hospital, and reinstated White House teas, garden parties, the Christmas reception, the annual Easter egg roll on the White House lawn, and the traditional New Year's Day reception. She also opened the White House to public tours. Until this time, a visitor could only tour the executive mansion after having secured an invitation through his Congressman.

The American public was afforded glimpses of its First Lady through her pro forma ceremonial activities. The public seemed to like this down-to-earth First Lady; Washington society, which found her to be too common, did not.

Press Relations. It seems possible that her work on the *Marion Star* made Mrs. Harding sensitive to reportorial needs. She was friendly to reporters and tried to be helpful. Shortly after her husband received the Republican nomination for President, the *New York Times* wrote, "Mrs. Harding was the only candidate's wife who came more than half way to meet newspaper reporters."[22] Mrs. Harding told the *New York Times* that she liked the Washington newspaper-women and gave them tips on upcoming stories whenever she could. She liked the newspaper fraternity because she felt they had never betrayed her.[23] She did not address any substantive issues, but she was well liked by reporters and always enjoyed a complimentary press.

Factors That Influenced the First Lady's Performance as Public Communicator

Relationship with Her Husband. The relationship between the Hardings could hardly be described as loving. Theirs was a stormy marriage, marked by frequent quarrels and unpleasantness. Florence Harding could be unbearable, nagging and scolding her husband. Unhappy and feeling the pressures and burdens of the presidency, Harding lapsed into moodiness and depression. Speaking of his wife to his mistress Nan Britton, he said, "She makes life hell for me."[24] Years after Harding's death, Charles Forbes recalled that on one occasion Harding had told him how unhappy he was and how empty his life had been. Then Forbes had gone with the President to the rear lawn of the White House and Harding had cried.[25]

For many years Harding had sought female solace outside his marriage. His affairs were legion, and one of his love trysts was purported to have produced a child.[26]

After Mrs. Harding's serious illness, her relationship with her husband seemed to improve. They were especially close just prior to Warren Harding's death.

Access to Presidential Decision Making. President Harding once remarked, "Mrs. Harding wants to be the drum major in every band that passes."[27] It is possible that the President was commenting on Mrs. Harding's desire to be a part of his administration.

Mrs Harding did, in fact, have input into presidential decisions. It is not known whether Warren Harding actively solicited his wife's views on various issues, but she gave her opinions regardless. There was never any outward indication that this wifely interference troubled Harding.[28]

When the President finished preparing his first message to Congress, Mrs. Harding reviewed the text of his address. She found a paragraph that committed the United States to membership in the League of Nations by vague inference.[29] As a Senator and presidential candidate, Harding had opposed the league. Mrs. Harding may have feared that the President would be seen as untrustworthy and unreliable if he delivered his speech as written. With the help of Harry Daughtery, the First Lady convinced the President to excise the objectionable paragraph.

In December 1921, the President allowed Mrs. Harding to choose which convicts would be given pardons.[30] For unexplained personal and political reasons, the First Lady vigorously opposed her husband's proposed pardon of Eugene V. Debs, who was serving a ten-year sentence for wartime pacifist activities. Mrs. Harding tried to persuade the President to reevaluate his position, but Harding stood his ground and had Debs released on December 24, 1921.[31]

On another occasion Harding prepared a congressional message urging a constitutional amendment that would limit the President to one six-year term of office. Mrs. Harding was furious, and argued that this was the equivalent of Harding refusing a second term. The President said he would withdraw his recommendation, but later told his secretary that he still planned to propose the six-year term before the conclusion of his own term of office.[32]

The First Lady influenced at least one decision that the President came to regret. She advocated the appointment of Charles Forbes as head of the Veteran's Bureau. Years later, Forbes was convicted of bribery and conspiracy.

Florence Harding was not above using her influence to spite people who had annoyed her in some way. Vindictive and prone to temper tantrums, she once told Alice Longworth "that she had a little red book which contained the names of people who had not been civil to her and Warren Harding since they came to Washington. These people were to realize that she was aware of their behavior."[33]

She disliked Vice President Calvin Coolidge and his pretty, socially accepted wife Grace. When a bill was introduced in Congress to buy and maintain a stately home as a residence for the Vice President, Mrs. Harding responded angrily; "I am going to have that bill defeated. Do you think I am going to have those Coolidges living in a house like that? A hotel apartment is plenty good for them!"[34] With or without the First Lady's intervention, the bill was defeated.[35]

Mrs. Harding appears to have been involved in the workings of the Harding administration. The First Lady maintained contact with administration officials, and frequently made suggestions that were implemented by government departments. The First Lady "frankly made it her business to know about major governmental developments."[36]

The President's and First Lady's Perceptions of Women. As a Senator, Harding was "utterly indifferent" to suffrage, but supported the measure because the people of Ohio and Senate Republicans endorsed it.[37]

As a presidential candidate, Harding invited women leaders to his home and "called for equal pay for women, an eight hour day, passage of maternity and infancy legislation, and creation of a federal department of social welfare."[38]

Warren Harding appointed eight women to high-level positions, and a total of fourteen women served in his administration.[39] Florence Harding was probably the only woman who had any direct influence on her husband's decision making.

Some writers feel that Florence Harding was as great a failure as First Lady as her husband was as President. One historian comments, "No more fitted to her position than her husband to his, she overdid it; she tried too hard to be a great lady."[40]

Mrs. Harding made no effort to be a public communicator beyond her ceremonial contacts. One might expect that with her background in newspapers and understanding of public curiosity she might have expanded the First Lady's role. Mrs. Harding was not interested in enlarging the First Lady's public role, but she did influence presidential decision making and thus increased the scope of the First Lady's private role. To this end, Florence Harding was successful as First Lady, influential in private and well liked by the public.

GRACE ANNA GOODHUE COOLIDGE

Grace Coolidge was a vibrant, lively woman who might have accelerated the transition of the First Lady from party giver to activist had she been afforded the opportunity. That was not the case, however, as Calvin Coolidge effectively silenced his wife by forbidding her to communicate with the public.

Route to the White House

Grace Anna Goodhue, the only child of Lemira and Andrew Issachar Goodhue, was born in Burlington, Vermont, on January 3, 1879.[41] Grace had a happy, uneventful childhood. In an action unusual for the late nineteenth century, she enrolled at the University of Vermont (thus becoming the first First Lady in the twentieth century to have a college education), where she evidenced greater interest in extracurricular activities than in academic pursuits. She was graduated from the university in 1902.

Over her mother's objections, the independent Grace went to Northhampton, Massachusetts, to become an apprentice teacher at the Clarke School for the Deaf. She learned sign language and lip reading, and taught both subjects to her students.

In Northampton, Grace was introduced to a young lawyer, Calvin Coolidge. Also a Vermonter by birth, Coolidge had come to Northampton following graduation from Amherst College in 1895. He had "read law" with a local law firm and had been admitted to the Massachusetts bar. When he met Grace, he had his own office on Main Street.

The romance between the taciturn Coolidge and the fun-loving Miss Goodhue progressed slowly. She was a pretty young woman who enjoyed all activities, especially skating, dancing and hiking. To please her, Coolidge tried skating and dancing with little success.

Her friends could not understand Grace's attraction to the tight-lipped lawyer. She genuinely liked people; indeed, one biographer writes, "Everyone who knew Grace Goodhue liked her immensely; those who knew Calvin Coolidge never knew quite what to make of him."[42] Coolidge had little to say, and looked out of place and uncomfortable everywhere. Still, the couple seemed to get along well.

Late in the summer of 1905, the dour, outwardly unsentimental Coolidge proposed to Grace in his own unique way. He said to her, "I am going to be married to you."[43] They were married on October 4, 1905.

The Coolidges returned to Northampton, and thus began Calvin Coolidge's steady if not spectacular rise in Massachusetts politics. After an initial setback he was elected a member of city council, city solicitor, and then mayor of Northampton. In 1907 he was elected to the Massachusetts House of Representatives, and in 1912 to the Massachusetts Senate.

While Calvin was establishing himself in politics, Grace stayed home and raised their two sons, John born in 1906, and Calvin, Jr., born in 1908. She was a companion to them, playing baseball and other children's games. Additionally, she was active in her church and knitted stockings for the Red Cross.

Encouraged by wealthy businessmen, Coolidge ran for and was elected to the positions of Lieutenant Governor in 1918 and Governor of Massachusetts in 1919. At Coolidge's inaugural ball, a friend commented that one of Coolidge's greatest assets was Mrs. Coolidge, saying, "She will make friends wherever she goes and she will not meddle with his conduct of the office."[44]

In 1919, Coolidge achieved national prominence when as Governor he intervened in the Boston police strike. His popularity helped him to win the Republican nomination for Vice President.

When Grace Coolidge went to Washington in 1921, she was said to have emerged as a great lady. A Coolidge biographer writes, "For the first time in her life, Grace Coolidge bloomed into all the beauty that her qualities of heart and mind had promised at Burlington, at Northampton and at Boston."[45]

The Vice President and his wife were important social as well as political figures, much sought after by hostesses. Grace was a great success in Washington. Her good humor, enthusiasm, and tact brought the Coolidges popularity and social acceptance.

The Coolidges were invited out often, and Washington society discovered the less than loquacious Mr. Coolidge. Many an unfortunate dinner partner suffered through silent meals as the Vice President remained mute. Often Grace functioned as a buffer, explaining her husband's silence or occasional acerbic comments to a hurt guest or friend. Coolidge appreciated his wife's efforts and realized how much she helped him. In a letter to his father he wrote; "She [Grace] is wonderfully popular here. I don't know what I would do without her."[46]

In the early morning hours of August 3, 1923, Calvin Coolidge was awakened by his father with the news of President Warren Harding's death. A few minutes later, Colonel John Coolidge, a notary public and justice of the peace, swore in his son as the thirtieth President of the United States.

The country was rocked by disclosures of corruption in the Harding administration. Coolidge felt it imperative that respect in government be restored. He did this by initiating investigations into the scandals but carefully separating himself from the resulting litigation. Moreover, he tried to inspire faith by being an especially dignified President. He insisted that the new First Lady also embrace this grave decorum and "carefully restricted her personal life, forbidding her from driving . . . or being flown. She was commanded to express no political views."[47] Mrs. Coolidge was also forbidden to dance in public.[48] Perhaps of greatest importance was President Coolidge's edict that the First Lady not be interviewed or quoted.[49]

One can only conjecture what Mrs. Coolidge thought about the restrictions that were placed on her activities. She expressed no anger or resentment in public, but she felt the edict "not to try anything new" (her husband's advice to her in the White House) had the "semblance of a death notice."[50] On another occasion, Mrs. Coolidge wrote to a friend, "I must not forget that I am to be guided by circumstances beyond my control."[51] Slowly, Coolidge's goal was realized and the country regained its faith in government, but the President never relaxed the strict regulations that he had imposed on his wife's behavior.

The greatest tragedy in the Coolidges' lives occurred on July 7, 1924, when young Calvin, aged sixteen, died from an infection incurred while playing tennis on the White House lawn. Calvin Coolidge was grief-stricken by his son's death, and wrote later in his autobiography, "When he went, the power and the glory of the presidency went with him."[52] Grace drew inward and spent more time alone. Friends found her to be grave and reserved.

Calvin Coolidge was elected to his own term as President in 1924, and enjoyed a great deal of success in both foreign and domestic affairs. The country was enjoying "Coolidge Prosperity"—a time of plenty—when the President released his now famous twelve-word message on August 2, 1927: "I do not choose to run for President in nineteen twenty-eight."[53]

No one had received any indication that Coolidge was considering an end to his public service, least of all his wife. When she was informed of her husband's deed, she exclaimed; "Isn't that just like the man! He never gave me the slightest intimation of his intention! I had no idea!"[54]

The reason for Coolidge's decision not to run is still a mystery. Health cannot be overlooked as a major possibility. The Washington humidity aggravated Mrs. Coolidge's sinusitus, and "she found the task of White House hostess increasingly wearing."[55] Coolidge feared that four more years in the White House would kill her. The Coolidges were still mourning the loss of Calvin, Jr., and this too probably blunted the President's enthusiasm for another term. There is also evidence to suggest that Coolidge knew that a depression was imminent and did not want to have to deal with it.[56]

The Coolidges returned to Northampton. Calvin Coolidge died of a coronary thrombosis on January 5, 1933. Grace Coolidge continued an active private life in public silence. She died in Northampton on July 8, 1957.

Major Communication Activities of the First Lady

Grace Coolidge's communication activities were entirely ceremonial in scope. She gave no formal speeches, campaigned for no candidates, and advocated no causes. She made brief remarks on a few ceremonial occasions, but there is no record of what she said and no information as to the authorship of her remarks.

The radio networks, still in their infancy and seeking legitimacy as channels of communication, had hoped to transmit Mrs. Coolidge speaking before she left the White House. There were numerous opportunities for broadcasts, however, the First Lady, probably at the insistence of President Coolidge, never did speak over the radio.

Advocacy. Almost forty years before Lady Bird Johnson initiated efforts to beautify Washington, Grace Coolidge expressed concern for the capitol city. She was very interested in the passage of the Public Buildings Act (approved in 1926) which appropriated $165,000,000 for the construction of certain badly needed federal buildings. There is no evidence to suggest that the First Lady publicly advocated this measure, and she certainly took no action to demonstrate a commitment to the legislation, but she did keep abreast of developments by speaking frequently with Charles Moore, Chairman of the National Commission of Fine Arts.[57]

The First Lady was also concerned that the White House did not contain any furniture that had been there when it was built. She helped initiate a program to obtain original pieces.[58]

Ceremonial Presence. In the 1920s official Washington society wielded enormous influence. Since the time of Andrew Jackson, visiting or "carding" had been one of the customs dictated by protocol.[59] Wives of men in official life were expected to "call on" or visit and leave their calling cards with other people active in public affairs. As the wife of the most important man in Washington, Mrs. Coolidge spent a great deal of time receiving visitors (she was not required to call on others) and entertaining at afternoon teas and dinners.

In addition to receiving, the President and First Lady were required by protocol to preside over "the season," a procession of official dinners and receptions beginning after Thanksgiving and concluding just before Lent. Among the events that comprised the social season of 1923–1924 were the Cabinet Dinner, the Diplomatic Reception, the Diplomatic Dinner, the New Year's Reception, the Judicial Reception, the Supreme Court Dinner, the Congressional Reception, the Dinner for the Speaker of the House, and the Army and Navy Reception.[60]

The press reported administration social events in minute detail. Prior to the Coolidges' first official function as President and First Lady (the Cabinet Dinner in December 1923), reporters speculated on the probable floral arrangements, menu, and clothing to be worn by those attending the event.

Mrs. Coolidge is mentioned in press accounts of the event, but little more is said about her other than the fact that her major contribution was directing the floral arrangements. There are also descriptions of the First Lady's dress. The *Washington Star* commented on Mrs. Coolidge as hostess: "Mrs. Coolidge with her gentle, retiring way, her artistic instinct and simple American hospitality, is giving a pleasing impression of herself."[61]

From August 1923 through March 1929, Mrs. Coolidge was a participant in approximately ninety-one ceremonial activities.[62] She was assisted in her duties by two secretaries who arranged the First Lady's schedule, planned social events, and answered mail.

Years later, Mrs. Coolidge revealed her feelings about White House entertaining and other duties when she wrote; "When I reflect upon my Washington career, I wonder how I ever faced it. I had been brought up very simply in a modest home where the amenities of social life were confined within narrow limits."[63]

Press Relations. Mrs. Coolidge had no press secretary, but social secretary Mary Randolph frequently responded to press inquiries. Randolph had to remind reporters that the First Lady could not be interviewed or quoted.

Despite these restrictions, Mrs. Coolidge enjoyed excellent relations with the press. She was almost invariably described in glowing terms. All the stories written about her were speculative in nature as they were written from afar. The President's no-interview, no-quote edict had one definite consequence: from August 1923 through 1929, only eight stories about the First Lady appeared in general circulation magazines.[64] The American public had little chance to become acquainted with its lively First Lady.

Factors That Influenced the First Lady's Performance as Public Communicator

Relationship with Her Husband. In his autobiography, Calvin Coolidge wrote of his wife; "We thought we were made for each other. For almost a quarter of a century she has borne with my infirmities and I have rejoiced in her graces."[65]

Calvin Coolidge loved his wife deeply and was loyal and devoted to her, but he expected a great deal in return. He felt that a woman's place was in the home and her natural concerns should be her husband and children. He felt no need to discuss his business affairs or political aspirations with his spouse. He expected her to subjugate her desires to his demands, which she did.

By Grace's own admission, Coolidge had little respect for her intellect, and less for her education. Years later Mrs. Coolidge observed; "Sometimes I wonder if Mr. Coolidge would have talked with me more freely if I had been of a more serious turn of mind. We seldom discussed current events, government, philosophy or religion."[66]

Access to Presidential Decision Making. A number of publications praised Grace Coolidge for accepting the role of wife and mother. One, analyzing Mrs. Coolidge's success, suggested that she had been successful as First Lady because she had not been a political wife. It concluded, "Certainly Grace never knew when a bill was to be signed or a candidacy approved."[67] A more accurate observation would be difficult to make. Grace Coolidge had absolutely no access to presidential decision making.

Mrs. Coolidge realized that she did not have the power to persuade the President to adopt a particular course of action, and she sensed that her husband would not be pleased if she offered her opinion on a political matter. She commented, "If I had manifested any particular interest in a political matter, I feel sure I should have been properly put in my place."[68]

The First Lady did not even have the right to determine her own schedule; the President dictated what she would do. He would make appointments for the two of them, and never tell his wife. Mrs. Coolidge finally told the President that she was going to have his secretary prepare a list of their engagements. Coolidge replied, "We don't give out that information promiscuously."[69]

If Mrs. Coolidge was frustrated by being excluded from her husband's political decision making, her ire and frustration were not apparent and she never spoke of it to friends. Years later she was able to write of her husband's decision not to run for reelection in 1928, "I am rather proud of the fact that after nearly a quarter of a century of marriage, my husband feels free to make his decisions and act upon them without consulting me or giving me advance information concerning them."[70] It is questionable whether Mrs. Coolidge had any interest in the issues of the day. That she could not have influenced them is certain.

The President's and First Lady's Perceptions of Women. Calvin Coolidge had sup-ported suffrage "because his district felt that way," but there is reason to believe that he would have opposed the measure personally.[71] Coolidge saw his wife and most women as wives and mothers; they played a very limited role in his world.

In the White House, Coolidge did nothing to advance the cause of women. He appointed only five women to high-level positions, twelve female appointees from previous administrations also worked in the upper echelons of power during the Coolidge years.[72] Grace Coolidge was an intelligent woman, but one doubts that she had the inclination or influence to educate her husband about women.

Grace Coolidge was denied the chance to be a more active, involved First Lady. Calvin Coolidge refused her access to the channels of communication that would have ultimately brought her to the public's attention. There were no speeches, no press conferences or interviews, and only limited contact with the public in ceremonial situations. The vivacity, charm, and good humor that might have made Mrs. Coolidge an effective public communicator and political asset were never realized.

ELIZABETH WALLACE TRUMAN

Following her husband's nomination as Franklin D. Roosevelt's vice presi-dential running mate in 1944, Bess Truman found herself being mauled by crowds of enthusiastic well-wishers. She turned to Harry Truman and asked, "Are we going to have to go through this all the rest of our lives?"[73] Harry Truman did not respond. He knew well the rigors of political life and understood the press and public's sudden interest in his wife.

Bess Truman was fifty-nine years old when her husband was nominated for Vice President. A plump, matronly, Midwestern housewife, she had lived a quiet life as the wife of a local politician, and later, of the junior Senator from Missouri. Now she found herself to be a news item. She disliked the attention and the glare of publicity, and would continue to feel distaste for it after she and Harry S Truman entered the White House nine months later.

Bess Truman was not happy about becoming First Lady, but resigned herself to her role and its demands. Unlike her predecessor Eleanor Roosevelt, she felt no desire to carve out her own career. She did not perceive herself as a public communicator; her views on issues were private. She felt strongly that the American people should hear unimpeded the views of President Harry S Truman, not Bess Truman. In accordance with this belief, there would be no press conferences, no speeches, and no radio broadcasts.[74] Ceremonial appearances would be selected with care.

The death of Franklin Roosevelt had made her First Lady, but "she would always remain Bess Wallace Truman of Independence by preference."[75]

Route to the White House

Elizabeth Virginia Wallace, the oldest child of Margaret (Madge) Gates Wallace and David Wallace, was born in Independence, Missouri, on February 13, 1885.[76] At Sunday school, the tomboyish Bess met Harry Truman, whose family had moved to Independence from Grandview, Missouri. Years later Harry Truman wrote in his *Memoirs* that when his family moved to Independence he met many children but "I became interested in one in particular. She had golden curls and has to this day, the most beautiful blue eyes."[77] Harry's admiration for Bess would continue for a lifetime, but through grammar and high school the two were just friends. As the daughter of a prominent Independence family, Bess never lacked for suitors, and the poor, bookish Harry Truman was not thought to have a serious chance of wooing the popular Miss Wallace.

After graduation from high school in 1901, Harry and Bess parted company. Harry had hoped to attend college, but his family could not afford higher education and it was imperative that he work. In 1906 he returned to Grandview to help his family run their farm.

Bess remained in Independence and helped her mother care for her younger brothers. Her aid became invaluable after David Wallace committed suicide in 1903. Bess dated a number of young men, and completed her education with a year of study at Miss Barstow's Finishing School for Girls in Kansas City.

Harry and Bess did not renew their acquaintance until a chance meeting five years after high school graduation.[78] After this meeting Harry frequently traveled to Independence to see Bess, and the two carried on a voluminous correspondence.

Mrs. Wallace heartily disapproved of Harry. He had no education or money, and his future seemed unpromising at best. A biographer notes, "It was preposterous to Madge Wallace that her daughter would marry a dirt farmer, and even worse, one who did not even own the farm he worked!"[79]

Over Mrs. Wallace's opposition, Bess and Harry announced their engagement just before he joined the army and was shipped overseas. Truman always maintained that he and Bess did not marry prior to the war because he did not want her to have to face the prospect of possible widowhood. More likely, Mrs. Wallace's dislike of Harry kept the young people apart.

Truman returned safely from the war, and on June 28, 1919, he and Bess were married. Mrs. Wallace never reconciled herself to the marriage, always believing that "Bess had clearly married beneath herself."[80] In spite of Mrs. Wallace's behavior and occasional snide comments, Harry Truman was always kind to Bess's mother.

The newlyweds moved into the Gates mansion at 219 North Delaware Avenue. Harry and a war buddy, Eddie Jacobson, decided to open a haberdashery together in Kansas City. The store did well the first year, but failed in 1921 as a result of a business slump.

Truman had always been interested in politics. Now unemployed and in debt, he accepted the support of the Pendergast family who ran the efficient and corrupt Kansas City political machine. He was elected county judge.

Bess was less than enthusiastic about Harry's new career. She was not enamoured of his cronies, whom she considered a coarse, unrefined lot, and she did not enjoy being a politician's wife. Her daughter Margaret Truman suggests that Bess may have disliked Harry Truman's vocation because of the attendant publicity.[81]

Truman lost the only election of his career when he was defeated for reelection as county judge in 1924. In February of that year, Bess gave birth to their only child, Mary Margaret.

Truman was involved in a few unsuccessful business ventures before deciding to reenter politics in 1926. Possibly in an effort to interest his wife in his work, he took Bess along with him to political meetings and speaking engagements as he campaigned for presiding judge of the county court. He was probably unsuccessful in sparking Mrs. Truman's interest, but he won the election.[82] In 1934 Tom Pendergast offered Truman his support for a senatorial bid, and Truman was subsequently elected.

Bess, Margaret, and Mrs. Wallace (who lived with the Trumans) were unhappy about moving to Washington. They had little money, and Bess feared "the coldness of an eastern city."[83] The family moved into a modest five-room apartment on Connecticut Avenue. Bess did the cooking and cleaning and faithfully attended the Senate wives' luncheons, but admitted that "they bore me."[84] She played canasta and bridge with other Senate wives and kept an eye on Margaret.

Finances were a major problem. The Trumans and Mrs. Wallace could not live on Harry's ten-thousand-dollar-a-year Senate salary. The senator placed his wife on his office payroll as a forty-five-hundred-dollar-a-year secretary. Disclosure of this action caused a storm of controversy after Truman had been nominated for Vice President. Asked by the press to clarify his wife's status, Truman responded: "She's a clerk in my office and that's the reason I've got her there. I never make a report or a speech without her editing it."[85] The storm subsided.

Following reelection to the Senate in 1940, Truman gained national prominence when he chaired the Committee to Investigate the National Defense Program. Later to be known as the "Truman Committee," the group investigated waste in the military. The work of the committee brought the junior Senator from Missouri to the attention of the White House. President Roosevelt told Democratic National Committee Chairman Robert Hannegan that he would be willing to accept either Harry Truman or William O. Douglas as his running mate in 1944. Satisfied with his work in the Senate, Truman told Hannegan numerous times that he did not wish to be Vice President. However, Hannegan was persistent, and finally, Truman capitulated and was nominated.

The morning after her husband's nomination, Mrs. Truman held a press conference. She told the assembled reporters that she was "reconciled" to her husband's nomination and that she would accompany him during the campaign and collaborate on his speeches "because we've done that so long, it's a habit."[86] Mrs. Truman herself would not deliver any speeches. A *Kansas City Journal* story quotes Mrs. Truman as saying, "I'm somewhat superstitious about women making speeches in behalf of their husbands. . . . I've never seen a candidate who let his wife take the platform to speak for him."[87]

Ill and preoccupied with World War II, Franklin Roosevelt delegated almost the entire task of campaigning for reelection to Harry Truman. Truman did not object and, accompanied by Bess, he traveled all over the country lambasting Governor Thomas Dewey and the Republicans.

Harry S Truman was sworn in as Vice President on January 20, 1945. Less than three months later, on April 12, Franklin Roosevelt died and Truman became the thirty-third President of the United States.

A volatile and emotional man, Harry Truman often had a difficult time convincing Congress and the American people that his positions on issues and his programs were worthwhile. "His Accidency," as Truman was labeled by the press was compared unfavorably with Franklin Roosevelt, and his popularity plummeted. As the 1948 election approached, many Democratic regulars expressed concern that the President would not be able to secure the nomination of his own party.

In his *Memoirs*, Truman remembered, "If I had heeded the desire of my family, I would have made plans to leave the White House at the end of my first term."[88] However, Truman did not go along with Bess and Margaret, and instead decided to wage a battle to win his own term as President. He won the presidential nomination at a near-funereal Democratic National Convention, and then prepared to meet his Republican challenger Thomas Dewey.

Virtually no one except Harry Truman believed that he had a chance to win the election of 1948. Undaunted, the feisty President climbed aboard his campaign train, the *Ferdinand Magellan*, and he, Bess, and Margaret were off on a 21,928-mile, 475-speech odyssey to persuade the voters to keep Harry Truman in the White House.[89]

Bess and Margaret were an integral part of the President's "whistle-stop" psychology. When the campaign train arrived at a scheduled stop, the President would come out on the rear platform and "give 'em hell," forcefully explaining why he should be elected, then he would tell his audience what was wrong with his Republican challenger. When he had finished his speech, he would say, "I want you to meet the Boss," and he would proudly lead the First Lady to the platform where she would smile and wave to the assembled throng.[90] Then Truman would say, "And here's the one who bosses her," and Margaret would appear.[91] The Truman women were popular with campaign crowds.

Confounding pollsters, politicians, and even his own family, Truman was elected by a popular vote of 24,105,587 to 21,970,017 for Dewey.[92] Harry Truman had accomplished the most stunning political upset of the century.

Truman's next four years in office were as turbulent as his preceding term as chief executive. By 1952, he and "the Boss" had spent eighteen years in Washington and looked forward to returning to Independence. On January 20, 1953, the Truman family gratefully became private citizens.

The former President and his wife returned to the house on North Delaware Avenue. Harry S Truman died on December 26, 1972. Bess Truman died at the age of ninety-seven on October 18, 1982.

Major Communication Activities of the First Lady

Harry Truman commented on his wife's perception of her role as First Lady: "She was entirely conscious of the importance and dignity of White House life. She was not especially interested however, in the formalities and pomp or artificiality which, . . . inevitably surround the family of a President."[93] Mrs. Truman chose to interpret her duties as First Lady as strictly ceremonial in scope. For a number of reasons discussed herein, even these duties were limited.

As stated earlier, Mrs. Truman was not interested in sharing her views on any issue with the public. She gave no speeches during her years in the White House. Occasionally she would utter very brief remarks, but her longest statement was under fifty words in length.

Mrs. Truman never voiced support for a project or idea, and never campaigned for a Democratic Party candidate. With the exception of ceremonial appearances, Bess Truman successfully avoided communicating with the public.

Ceremonial Presence. Archivists at the Truman Library estimate that from April 1945 through January 1953 Mrs. Truman was involved in 640 activities.[94] These activities included attendance at luncheons, receptions, fashion shows, teas, dinners, parties, plays, and concerts, meetings with organizations, honorary chairmanships of fund-raising events, and serving as the President's representative at dedications and funerals. She also coordinated the events of the official Washington social season, the first since the beginning of World War II, and acted as hostess at state dinners.

Mrs. Truman was relatively inactive, participating in an average of ninety-one activities per year. Perhaps she wanted to have more contact with people, but her entertaining was curtailed by several factors. There were still food shortages following World War II, and only a limited number of people could be invited to the White House for luncheons or dinners. After President Truman was elected to his own term of office in 1948, it was discovered that the White House needed to be rebuilt. The Trumans took up residence at Blair House. Large-scale entertaining at the smaller edifice was not possible. During the years of White House renovation, state dinners and receptions were staged at the Mayflower Hotel. The worsening situation in Korea brought a near moratorium on already limited entertaining in 1950.[95] Possibly the major reason for Mrs. Truman's lack of activity was that she felt her primary duty was to be a wife and mother, futhermore, she detested receiving lines and found the experience of meeting new people to be very difficult.[96]

In spite of her shyness, Mrs. Truman worked diligently to become a gracious hostess, and developed a reputation as one who had a facility for small talk and never forgot a name.[97] Edith Helm, Mrs. Truman's social secretary, noted, "All over Washington I heard from people—many of them no friends of the Truman administration or its ways—nothing but praise of Mrs. Truman, her dignity and her unfailing cordiality when hostess at the White House."[98]

Press Relations. Reporters were distressed and annoyed when her staff announced that the First Lady would not hold press conferences or grant interviews, both standard practices during the Roosevelt years.[99] A 1946 article in the *New York Times* discussed the First Lady's reasons for her position: "She simply stood out . . . against any such direct question and answer dealings between her and a public which she regards as wholly her husband's."[100] *Newsweek* presented a different view, wondering if Mrs. Truman truly cared about issues: "Mrs. Truman never expresses opinions about public questions, even among intimates."[101] Instead of press conferences, her secretaries, Miss Reathel Odum and Mrs. Helm conducted fortnightly question-and-answer sessions with the press at which they distributed copies of Mrs. Truman's schedule.

Mrs. Truman apparently was not enthusiastic about the press, and held it in low regard. On one occasion, a reporter persistently called Miss Odum to ask why Margaret Truman was in Independence and not in Washington. Odum put the question to the First Lady who responded that Margaret was "finishing a course in voice lessons—better tell her [the reporter]. God only knows what they may be saying—I'd prefer telling her it's none of their d———business."[102]

A summation of Mrs. Truman's press relations was offered by Bess Furman of *The New York Times* who wrote, "Aside from letting it be known that she had never really wanted to live in the White House, her reaction was 'no comment.' "[103]

Relationship with Her Husband. Bess and Harry Truman were devoted to each other. During fifty-three years of marriage, each was the others' best friend and partner. An enduring testament to their love is Harry's voluminous correspondence spanning the years 1910 through 1959.[104] The 1,300 letters that were opened to researchers in 1983 present a portrait of Harry Truman as suitor, ambitious young man, and soldier, and later as husband, politician, and President. In the letters Harry is always solicitious and protective of Bess, and on many occasions he expresses his love. During the White House years, while still proclaiming his commitment to his wife, the letters touch on momentous issues of the day and the dilemmas Harry confronted as Chief Executive.

The Trumans courted for over three years before Bess agreed to Harry's proposal of marriage. When she did say she would marry him, Harry Truman was speechless. Later he wrote to Bess; "I guess you thought I didn't have much sense Sunday, but I just couldn't say anything. . . . It doesn't seem real that you should care for me. I have always hoped you would but some way feared very much you wouldn't."[105] In another letter he proclaimed his love but admitted to being unable to express it face-to-face. Truman wrote:

You really didn't know I had so much softness and sentimentality in me, did you? . . . I'd die if I had to talk it. I can tell you on paper how much I love you and what one grand woman I think you, but to tell it to you I can't.[106]

His devotion to his wife never wavered or changed. In a March 1947 letter Harry tells Bess that he has heard a song that had held special significance for them when they became engaged. He asks his wife: "Do you remember it [the song]? I'll never forget it because it hit me right where I lived. It does yet."[107] On their twenty-ninth wedding anniversary Harry reflected: "Twenty-nine years! It seems like 29 days. . . . [Y]ou still are on the pedestal where I placed you that day in Sunday school, 1890. What an old fool I am."[108]

Needless to say, Harry Truman idolized "the Boss," and endeavored to protect her and Margaret from gossip and rude behavior. As a politician he fully expected to be criticized for his actions, but comments about his family enraged him.

Congresswoman Clare Booth Luce suggested that Mrs. Truman was unworldly and unsophisticated.[109] The president was furious and had Mrs. Luce excluded from White House guest lists during his administration. General Harry Vaughn, the president's military aide, commented that "Harry regarded that [insulting Bess] as the equivalent of spitting on the flag."[110] On another occasion the President almost provoked an international incident when he planned to have an ambassador recalled for what he perceived as rude behavior to Mrs. Truman.[111]

Mrs. Truman did her best to protect the President. She would try to calm or mollify him when he became overly excited. The White House staff heard her repeat one phrase over and over again to the President: "You didn't have to say that."[112] Of the many presidential couples, the Trumans were perhaps the most devoted and protective of each other.

Access to Presidential Decision Making. There is evidence to support the contention that Mrs. Truman influenced her husband's decision making. Virtually no doubt exists that Mrs. Truman functioned as her husband's speech editor and consultant. In addition to Harry Truman's 1944 comment about his wife's role in preparing his public discourse, George Elsey, who served as an administrative assistant in the Truman administration, has said: "The President would comment at times to us in a final speech session that Mrs. Truman had suggested a different phraseology. . . . We were delighted. . . . Mrs. Truman had a sharp ear and a good ear for matters of this sort."[113] Harry Truman's letters to his wife also confirm that the First Lady was au courant with public-policy matters. He wrote her every day from the Potsdam Conference, and felt free to comment on Winston Churchill, Josef Stalin, and his hopes for ending World War II. When he returned home, he reported on other matters. In 1947 he wrote, "We [the cabinet] had a real honest to goodness discussion of policy toward Germany and Japan, as well as a discussion on a food and grain purchase program."[114] In another letter he was optimistic about the Berlin situation: "Had a good cabinet meeting, short and to the point. Marshall [General George C. Marshall, Secretary of State] reported on Berlin situation. Looks good."[115] Frequently the President would express opinions about various people and institutions in his letters, and it was not uncommon for him to vent his spleen in writing.[116]

Truman scholar Robert H. Ferrell has said that some of the letters that Mr. Truman wrote contain material that would "practically amount these days to secrets of state."[117] At the very least, Mrs. Truman learned about decisions or policies before the American public.

Mrs. Truman's involvement in her husband's decision making seems to have been more complex than serving as speech editor or being the recipient of letters. In 1963 the former President told a reporter that his wife was "a full partner in all my transactions—politically and otherwise."[118] He went on to acknowledge that she was able to provide an objective view of problems. "Her judgment was always good. She never made a suggestion that wasn't for the benefit of the country and what I was trying to do. She looks at things objectively and I can't always."[119] Margaret Truman confirms that her parents discussed the issues, problems, and personalities that Harry Truman confronted as President.[120] Finally, Mrs. Gerald Ford, a young congressional wife at the time, observed that Mrs. Truman "certainly told President Truman exactly what she thought and everybody knew it and everybody knew he listened."[121]

Mrs. Truman probably played a limited role in Harry Truman's decision making. The First Lady had access to current and sometimes sensitive information, discussed various matters with her husband, and helped him to frame his thoughts for public presentation. The President respected Mrs. Truman's common sense and objectivity, and given the available evidence, he is likely to have sought her counsel on a wide variety of issues.

The President's and First Lady's Perceptions of Women. President Truman appointed eighteen women to high-level positions within his administration. Twenty-one women appointed during other administrations continued to serve in various capacities during President Truman's White House tenure.[122]

Privately, Mr. Truman seems to have had traditional perceptions about women. In 1947 he criticized Eleanor Roosevelt when he wrote to Bess: "Also had a saucy letter from Eleanor on the same subject [appointment of a Democratic National Chairman]. Thank heaven there are no pants wearing women in my family. Harry Vaughn says she wears the coat and vest too."[123]

Little is known of Mrs. Truman's perception of women, but it is likely that in spite of her own experience as presidential confidante, she saw them mainly in the roles of wife and mother.

Bess Truman chose not to communicate with the American public in any capacity except for limited ceremonial activities. Though she was kindly and gracious, the country never got to know its First Lady. There was disappointment over Mrs. Truman's lack of public persona, but she was not swayed.

Mrs. Truman chose to be active in private spheres, probably influencing her husband on many issues. To the world she seemed to be Harry Truman's help-mate; he knew that she was much more.

MARY EISENHOWER

Unlike Bess Truman, Mamie Eisenhower genuinely enjoyed her tenure as First Lady. Former White House Chief Usher J. B. West wrote, "She adored the pomp and circumstance and grandeur that went along with the nation's top job."[124] Though her White House schedule often tired her, she enjoyed host-essing state dinners and welcoming the thousands of people who came to visit the executive mansion.

Mamie Eisenhower was especially well prepared for her role as First Lady. A former army wife, she had lived all over the world, supervised large households, and entertained and lived by the rigid rules of military protocol. Dwight D. Eisenhower was a hero, and Mamie had learned to deal with the accompanying adulation and attention.

Mrs. Eisenhower was more enthusiastic about her role as public communicator than was Bess Truman. There still would be no speeches or radio broadcasts by the First Lady, but Mrs. Eisenhower promised occasional press conferences. More outgoing than her predecessor, there seemed to be the likelihood of increased communication activities.

Route to the White House

Mary Geneva Doud was born in Boone, Iowa, on November 14, 1896.[125] Her parents, Elvira Carlson Doud and John Shelton Doud, had four daughters, but only Mary, nicknamed Mamie, and her youngest sister Mabel, nicknamed Mike, survived to adulthood.

John Doud amassed a fortune in the meat-packing business, and at the age of thirty-six retired with his family to Denver, Colorado. Mamie enjoyed a well-to-do upbringing there. She attended a private elementary school and completed her education at Denver's fashionable finishing school, Miss Woolcott's. Mamie was only an average student, but she was always popular and well liked.

The affluent Douds purchased a home in Texas, and it was in San Antonio that they spent the winter months. In October 1915 the Douds visited with friends at nearby Fort Sam Houston. The friends introduced Mamie to one of the post's newest officers, a recent West Point graduate, Second Lieutenant

Dwight Eisenhower. Eisenhower wrote of the meeting, "The one who attracted my eye instantly was a vivacious and attractive girl, smaller than average, saucy in the look about her face and in her whole attitude."[126] Mamie was equally smitten, remembering later that her future husband was "just about the handsomest male I had ever seen."[127]

Mamie had many beaux, but Eisenhower quickly disposed of his competition. He and Mamie were married in the Douds' home in Denver on July 1, 1916. Mamie was nineteen, and Ike was twenty-five.

The Eisenhowers' first home was Ike's former bachelor quarters at Fort Sam Houston. Accustomed to luxury, the young bride was not quite prepared for army life in cramped surroundings. She knew nothing about cooking, cleaning, or budgeting. In time, however, she learned what was necessary.

Mamie also had to learn about her new husband's priorities. Shortly after the wedding, Ike had to leave on maneuvers. Mamie balked at the news, but Ike explained to her: "My country comes first and always will. You come second."[128] Ike's priorities never changed.

Having grown up in a sophisticated environment, Mamie was able to help Ike broaden his rather narrow horizons. John Eisenhower noted, "She takes full credit for smoothing the edges off the rough and ready Kansan and for teaching him some of the polish that later put him in good stead."[129] One Eisenhower associate remarked that "Ike would have been Colonel Dwight D. Eisenhower, if it weren't for Mamie."[130]

Ike was away when their first child, Doud Dwight, was born on September 24, 1917. A few months after the baby's birth, "Icky," as he was nicknamed, and Mamie joined Ike and began a nomadic army existence, moving from post to post.

Just after Christmas 1920, Icky became seriously ill with scarlet fever; he died in early January 1921. Forty-seven years later, the pain of the little boy's loss still haunted Eisenhower, and he wrote, "This was the greatest disappointment and disaster in my life, the one I was never able to forget completely."[131] Mamie was inconsolable for months.

Mamie was especially depressed when duty required her husband to be absent from home for increasingly long periods of time. Occasionally she would return to Denver to visit with her parents for extended periods. The Eisenhower's lethargy lifted with the birth of a second child, John, in August 1923.

Over the next eighteen years, Mamie made homes for Ike and John in the Canal Zone, the Phillipines, Paris, and Washington, D.C. Eisenhower, whose promotions had come frustratingly slow, was promoted to brigadier general in 1941. Two years later he was named Supreme Commander of the Allied Expeditionary Forces. With the exception of twelve days together, this assignment kept Ike and Mamie apart for the duration of World War II.

With Ike stationed in Europe and John a cadet at West Point, Mamie took an apartment at the Wardman Park Hotel in Washington. She spent the war years in a state of depression, worrying about her husband and son, playing cards, and working in a USO canteen.

From other army wives Mamie heard rumors of a romance between her husband and his driver in Europe, Kay Summersby. Former President Harry Truman told an interviewer that Eisenhower wrote to the U.S. Chief of Staff, General George Marshall, and requested permission to divorce Mamie and marry Miss Summersby. It is probable that the relationship between Eisenhower and Miss Summersby was simply a flirtation, but the unsubstantiated rumors of infidelity augmented Mamie's depression.[132]

General Eisenhower returned from the war a hero. He was courted by both the Republican and Democratic parties as a potential presidential candidate in 1948, but he declined their offers, resigned from the army, and accepted the presidency of Columbia University.

Eisenhower's tenure as President of Columbia was short-lived. In 1950 he resigned his position with the university and returned to the military, this time as Supreme Commander of the Allied Powers in Europe.

In 1952 the clamoring for Eisenhower to run for President became irresistible, and he returned to the United States to declare himself a candidate for the Republican nomination. Mamie opposed a presidential race, "for it would mean her cherished privacy would be gone forever."[133] In spite of her opposition, Eisenhower waged a fight for the nomination and later won the right to be the Republican standard-bearer. He and Mamie began an exhaustive campaign that took them all over the country by train.

Mamie was popular with the crowds that came out to meet the Eisenhower campaign train. Borrowing Harry Truman's idea, General Eisenhower would draw his wife forward at the conclusion of his remarks and say, "And now I want you to meet my Mamie."[134] These theatrics always brought cheers from the assemblage. Mrs. Eisenhower smiled and waved, but like Mrs. Truman, she never uttered a word.

A rumor suggesting that Mamie was an alcoholic, circulated during the campaign. One historian writes that Eisenhower was questioned about Mamie's problems with alcohol during the 1952 Republican National Convention. He replied that his wife had "pretty well renounced hard liquor—on which she had clearly been dependent . . . in the interests of her husband's political career. 'I don't think Mamie's had a drink in something like eighteen months,' " he said.[135]

Mrs. Eisenhower may have been dependent on liquor, but she also suffered from health problems that might have given the impression of alcohol abuse. She had sustained heart damage from a bout with rheumatic fever as a child. In addition, she suffered from Ménière's disease, an inner ear problem. The combination of the two afflictions caused Mrs. Eisenhower to tire easily and to suffer from dizziness. She missed engagements, and when she was able to attend, she required assistance in climbing stairs and other activities.[136] The rumor of alcoholism continued to plague her for the duration of the campaign and for all her years in the White House. However, it appeared to have little effect on the Eisenhower campaign. On Election Day the former general swept into office with 55 percent of the popular vote.[137]

On September 24, 1955, President Eisenhower suffered a moderate heart attack while vacationing in Denver. As he recovered, Mamie tried to cheer him and responded personally to almost twenty thousand get-well wishes.

Shortly after the President's recovery, he decided to seek a second term of office. He and Mamie campaigned across the country once again, and on Election Day, the President defeated Adlai Stevenson by a greater plurality than in 1952, taking 57 percent of the popular vote.[138]

Both the President and the First Lady were glad to retire to their Gettysburg, Pennsylvania, farm at the conclusion of Eisenhower's term in January 1961. Eisenhower's retirement was not as lengthy as he had hoped; he died of heart disease in Walter Reed Hospital on March 28, 1969. Mamie Eisenhower suffered a stroke in September 1979. She died on December 1, 1979.

Major Communication Activities of the First Lady

Mrs. Eisenhower did not see herself as a communicator or an independent presence in the White House. She advocated no causes, and gave only one very brief speech during this time.[139] Although she accompanied her husband on the campaign trail in 1952 and 1956, she said nothing. The press conferences she promised never materialized. Mrs. Eisenhower saw her role as being wholly ceremonial; this was the forum she selected for meeting the American public.

Ceremonial Presence. President Eisenhower wrote: "I personally think that Mamie's biggest contribution was to make the White House livable, comfortable and meaningful for the people who came in. She was always helpful and ready to do anything. She exuded hospitality."[140]

Mrs. Eisenhower was considerably more active than Mrs. Truman in terms of ceremonial activities. She was involved in approximately 878 activities from January 20, 1953, to January 20, 1961.[141]

To the delight of Washington hostesses, Mrs. Eisenhower resurrected the formal social season. Their enthusiasm was short-lived when traditional social events were curtailed because both the President and First Lady became ill in 1955. Mamie Eisenhower genuinely enjoyed her duties. A truly considerate hostess, she went "wholeheartedly into the business of satisfying the social, charitable and discreetly political demands made upon her."[142]

Press Relations. Mamie Eisenhower's relations with the press were cordial. Information about her activities was released by her social secretary. Mrs. Eisenhower had promised to hold occasional press conferences, but held only one, on March 11, 1953. Helen Thomas, United Press International's White House Bureau Chief, attended the news conference, and remembered that Mrs. Eisenhower "held her own beautifully . . . but that the First Lady . . . certainly did not want to discuss anything substantive."[143] Various questions were raised at the news conference, but a majority of queries concentrated on the social side of the White House. The First Lady politely sidestepped any political questions.

Bonnie Angelo of *Time* recalled that during the Eisenhower administration the press was used in a perfunctory way. "We were allowed to come to White House functions, but we had no access to the First Lady."[144] Marie Smith of the *Washington Post* noted that if reporters got physically close enough to Mrs. Eisenhower to ask a question, she was friendly and willing to answer, "but her social secretary would quickly say, 'that's all, that's enough.' "[145]

Mrs. Eisenhower maintained a pleasant relationship with the press. Though the news she generated was of a purely social nature, her warm and cordial manner produced a consistently complimentary press.

Factors That Influenced the First Lady's Performance as Public Communicator

Relationship with Her Husband. The Eisenhower's relationship was strongly influenced by the military. Mamie Eisenhower was expected to be a good soldier, following her husband dutifully from camp to camp, and accepting the fact that his duty to his country would often separate them. She experienced "long periods of monotony followed by sudden domestic upheavals."[146] Mamie Eisenhower's devotion to her husband and his career was total. One reporter opened an article about Mamie by writing: "She's a career woman. Her career is Ike."[147] John Eisenhower commented, "She felt her role was to push him [Eisenhower] forward and to give him all the emotional support he needed."[148]

Mamie Eisenhower exerted a humanizing influence on her husband's life. She provided him with a release from his responsibilities, but she very rarely aided him in their execution.

Access to Presidential Decision Making. Mrs. Eisenhower was once quoted as saying, "Ike fights the wars, I turn the lambchops."[149] Mrs. Eisenhower played a minor role in her husband's official life. She rarely if ever tried to influence any of his decisions. Her lack of impact in substantive matters never bothered her. She apparently delighted in being a traditional wife and helpmate.

The President occasionally consulted his wife regarding White House business, especially economic and budget matters. Mrs. Eisenhower had always managed their accounts, so it seemed natural that the President would show her the national budget, which he viewed "as an enlarged version of a household budget."[150] The President also found his wife to be a perceptive judge of people.

Mrs. Eisenhower had minimal influence on public policy matters. Dwight D. Eisenhower had spent a lifetime giving commands without his wife's aid. It would seem that he always put his own judgment before hers.

The President's and First Lady's Perceptions of Women. Dwight D. Eisenhower had always dealt with men in military and university settings; women played minor roles in both institutions. However, as President, Eisenhower surprised many people by appointing twenty-seven women to high-level positions. Thirteen women appointed by Eisenhower's predecessors continued to serve in various capacities, thus pushing the number of women in high-level positions in the Eisenhower administration to forty.[151]

Mrs. Eisenhower seemed to perceive women as wives and mothers who had little input or interest in the affairs of men. Like Mrs. Truman, Mamie Eisenhower interpreted her duties as being strictly ceremonial in scope. Helen Thomas observes, "She wasn't a person who was engaging her energies in anything else except being a wife and First Lady in a very pro forma sense."[152]

Mrs. Eisenhower was not concerned with publicly projecting her views on any issue or political candidate. She seems to have seen herself as the nation's hostess; for eight years she graciously dispensed the hospitality of the White House to thousands of visitors.

A number of factors probably determine how active a woman will be in the White House. Age, state of health, family obligations, and the President's attitude toward the degree of his wife's participation in his affairs are all determinants. Does the President really want his wife to be active? If not, will he endeavor to restrict her activity? Of greatest importance perhaps is the social and historical context of the First Lady's White House tenure. Do the times permit or encourage her to be active?

Florence Harding, Grace Coolidge, Bess Truman, and Mamie Eisenhower were inactive communicators. They never addressed the public on an issue, almost never held press conferences, and never made radio broadcasts. All were visible presences and hostesses, but maintained almost total public silence.

Florence Harding was sixty years old when she became the First Lady. She enjoyed her ceremonial responsibilities immensely, but made no attempt to enlarge the traditional scope of the First Lady's public activities by initiating new communication activities. Mrs. Harding attempted to influence her husband's decision making as President, and inadvertently began to expand the private role of the President's wife. Warren Harding did not encourage—nor could he discourage—his wife from taking an active private role.

When Grace Coolidge arrived at the White House in 1923, she was young, forty-four years of age, and possessed the personality and ability to expand the First Lady's role. This was not to be. Grace Coolidge was the beneficiary of a nineteenth-century upbringing, and she scrupulously obeyed her husband's commands. Calvin Coolidge restricted his wife from communicating with the public and from playing any role in his affairs. In 1924 Calvin, Jr., died, blunting Grace's own enthusiasm for her position. The First Lady remained a pleasant, passive hostess.

While reflecting a similar nineteenth-century upbringing, Bess Truman and Mamie Eisenhower were also typical of women in the post–World War II America of the 1950s. They perceived their White House responsibilities as an extension of domestic responsibilities, supervising the physical plant of the White

House, being good wives, and aiding their husbands' careers while remaining in the background. To a great extent, the profile of the American woman and that of the First Lady in the late 1940s and 1950s were the same.

Bess Truman was sixty years of age when she became First Lady. She had never worked outside her home with the exception of the time when she was employed in Harry Truman's Senate office. When she came to the White House, Mrs. Truman still had family obligations; Margaret was in college and she was also caring for her aged mother. Bess was shy and shunned contact with the public. Harry Truman did not ask her to play a greater role in his administration.

Mamie Eisenhower was not a well woman, suffering through a variety of illnesses and undergoing surgery while living in the White House. She was fifty-seven years of age when she became First Lady, younger than Bess Truman but after thirty-seven years as a military wife not predisposed to become involved in her husband's affairs. Like Harry Truman, Dwight Eisenhower did not encourage his wife to be more active or involved in his administration.

In spite of a lack of activity, both women were popular. A 1948 Gallup Poll found that Mrs. Truman ranked number five out of a group of ten most admired women in the world.[153]

Overall, Mrs. Eisenhower ranked higher than Mrs. Truman. In her first poll, in January 1953, Mrs. Eisenhower was rated as number three of the five most admired women.[154] After this, she never ranked lower than number four of ten.[155]

Changes during the Eisenhower administration would be forthcoming, of course. As Mamie Eisenhower entered the White House, the influence of Washington society was in decline. For a short period during Mrs. Eisenhower's tenure as First Lady, Washington hostesses had a chance to entertain and be entertained in a grand style at the White House. The respite was brief, for illness caused the Eisenhowers to severely curtail their official entertainment. By the time Jacqueline Kennedy became mistress of the executive mansion in 1961, the strict protocol of years past had diminished and the social season was almost nonexistent. The First Lady would not be required to give as many dinners and receptions, she could concentrate her efforts elsewhere.

The development of television, the expansion of the news media, and a growing interest in the First Family would occur. Demands for press conferences and interviews would multiply. The Reader's Guide to Periodical Literature lists twenty-two articles written about Bess Truman from April 1945 to January 1952. The number of articles more than doubled—forty-eight in all—during Mamie Eisenhower's tenure from January 1953 to January 1961.

Bess Truman and Mamie Eisenhower consciously chose not to be public communicators. During their time in the White House, the First Lady's role reverted to the ceremonial responsibility of the years of earlier First Ladies. The First Lady would not remain simply a hostess for the nation, but at that time the American people did not disagree with this interpretation of responsibilities. Soon it would be almost impossible to isolate oneself in the White House and shun public contact as Bess Truman did. Though they were typical of the time, Bess Truman and Mamie Eisenhower were the last of that era.

NOTES

1. Biographical material has been culled from a number of sources, including Sol Barzman, *The First Ladies* (New York: Cowles, 1970), pp. 265–274; Marianne Means, *The Woman in the White House* (New York: Random, 1963), pp. 165–188; and Francis Russell, *The Shadow of Blooming Grove: Warren G. Harding in His Times* (New York: McGraw-Hill, 1968), pp. 37–113.

2. Russell, *Shadow*, p. 83.

3. Russell, *Shadow*, p. 85, Barzman, *First Ladies*, p. 267.

4. Samuel Hopkins Adams, *Incredible Era: The Life and Times of Warren Gamaliel Harding* (Boston: Houghton, Mifflin, 1939), p. 25.

5. Jack Warwick, "Growing up With Harding," *Northwest Ohio Quarterly*, 31:2, (Spring 1959), p. 89, cited in Randolph C. Downes, *The Rise of Warren G. Harding* (Columbus, Ohio: Ohio State University Press, 1970), pp. 18–19.

6. Russell, *Shadow*, p. 260.

7. Harry M. Daugherty and Thomas Dixon, *The Inside Story of the Harding Tragedy* (New York: Churchill, 1932), p. 10.

8. Adams, *Incredible Era*, p. 120.

9. Russell, *Shadow*, p. 313.

10. Apparently Mrs. Harding's concerns about her husband's health were well-founded. Harding admitted to a friend that his blood pressure was elevated and he had traces of sugar in his urine: Russell, *Shadow*, pp. 331–332; Downes, *Rise of Warren G. Harding*, p. 306.

11. Russell, *Shadow*, p. 354.

12. "Mrs. Harding's Foreboding," *New York Times*, June 11, 1921, p. 3.

13. Means, *Woman in the White House*, p. 187.

14. Means, *Woman in the White House*, p. 187.

15. Adams, *Incredible Era*, p. 184.

16. John L. Moore (ed.), *Guide to U.S. Elections* (Washington, D.C.: Congressional Quarterly, 1975), p. 286.

17. Russell, *Shadow*, p. 556.

18. This point is taken by Gaston Means in his sensational and generally meretricious book. Gaston B. Means and May Dixon Thacker, *The Strange Death of President Harding* (New York: Guild, 1930).

19. Russell, *Shadow*, pp. 605–606.

20. Barzman, *First Ladies*, p. 272.

21. The estimate of the number of Mrs. Harding's activities was achieved by scanning the *New York Times* and the *Washington Post*.

22. "Mrs. Harding Fears Impending Tragedy," *New York Times*, June 13, 1920, p. 7.

23. "Mrs. Harding Fears Impending Tragedy," p. 7.

24. Russell, *Shadow*, p. 467.

25. Russell, *Shadow*, p. 487.

26. Paternity is extremely questionable; Warren Harding is thought to have been

sterile as the result of a case of mumps contracted as a boy: Russell, *Shadow*, p. 311. Nan Britton was known to have been involved with numerous men: Russell, *Shadow*, pp. 466, 606, 607.

27. Barzman, *First Ladies*, p. 272.

28. Robert K. Murray, *Warren G. Harding and His Administration* (Minneapolis: University of Minnesota Press, 1969), p. 420.

29. Russell, *Shadow*, p. 455.

30. Means, *Woman in the White House*, p. 169.

31. No source is entirely clear on why Mrs. Harding opposed Debs's release so vehemently. Russell believes personal reasons motivated her opposition, but fails to discuss it further: Russell, *Shadow*, p. 487. Eúgene Trani and David Wilson write that the First Lady thought the decision was unwise politically: Eugene P. Trani and David L. Wilson, *The Presidency of Warren G. Harding* (Lawrence, Kansas: Regents Press, 1977), p. 102.

32. Russell, *Shadow*, p. 486.

33. Alice Roosevelt Longworth, *Crowded Hours* (New York: Scribner, 1933), p. 323.

34. Russell, *Shadow*, pp. 451–452.

35. Russell, *Shadow*, p. 452.

36. Murray, *Warren G. Harding*, p. 420.

37. Andrew Sinclair, *The Available Man: Warren Gamaliel Harding* (New York: MacMillan, 1965), p. 104.

38. Chafe, *American Woman*, p. 27.

39. Karen Keesling and Suzanne Cavanagh, "Women Presidential Appointees Serving or Having Served in Full-Time Positions Requiring Senate Confirmation 1912–1977" (Congressional Research Service, Library of Congress, March 23, 1978), p. 20.

40. Adams, *Incredible Era*, p. 215.

41. Background material has been culled from a number of sources, including Barzman, *First Ladies*, pp. 275–283; Margaret Bassett, *American Presidents and Their Wives* (Freeport, Maine: Bond Wheelwright, 1969), pp. 307–315; and Ishbel Ross, *Grace Coolidge and Her Era* (New York: Dodd Mead, 1962), pp. 1–86.

42. Donald McCoy, *Calvin Coolidge: The Quiet President* (New York: MacMillan, 1967), p. 31.

43. Ross, *Grace Coolidge*, p. 17.

44. Barzman, *First Ladies*, p. 279.

45. William Allen White, *A Puritan in Babylon: The Story of Calvin Coolidge* (New York: MacMillan, 1938), p. 323.

46. Claude M. Feuss, *Calvin Coolidge: The Man from Vermont* (Hamden, Conn.: Archon, 1965), p. 287.

47. McCoy, *Quiet President*, p. 161.

48. McCoy, *Quiet President*, p. 160.

49. Mary Randolph, *Presidents and First Ladies* (New York: Appleton-Century, 1936), pp. 25–26.

50. Ross, *Grace Coolidge*, p. 94.

51. McCoy, *Quiet President*, p. 161.

52. Calvin Coolidge, *The Autobiography of Calvin Coolidge* (New York: Cosmopolitan, 1939), p. 190.

53. "National Sensation Caused by Brief Presidential Statement," *New York Times*, August 3, 1927, p. 1.

54. Feuss, *Man from Vermont,* p. 395.

55. McCoy, *Quiet President,* p. 389.

56. White, *Puritan,* p. 366n.

57. Feuss, *Man from Vermont,* p. 385.

58. Grace Coolidge, "Making Ourselves at Home in the White House," *American Magazine,* 108 (November 1929), pp. 160–163.

59. Carol Felsenthal, *Alice Roosevelt Longworth* (New York: Putnam, 1988) p. 123n.

60. The list of social functions for 1923–1924 was culled from President and Mrs. Coolidge's Social and Personal Newspaper Clippings, Box 1, December 4, 1923–March 9, 1924, the Coolidge Memorial Room, Forbes Library, Northampton, Massachusetts.

61. Mrs. Coolidge Wins Place in Hearts of the People by Gentle, Winning Ways," *Washington Star,* December 9, 1923, Box 1, Coolidge Memorial Room, Forbes Library, Northampton, Massachusetts.

62. This is an estimate of the volume of Mrs. Coolidge's ceremonial activites. It was achieved by scanning the *New York Times* for the years 1923–1929.

63. Grace Coolidge, "The Real Calvin Coolidge," *Good Housekeeping,* 100 (April 1935), p. 41.

64. The figure was obtained by surveying the *Reader's Guide to Periodical Literature* for the period of 1923–1929.

65. Calvin Coolidge, *Autobiography,* p. 93.

66. Grace Coolidge, "The Real Calvin Coolidge," *Good Housekeeping,* 100 (June 1935), p. 42.

67. "The Other Presidents," *Good Housekeeping,* 97 (February 1932), p. 141.

68. Feuss, *Man from Vermont,* pp. 489–490.

69. Feuss, *Man from Vermont,* p. 490.

70. Grace Coolidge, "When I Became the First Lady," *The American Magazine,* Vol. 208, September, 1929, p. 106.

71. Feuss, *Man from Vermont,* p. 102.

72. Keesling and Cavanagh, "Women Presidential Appointees," pp. 16, 21–22.

73. Bassett, *American Presidents,* p. 366.

74. "Truman's to Keep White House Aides," *New York Times,* May 7, 1945, p. 30.

75. Barzman, *First Ladies,* p. 307.

76. Biographical material has been culled from the following sources: Barzman, *First Ladies,* pp. 306–315; Bassett, *American Presidents,* pp. 361–368; Robert H. Ferrell, *Dear Bess: The Letters from Harry to Bess Truman 1910–1959* (New York: Norton, 1983); Means, *Woman in the White House,* pp. 215–241; Merle Miller, *Plain Speaking: An Oral History of Harry S Truman* (New York: Putnam, 1973), pp. 42–264; Harry S Truman, *Memoirs Volume I: Years of Decision* (Garden City, N.Y.: Doubleday, 1955); and Margaret Truman, *Bess W. Truman* (New York: MacMillan, 1986).

77. Harry S Truman, *Memoirs Vol. I,* p. 116.

78. Margaret Truman, *Harry S Truman* (New York: Pocket, 1974), p. 55.

79. Alfred Steinberg, *The Man From Missouri: The Life and Times of Harry S Truman* (New York: Putnam, 1962), p. 37.

80. Miller, *Plain Speaking,* pp. 105–106.

81. Margaret Truman, *Harry S Truman,* p. 330.

82. Steinberg, *Man from Missouri,* p. 85.

83. Barzman, *First Ladies,* p. 311.

84. Means, *Woman in the White House,* p. 239.

85. " 'No Secret' Truman Says of Wife's Job in Senate," *New York Times,* July 27, 1944, p. 11.

86. "It Was Fun to Win Says Mrs. Truman," *New York Times,* July 23, 1944, p. 29.

87. Will Davis Rinkle, "Mrs. Truman Spurns Active Campaign Role," *Kansas City Journal,* undated, Vertical File, "1920–April 1945," Harry S Truman Library, Independence, Missouri (hereafter cited as HST Library).

88. Harry S Truman, *Memoirs Volume II: Years of Trial and Hope 1946–1952* (Garden City, N.Y.: Doubleday, 1956), p. 170.

89. Steinberg, *Man from Missouri,* p. 323.

90. Cabell Phillips, *The Truman Presidency* (Baltimore, Md.: Penguin, 1966), p. 239.

91. Phillips, *Truman Presidency,* p. 239.

92. John L. Moore, (ed.), *Guide to U.S. Elections,* p. 293.

93. Harry S Truman, *Memoirs Vol. I.,* p. 45.

94. Letter, Benedict K. Zobrist to the author, January 15, 1982.

95. J. B. West, *Upstairs at the White House* (New York: Warner, 1974), p. 114.

96. Lillian Rogers Parks, *My Thirty Years Backstairs at the White House* (New York: Fleet, 1961), pp. 79–80.

97. Means, *Woman in the White House,* pp. 217, 225.

98. Edith Benham Helm, *The Captains and the Kings* (New York: Putnam, 1954), p. 266.

99. J. Leonard Reinsch interviewed by J. R. Fuchs, Atlanta, Ga., March 13 and 14, 1967, Harry S Truman Oral History Project, p. 65 (hereafter referred to as HSTOHP), HST Library; Bess Furman, *Washington Bi-Line* (New York: Knopf, 1949), p. 325.

100. Bess Furman, "Independent Lady from Independence," *New York Times,* June 9, 1946, p. 17.

101. "First Lady," *Newsweek,* 27 (January 7, 1946), p. 26.

102. Memo, Reathel Odum to Mrs. Truman, October 14, 1946, in "Mrs. Truman, 1945, Correspondence," Reathel Odum Papers, Box 4, HST Library.

103. Furman, *White House Profile,* (Indianapolis: Bobbs Merrill, 1951), p. 338.

104. The correspondence might have been even greater, but Mrs. Truman destroyed a quantity of her husband's letters in 1955. For a description of this incident see Ferrell, *Dear Bess,* p. vii.

105. Letter, Harry Truman to Bess Wallace, November 4, 1913, quoted in Ferrell, *Dear Bess,* p. 141.

106. Margaret Truman, *Bess W. Truman,* p. 50.

107. Letter, Harry S Truman to Bess Truman, undated but located in the March 1947 folder, HST Papers, Box 9, Correspondence from Harry S Truman to Bess W. Truman, March 1947, HST Library.

108. Letter, Harry S Truman to Bess Truman, June 28, 1948, HST Papers, Box 9, June 1948, HST Library.

109. Jhan Robbins, *Bess and Harry: An American Love Story* (New York: Putnam, 1980), p. 128.

110. Robbins, *Bess and Harry,* p. 114.

111. Phillips, *Truman Presidency,* p. 138.

112. Parks, *My Thirty Years,* p. 278.

113. George M. Elsey interviewed by Charles T. Morrissey and Jerry N. Hess, Washington, D.C., February 10 and 17, 1964, p. 189, HSTOHP, HST Library.

114. Letter, Harry S Truman to Bess Truman, July 19, 1947. HST Papers, Box 9, Correspondence from Harry S Truman to Bess Truman, July, 1947, HST Library.

115. Letter, Harry S Truman to Bess Truman, August 6, 1948. HST Papers, Box 9, Correspondence from Harry S Truman to Bess W. Truman, August, 1948, HST Library.

116. Monte M. Poen, ed., *Strictly Personal and Confidential: The Letters Harry Truman Never Mailed* (Boston: Little, Brown, 1982).

117. Robert H. Ferrell quoted in Edwin McDowell, "1,300 Letters of Truman's Made Public," *New York Times*, March 14, 1983, p. 1.)

118. Means, *Woman in the White House*, p. 217.

119. Means, *Woman in the White House*, p. 217.

120. Margaret Truman, *Bess W. Truman*, p. 286.

121. Mrs. Gerald R. Ford interviewed by the author, Vail, Colorado, July 17, 1979.

122. Keesling and Cavanagh, *Women Presidential Appointees*, pp. 9, 15, 28–30.

123. Letter, Harry S Truman to Bess Truman, September 22, 1947, HST Library.

124. West, *Upstairs*, p. 133.

125. Biographical material has been culled from the following sources: Barzman *First Ladies*, pp. 317–327; Bassett, *American Presidents*, pp. 377–382; Piers Brenden, *Ike: His Life and Times* (New York: Harper, 1986); Julie Nixon Eisenhower, *Special People* (New York: Simon, 1977), pp. 187–217; and Means, *Woman in the White House*, pp. 242–261.

126. Dwight D. Eisenhower, *At Ease: Stories I Tell to Friends* (Garden City, N.Y.: Doubleday, 1967), p. 113.

127. Steve Neal, *The Eisenhowers: Reluctant Dynasty* (Garden City, N.Y.: Doubleday, 1978), p. 35.

128. Julie Nixon Eisenhower, *Special People*, p. 197.

129. Neal, *The Eisenhowers*, p. 38.

130. Kevin McCann quoted in Nick Thimmesch, "Mamie Eisenhower at 80," *McCalls*, 140 (October 1976), p. 212.

131. Eisenhower, *At Ease*, pp. 181–182.

132. President Truman told Merle Miller that General Marshall was so outraged at Eisenhower's request that he threatened to bust him out of the army and make the rest of his life a living hell if he pursued a divorce: Miller, *Plain Speaking*, p. 340. Neal argues that scholars have found no evidence that Eisenhower ever wrote the aforementioned "divorce" letter to General Marshall. He points to Ike and Mamie's wartime correspondence as proof that the couple missed each other and never mentioned divorce. Moreover, Eisenhower requested, but was denied permission to have Mamie join him in England: Neal, *The Eisenhowers*, pp. 175–179. John Eisenhower believes that the divorce letter referred to by President Truman was a "spiteful falsehood." He writes, "There is no evidence that divorce ever seriously crossed Dad's mind, even in the loneliest moments across the Atlantic": John S. D. Eisenhower, ed., *Letters to Mamie by Dwight D. Eisenhower* (Garden City, N.Y.: Doubleday, 1978), p. 12. Also see Brendon, *Ike*, pp. 191–192.

133. Neal, *The Eisenhowers*, p. 271.

134. Means, *Woman in the White House*, p. 253.

135. Brendon, *Ike*, p. 214.

136. Peter Lyon, *Eisenhower: Portrait of the Hero* (Boston: Little, Brown, 1974), p. 338; Means, *Woman in the White House*, p. 248.

137. John L. Moore (ed.), *Guide to U.S. Elections*, p. 294.

138. John L. Moore (ed.), *Guide to U.S. Elections*, p. 295.

139. "Mamie's Working Hard for Ike—Receptions, Handshakes," *U.S. News and World Report*, 35 (August 21, 1953), p. 54.

140. Neal, *The Eisenhowers*, p. 400.

141. This estimate is based on a survey of the *New York Times* and material furnished by the Eisenhower Library.

142. Nona Brown, "Being First Lady is a Man Sized Job," *New York Times*, May 18, 1953, p. 79.

143. Helen Thomas, interviewed by the author, Washington, D.C., June 6, 1979.

144. Bonnie Angelo, interviewed by Norma Ruth Holly Foreman, Washington, D.C., January 20, 1968. Quoted in Norma Ruth Holly Foreman, "The First Lady as a Leader of Public Opinion: A Study of the Role and Press Relations of Lady Bird Johnson" (unpublished doctoral dissertation, University of Texas at Austin, 1971), p. 84.

145. Marie Smith, interviewed by Norma Ruth Holly Foreman, Washington, D.C., January 20, 1968. Quoted in Foreman, "First Lady as Leader," p. 84.

146. Brendon, *Ike*, p. 42.

147. Elizabeth Henney, "Presenting: Mrs. Eisenhower," *Washington Post*, August 2, 1942, quoted in Martin M. Teasley, "Ike was Her Career: The Papers of Mamie Doud Eisenhower," *Prologue*, Vol. 19, Summer, 1987, p. 107.

148. John Eisenhower, *Strictly Personal* (Garden City, N.Y.: Doubleday, 1974), p. 10.

149. "Mrs. Dwight D. Eisenhower," Sketch 4057, February 1, 1960 (New York: the Associated Press Biographical Service), p. 2.

150. Means, *Woman in the White House*, p. 247.

151. Keesling and Cavanagh, "Women Presidential Appointees," pp. 1, 2, 32–35.

152. Helen Thomas interview, June 6, 1979.

153. George Gallup, *The Gallup Poll: Volume I, 1935–1948* (New York: Random, 1972), p. 775.

154. Gallup, *The Gallup Poll: Volume II, 1972–1977* p. 1113. Wilmington, Scholarly Resources, 1978.

155. Gallup, *The Gallup Poll: Volume II*, pp. 1220, 1299, 1462, 1584. Also see George Gallup, *The Gallup Poll: Volume III, 1959–1971* (New York: Random, 1972), pp. 1647, 1696.

3

THE EMERGING SPOKESWOMEN

Lou Hoover
Jacqueline Kennedy
Pat Nixon

Three women were moderately active as First Ladies and public communicators in the period of 1920 through 1989. Lou Hoover, Jacqueline Kennedy, and Pat Nixon expanded the ceremonial role of the First Lady, but were clearly more than mere presences in the White House. They began to change the First Lady's role from that of party-giver to emerging spokeswoman and involved, visible helpmate.

There is reason to believe that this group of First Ladies devoted some thought to how they could communicate their ideas and concerns to the American people. All seemed to have an awareness of their potential national audience and the benefits to be reaped by gaining its support.

To this end, there was a slight increase in rhetorical activity over that of their predecessors, the White Housekeepers," in rhetorical activity. While only Lou Hoover delivered formal speeches, the other two women also made occasional brief remarks or statements. Lou Hoover and Jacqueline Kennedy used the emerging communication mediums of radio and television respectively to transmit their ideas. Mrs. Kennedy and Mrs. Nixon used the press to publicize their White House projects.

The incipient spokeswomen were also more active privately. Mrs. Hoover influenced presidential decision making and was probably encouraged to take an active role as First Lady. Neither Mrs. Kennedy nor Mrs. Nixon was discouraged from pursuing such a course of action.

The activities of the incipient spokeswomen did not have the impact of those of the more active political surrogates and independent advocates, but they helped expand a largely ceremonial role to one of growing influence and consequence.

LOU HENRY HOOVER

The country was still enjoying prosperity when Herbert and Lou Hoover arrived at the White House on Inauguration Day, March 4, 1929. Wealthy and sophisticated, they had spent almost three decades circling the globe engaged in mining and, later, public service. For almost their entire marriage they were partners in numerous endeavors.

Route to the White House

Lou Henry, the first child of Charles Delano Henry and Florence Weed Henry, was born in Waterloo, Iowa, on March 29, 1875.[1]

In 1884, the family moved to Whittier, California, in an effort to ease Florence Henry's asthma. Lou and her younger sister Jean grew up in a home that blended work and recreation. Mrs. Henry taught them how to cook and sew, but also encouraged interest in music and the arts. Mr. Henry introduced the girls to the outdoors, instructing them in horseback riding, camping, hunting, woodcraft, and geology.

In 1890 the family moved to Monterey, California, again in search of a climate more beneficial to Mrs. Henry. Lou decided to prepare for a career in teaching, and in the fall of 1891 she enrolled in the State Normal School in Los Angeles. She only remained a year before transferring to the San Jose Normal School, from which she was graduated in 1894.

During the summer of 1894, Lou attended a lecture that was to change her life. "The Bones of the Earth," a lecture presented by Professor John Casper Branner, Chairman of the Department of Geology and Mines at Stanford University, revived Lou's early interest in geology.[2] In the fall of 1894 she enrolled at Stanford as a geology major. She was the only woman in the discipline, and often found herself defending her decision to major in that area.

One afternoon Dr. Branner was showing Lou some rock specimens when Herbert ("Bert") Hoover, his laboratory assistant, entered the laboratory. The professor introduced his two students, and then said: "Miss Henry thinks... that this rock belongs to the precarboniferous age. What do you think Hoover?"[3] Hoover blushed and said nothing.

After their initial meeting, Lou and Herbert spent a great deal of time together on geological field trips, hiking, and going to parties. When Hoover graduated from the university in 1895, they reached an informal understanding that they were engaged.

Herbert Hoover's first job was a two-dollar-a-day "mucker," pushing gold ore carts in California. In 1897 he was appointed manager of the Australian gold mining interests of the British firm of Bewick, Moreing and Company. When he was appointed chief engineer for the Chinese Bureau of Mines a year later, he cabled Lou in Monterey. "Would she marry him and live in China? The answer which came back was a single word, 'yes.' "[4]

Lou was graduated from Stanford in 1898. Though reared as an Episcopalian, she decided to embrace her soon-to-be husband's Quaker faith. They were married in the Henry's home on February 10, 1899. The next day, the young couple embarked for China.

The Hoovers landed at Tientsin, China, and took up residence in a house in the foreign settlement of the city. Lou entertained, began to collect Ming porcelain, and studied Chinese. She helped Bert "in the collecting, translating and summarizing of all the literature available on Chinese mining."[5] She had hoped to accompany her husband on his travels in China but was prohibited from doing so by the Chinese government because they deemed some of the trips too rough and dangerous for women.

In June 1900, China exploded with the outbreak of the Boxer Rebellion. The dowager Empress Tzi Hsi encouraged the Chinese to rid themselves of foreign influence. The foreign settlement at Tientsin became a target for shelling and other attacks. Hoover oversaw the building of a barricade around the besieged settlement. Lou dodged bullets as she rode her bicycle to the settlement hospital to help nurse the wounded. In mid-July, a combined force of English, American, Japanese, German, Russian, and French troops lifted the siege on the settlement. The Hoovers left for London.

At the age of twenty-seven, Herbert Hoover became a junior partner in Bewick, Moreing and Company. He and Lou were headquartered in London, the site of the Bewick, Moreing home office, but were dispatched all over the world to carry out various assignments.

Whenever possible, Lou accompanied Bert. Two children were born during these years of wandering: Herbert Clark in 1903 and Allen Henry in 1907. The children always traveled with their parents. Herbert, Jr., had been around the world three times before he was four years old.[6]

While in London, the Hoovers became interested in Agricola's sixteenth-century treatise on mining, De Re Mettallica. For the next five years they painstakingly translated the entire work. Lou translated the Latin of the volume while Bert identified the minerals and elements with laboratory tests. The Hoovers published the work privately, sending most of the edition to friends, scientists, and schools of geology and mining. The rest were sold at a nominal price.[7]

In 1908, Hoover sold his share in Bewick, Moreing and Company and set out on his own as an independent consulting mining engineer. During the next six years, he became chief consulting engineer and managing director of twenty mining companies. He amassed a fortune.

In the summer of 1914, when World War I broke out, the Hoovers were vacationing in London. Two hundred thousand Americans were stranded in Europe with no access to funds because almost "every government in the world declared a moratorium on finance; no one could secure a dime from the banks."[8] Most tourists traveled to London to try to obtain the monies necessary to book passage to the United States. Hoover set up a credit agency that extended loans totalling over one and a half million dollars to more than eight thousand Americans over six months of operation.[9] Lou organized an effort to clothe, feed, house, and entertain the tourists until they were able to leave England. Herbert Hoover wrote: "Mrs. Hoover's Women's Committee took over the job of caring for the unaccompanied women and children. A good deal of their work consisted in holding the hands of the frightened."[10] He also noted that thirty to forty thousand people sought the services of the committee.[11]

Hoover now turned his outstanding organizational abilities to feeding the people of occupied Belgium. Working as a "neutral volunteer," he was able to persuade the belligerent nations to allow food-laden ships of the Commission for Relief in Belgium to sail the Atlantic unmolested.

Lou was not idle during this crisis. She opened her home to volunteers who had come to aid her husband in the distribution of food. To raise money for food, she assisted the Belgians in organizing a marketing system to sell Belgian lace throughout the United States and England. Her principal war activity was with the American Women's Hospital at Paignton, which she helped organize and manage for the duration of the war.[12]

In 1917, President Wilson asked Hoover to return to the United States to head the United States Food Administration. Hoover endorsed a program of voluntary food conservation rather than rationing. "Food will win the war" became a popular slogan, and people began to "Hooverize," which was synonymous with the food conservation effort.[13]

Hoover enlisted his wife's aid in guaranteeing the success of his program. She gave speeches to various groups endorsing the Food Administration program. Additionally, Lou assisted the hundreds of young women working for the Food Administration and other agencies in securing housing in Washington by organizing the Food Administration Girls Club.[14]

This was also the year that Lou became actively involved in Girl Scouting, serving as leader to Washington's Troop Eight. She and her troop grew a victory garden to demonstrate support for food conservation.

In March 1921, Herbert Hoover began his duties as Secretary of Commerce in the administration of President Warren G. Harding.[15] The cabinet years were hectic but satisfying for Lou Hoover. She became National President of the Girl Scouts in 1922. The following year saw her elected Vice President of the National Amateur Athletic Federation (she would continue her association with this organization until 1940). She organized a woman's division of the federation and set up an advisory committee composed of the directors of physical education at women's colleges in the United States. The purpose of this committee was to promote physical training for girls in every institution.[16] Mrs. Hoover, however, "opposed highly competitive professional athletics for women for physiological reasons and believed it would destroy play for play's sake."[17]

When the Teapot Dome scandal was disclosed, Lou called a conference on law enforcement. In her opening address she told 1,500 delegates that it was up to women to "arouse the whole country to an understanding of the dangerous significance of continued evasion of the law."[18]

After President Coolidge announced his intention not to run in 1928, the Republicans turned to Hoover as their candidate. He was nominated on the first ballot at the Republican National Convention in Kansas City.

Promising "a chicken in every pot," Hoover campaigned vigorously, crossing the country by train. Lou was an enthusiastic if relatively quiet campaigner, standing beside her husband uttering a few phrases whenever the occasion demanded a response. She was extremely popular with the crowds they drew.[19] Herbert Hoover was elected the thirtieth President of the United States, carrying forty of forty-eight states with a popular vote of 21,411,911.[20]

Herbert Hoover had been one of a small group of people who warned publicly against stock and real estate speculation as early as 1926.[21] When he became President, Hoover tried to reverse the inflationary policies of his predecessors. He asked newspapers and magazines to warn their readers against speculation, and persuaded Secretary of the Treasury Andrew Mellon to suggest to investors that they convert their stocks into bonds.[22] These efforts were to no avail, and in the eighth month of Herbert Hoover's administration, the stock market crashed.

Hoover worked hard to try to reverse the effects of the crash. He put in long hours and refused to take vacations. His only respite was brief weekends at his Virginia retreat, Camp Rapidan.

As she had done so many times during their marriage, Mrs. Hoover tried to ease her husband's burden by standing in for him on ceremonial occasions whenever possible, supporting his Depression relief programs in statements and speeches, and encouraging him during difficult times.

The First Lady campaigned with the President for his reelection in 1932. While Hoover was not surprised by his defeat, Lou Hoover was bitter and angry that the country had repudiated this man who had given so much of his life to public service.[23] A friend remarked, "it was a great shock to Mrs. Hoover, and I don't think she ever got over it, because she was so fond of him and she didn't like anything to go against him."[24]

The Hoovers retired to New York but continued to lead active lives. Mrs. Hoover worked with the Girl Scouts, and in 1940 became honorary chairman of the American Women's Division of the Commission for Relief in Belgium. Lou Hoover died of a heart attack in New York on January 7, 1944. Herbert Hoover succumbed on October 20, 1964.

Major Communication Activities of the First Lady

Lou Hoover was the first First Lady in the twentieth century to give formal speeches. She gave a total of fifteen speeches, supporting her husband's Depression relief programs, discussing the Girl Scouts and other youth organizations, and addressing a number of groups on ceremonial occasions. The whole country was able to listen to her statements, for Mrs. Hoover was the First Lady to broadcast her addresses over the radio.[25]

Some of Mrs. Hoover's actions were reminiscent of those of less active First Ladies. She accompanied her husband during the presidential campaigns of 1928 and 1932, but said nothing. The First Lady's press relations were strained because she instituted a no-interview, no-quote policy.

Despite her press policy and lack of participation in campaigning, Lou Hoover began the metamorphosis of the First Lady from silent partner to a more active, publicly involved partner.

Advocacy. As First Lady, Mrs. Hoover's best known association was with the Girl Scouts. For almost three decades, beginning in 1914, she was actively involved in the organization serving as National President, Vice President, and Chairman of the Board. Working with Girl Scout founder Juliette Low, Mrs. Hoover raised money and dramatically increased membership in the organization from 13,000 in 1917 to 840,000 girls by 1924. She supported the concept of summer day camp and sponsored the first national Girl Scout cookie sale.[26]

Mrs. Hoover believed that scouting developed vigor, fearlessness, and initiative in women.[27] Scouts, she felt, should engage in outdoor activities and community service.[28] Futhermore, the First Lady felt that the homemaking component of the Girl Scout program was important, and often expressed sentiments similar to those described to reporters when she attended the 1930 Girl Scout National Convention: "The housewife who stands at the kitchen sink washing dishes three times a day is not a bit less courageous than the big game hunter."[29] Almost half of her White House speeches were delivered to Girl Scout audiences.

Mrs. Hoover's efforts did not end with raising money, giving speeches, and making executive decisions about the National Girl Scouts organization. She visited and received troops of Girl Scouts at the White House, inspected their campsites, and joined them in their activities.

Though she engaged in no other activities to dramatize her commitment, Mrs. Hoover was concerned with women's efforts to relieve the severity of the Depression and delivered two speeches on the topic. In the first speech, in March 1931, she praised the achievements of women and girls in the difficult time of unemployment and drought.[30] In November 1932, she strongly urged that all women become involved in some Depression relief work. She discussed services that volunteers might render to those in distress. She said women could help "in finding those who, because they have never needed aid before are ashamed to ask for it, and in determining how these people may be aided without hurting their pride."[31] Additionally, they could aid relief efforts "by adding assistance to any movement, legislative or otherwise, designed to keep the hospitals and visiting nurse associations maintained."[32]

Two other activities of Mrs. Hoover's term in the White House were conducted in public silence and did not come to light until years after her death. Both the President and the First Lady donated money to a variety of causes. On one occasion the President gave his wife a large sum of money (approximately one million dollars) and told her that she could use it in any manner she wished as he desired no accounting of how it was spent. During the Depression, Mrs.

Hoover received countless letters from people all over the country asking for money. She had her secretaries discreetly investigate the claims.[33] If they were genuine, Mrs. Hoover arranged for the person to receive money from her but via an anonymous source or social agency. Mrs. Hoover's philanthropy continued through the Depression; she was responsible for the college education of many young people.[34]

The Hoovers' philanthrophy took another form. At the beginning of his term as President, Mrs. Hoover realized that her husband would occasionally need to escape the pressures of Washington and she began to look for an appropriate retreat. She found the location she had hoped for in the Blue Ridge Mountains of Madison County, Virginia, on the Rapidan River. Mrs. Hoover thus designed Camp Rapidan, a rustic vacation spot for the President of the United States.

When the Hoovers began camping on the Rapidan, they found that there was no school for the children of the region to attend. They "built a school and hired and paid a teacher to conduct classes."[35]

After they left Washington, the Hoovers donated Camp Rapidan and the school to the Shenandoah National Park with the proviso that the Park Service maintain the school and that the camp always be available for use by Girl or Boy Scout groups.[36]

The White House itself was one of Mrs. Hoover's concerns. When the Hoovers took up residence at 1600 Pennsylvania Avenue, they were disappointed with both their private rooms and the state rooms. Mrs. Hoover, like Mrs. Coolidge, was dismayed that the executive mansion contained very few pieces of furniture that dated back to the original occupants.

The First Lady began the restoration of the Lincoln Bedroom and the Monroe (Red) Room, and the first systematic cataloging of White House furnishings. Mrs. Hoover hired and personally subsidized Mrs. Dare McMullin to aid her in writing a book about the furnishings. The book was not completed until the Hoovers had left the White House; it was never published.[37]

Ceremonial Presence. As First Lady, Mrs. Hoover continued to be as active as she had in years past. She faithfully fulfilled the social and ceremonial obligations incumbent upon the mistress of the White House, and participated in approximately 481 activities from March 1929 to March 1933.[38]

While she welcomed all groups and delegations to the executive mansion, Mrs. Hoover was especially partial to aggregations of children and young people and any activities that would benefit them. One-third of Mrs. Hoover's ceremonial activities had some connection with youth.

Mrs. Hoover was not enamoured of some of the customs of social Washington. Years before, as the wife of the Secretary of Commerce, she had successfully led a quiet revolt against the practice of "leaving cards." Mrs. Hoover found the custom to be a waste of time and successfully persuaded the wives of other Harding cabinet members to abandon the ritual.[39]

As First Lady, Mrs. Hoover wished to changed other customs, but felt guilty about tampering with tradition. Some of the events of the official social season might have been discontinued if she had been less respectful. President Hoover acknowledged this when he wrote: "Mrs. Hoover's rigid sense of duty would not permit abolishing formal receptions. To her, it was part of the job."[40] The social season remained more or less intact.

There were two changes that Mrs. Hoover did make, however. She abolished the annual New Year's Day Reception, at which any citizen could shake the hand of the President, because she felt it was too much of a drain on the Chief Executive's energy. She also invited pregnant women to stand on her reception lines. Previously, a pregnant woman was expected to "retire" from public life once her condition became obvious.[41]

Mrs. Hoover's desire to discharge her social responsibilities fully resulted in a single but ugly controversy during her tenure as First Lady. On June 12, 1929, the First Lady invited the wife of black Congressman Oscar DePriest to tea at the White House. The invitation extended to Mrs. DePriest was not extraordinary; the First Lady received the wives of congressmen at the White House every year. However, a black person had only been invited to the White House once before, in 1901 when President Theodore Roosevelt had asked Booker T. Washington to lunch. That visit too had stirred controversy, but not as much as was to develop over the DePriest visit. Prior to the visit, Mrs. Hoover carefully divided the congressmen's wives into various groups and confirmed that those invited with Mrs. DePriest would not be offended by the black woman's presence. The event itself took place as scheduled and proceeded without incident.

The Southern press and various Southern congressional delegations did not look favorably on Mrs. Hoover's actions. *The Mobile Press* (Mobile, Alabama) expressed the opinion that in inviting Mrs. DePriest to the White House, Mrs. Hoover had "offered to the South and to the nation an arrogant insult."[42] *The Commercial Appeal* (Memphis, Tennessee) excoriated Mrs. Hoover, and suggested, "It might be advisable to drop the 'White' from the White House now that the DePriest tea party has added another tint."[43] *The Birmingham Age-Herald* (Birmingham, Alabama) drew a distinction between the White House visit of Booker T. Washington and Mrs. DePriest. "What was a meeting between Roosevelt and Washington contrasts with this later exclusively and intrinsically social event."[44]

The Georgia House of Representatives passed a resolution expressing "regret over recent occurances [sic] in the official and social life of the national capital, which have a tendency to revive and intensify racial discord."[45] The Texas and Florida Houses joined their confreres in Georgia by passing resolutions rebuking Mrs. Hoover for her actions.

The Eastern press almost unanimously lauded Mrs. Hoover's decision to entertain Mrs. DePriest. An editorial in the *Nation* concluded, "Mrs. Hoover is to be congratulated for the human decency of her act and for the dignified silence she has maintained since."[46]

President Hoover staunchly supported his wife. He wrote that she had been deeply hurt by the speeches, editorials, and resolutions condemning her actions.

Nonetheless, she stood behind her decision and "her tears . . . did not melt her indomitable determination. I sought to divert the lightning by at once inviting Dr. Moton of Tuskeegee to lunch with me. The White House was thus 'defiled' several times during my term."[47]

After a few weeks, other news stories took precedence over the DePriest visit; and gradually it was forgotten. With the exception of this controversy, Mrs. Hoover's days proceeded without incident.

Approaches to Communication

Preparation for Speaking. There is no information on Mrs. Hoover's preparation for speaking, but it is safe to assume that she had not received any formal speech training. However, she did acquire extensive "on-the-job" training, and had delivered over sixty speeches before entering the White House.[48] Many of the speeches were devoted to the Girl Scouts, but there were additional discourses on the Belgian Relief, saving food, and women in athletics. As First Lady, Mrs. Hoover gave approximately fifteen speeches, for which she prepared her own remarks.[49]

Communication Style and Delivery. Mrs. Hoover's speeches were simple and straightforward; they lacked any imagistic or stylistic devices. The First Lady used unembellished language to make her point.

Mrs. Hoover spoke rapidly with a slight regional accent. Her radio speeches had a distinctive "tinny" quality; this may have been due, at least in part, to the quality of early audio equipment. As few women used radio, the equipment was not yet adjusted to their vocal range.

Press Relations. After traveling with the Hoovers during the 1928 presidential campaign, reporter Bess Furman commented, "Mrs. Hoover was no particular help to the press."[50] Mrs. Hoover found the press to be a necessary evil; she tolerated their intrusion but generally ignored reporters.

As First Lady, Lou Hoover refused to grant interviews or to be quoted. A major reason for this could be that Mrs. Hoover held the press and its accuracy in low regard. On one occasion she told reporters "that she had even had a three column obituary printed 27 years previous when she had been reported dead in the Boxer Rebellion."[51] The Hoover Library retains a file entitled "Misrepresentations" which contains Mrs. Hoover's handwritten reactions to numerous erroneous news stories.[52] In a particularly candid letter to a friend, Mrs. Hoover criticized journalism and journalists: "Our modern journals and editors are, of course, most to blame [for rumors and half-truths]. Do we know any of them who insist upon truth in their pages at any sacrifice?"[53]

Mrs. Hoover permitted reporters to cover state functions in much the same manner as had her predecessors. Prior to these events, reporters were permitted to view the table decorations, refreshments, and guest lists. Then they returned to their desks to write their stories. Very few reporters ever had the opportunity to report on Hoover White House functions firsthand.[54]

Even during the 1932 presidential campaign, when she and her husband might have benefitted from their help, Mrs. Hoover remained aloof from reporters. This greatly annoyed those reporters covering the First Lady, as Mrs. Franklin D. Roosevelt was granting interviews daily on the Roosevelt campaign train.[55]

A historian expresses the opinion that Mrs. Hoover would have benefitted from more effective press relations and writes, "The American people were provided only the barest glimpse of her naturalness and gregariousness, which might have mitigated the impression of indifference and severity for their [the Hoover] years in the White House."[56]

Factors That Influenced the First Lady's Performance as Public Communicator

Relationship with Her Husband. The Hoovers had a genuinely symbiotic relationship for all the years of their marriage. They traveled the world together, raising their children, working, and dispensing aid wherever and whenever it was needed.

The Hoovers' personalities complemented one another, and "her outgoing social graces compensated for his awkward shyness."[57] A linguist, horsewoman, antique collector, and hostess, Lou brought a humanizing influence into her husband's life.

In the White House, Mrs. Hoover became especially protective of the President. Alonzo Fields, a White House butler, noted that if the First Lady felt the President was being drawn into a conversation he would rather avoid, she would change the topic "in a flash."[58] A former secretary remarked: "Above all, she was supportive of her husband and his interests came first. . . . [S]he never accepted any engagement . . . without being sure that her husband would not need her."[59]

Herbert Hoover could accept criticism of his ideas and policies, but Lou could not. Later the President wrote: "She was oversensitive, and the stabs of political life, which, no doubt, were deserved by me hurt her greatly. She was deeply religious, and to her such actions were were just plain wickedness."[60] The Hoovers were equal partners in an interesting and productive life together.

Access to Presidential Decision Making. While the First Lady might not have made suggestions about foreign affairs, she probably shared her perspectives on domestic policy with the President. She enthusiastically supported his measures to combat the Depression, and made numerous statements and speeches to publicize her support. It is likely that President Hoover discussed prospective appointees with the First Lady and listened carefully to her evaluations.[61]

The Hoover's marital relationship itself presents the strongest reason for believing that the First Lady influenced the President's thinking. They were equals, they were partners, and they depended on each other.

The President's and First Lady's Perceptions of Women. Herbert Hoover's perception of women was probably influenced by his religious beliefs and by his wife. As a Quaker, Hoover believed that women were equal to men. Lou Hoover, an original and independent woman, helped to reinforce her husband's religious beliefs.

Mrs. Hoover felt that women could accomplish any task. She was an early but gentle advocate of feminism,[62] and while the First Lady's "feminist activities would be considered moderate by today's standards, they were advanced and innovative for her time."[63] Prior to and during her time as First Lady, Mrs. Hoover supported the idea of women in athletics, encouraged women to vote, and felt that women could influence politics in a positive way. "She also urged women to . . . choose independent careers even if they were married, once telling a 1926 Girl Scout convention that the woman who uses her children as an excuse for not pursuing professional interests was lazy."[64] One of Mrs. Hoover's friends presents a slightly different perspective. She observes: "I think she was an active feminist but she didn't carry a hatchet. . . . She was an active woman in active women's liberation but not an aggressive one."[65]

Herbert Hoover had respected and utilized the talents of women in his many endeavors, including the Food Administration, the Commerce Department, and the Mississippi Flood Relief Program. As President, Hoover signed legislation favorable to women and appointed them to positions within his administration.

In December 1932, President Hoover signed Executive Order 5984, Amendment of Civil Service Rule VII. This rule concerned certification of nominees for Civil Service vacancies and specified that the selection process should be carried out "without regard to sex."[66] Archivists at the Hoover Library believe that this was the first time any executive order or legislation contained this phrase; it was a modest victory but showed that the movement to eliminate sex discrimination had begun.[67]

Twenty women served in high-level positions during Herbert Hoover's White House tenure. Seven women were selected by Mr. Hoover; thirteen had been appointed to their positions in previous administrations.[68] An additional thirty-five women were appointed to government commissions.[69]

Lou Hoover became the first First Lady in the twentieth century who could genuinely be called a public communicator. She was interested in communication, and used written articles, speeches, and radio broadcasts to share her views. The use of the new medium of radio is significant because the First Lady lent legitimacy to this tool of communication and could use it to address a national constituency.

Mrs. Hoover selected no major projects or causes, but pursued a number of interests in public silence. She was an advocate of women and probably influenced presidential decision making.

Lou Hoover was not as innovative or involved in her husband's administration as her successor, Eleanor Roosevelt. She did, however, begin to expand the role of First Lady from party-giver to doer. Her attempts to enlarge the scope of the First Lady's communication efforts were successful, and so eased the way for Mrs. Roosevelt.

JACQUELINE BOUVIER KENNEDY

Nineteen-sixty marked a turning point in the history of the First Lady as public communicator. Television played a significant role in the presidential election that year; the American people saw, heard, and became familiar with candidates John F. Kennedy and Richard M. Nixon. The new medium also generated increased interest in the candidates' wives.

After his victory, John F. Kennedy became the first television President and Jacqueline Kennedy became the first television First Lady.[70] Both Kennedys were well-suited to television and used the medium effectively. Their youth, good looks, style, and sense of confidence projected well.

Public and media interest in the Kennedys was intense. To deal with the increasing barrage of media requests, Jacqueline Kennedy appointed the first press secretary to the First Lady, an acknowledgment of the growth and increasing importance of all media.

A reluctant First Lady, Jacqueline Kennedy spent much of her White House tenure attempting to avoid communicating. However, she had projects that she hoped to advance and some contact with the public was necessary.

Route to the White House

On July 28, 1929, a daughter, Jacqueline Lee, was born to Janet Lee Bouvier and John Vernau Bouvier III of Easthampton, Long Island and New York City, New York.[71] The Bouviers were wealthy, sophisticated members of the social register. They lived in a world of horse shows, fox hunts, formal balls, and grand tours of Europe.

Young Jacqueline had the sort of youth befitting one of position and affluence. By the age of two, her name was already being mentioned in society columns.[72] Her mother was a skilled horsewoman and Jacqueline was instructed in the fine points of equestrian art. At age five she was riding in horse shows with her mother. She attended Miss Chapin's, a fashionable school in New York. She was a bright, independent, solitary student who enjoyed reading, writing, and poetry.

John "Black Jack" Bouvier was the most important person in Jacqueline's life. She adored her dark, swarthy, playful father. The relationship between the two was warm and loving. Unfortunately, the relationship between Janet and Jack was deteriorating as rumors of her husband's infidelities reached Janet's ears. Her parents' separation and subsequent divorce in 1940 was very painful for Jacqueline. Still devoted to her father, she looked forward to their weekends together. Their meetings became infrequent when Janet wed wealthy Washington, D.C., stockbroker Hugh D. Auchincloss.

At the age of fifteen, Jacqueline was sent to the exclusive Miss Porter's School in Farmington, Connecticut. She had grown into a beautiful young woman with a penchant for languages, acting, painting, and writing. Her yearbook at Miss

Porter's noted that Miss Bouvier's ambition was "not to be a housewife."[73] Jacqueline was presented to society in a social debut in 1947.

She began her college education at Vassar in the fall of 1947. She spent two years there and then won *Vogue's* Prix de Paris, which included a year's scholarship to the Sorbonne in Paris. The year abroad affected Jacqueline immeasurably. She became fluent in French, studied French art and history, and became passionately pro-French.[74] She returned to the United States to complete her education and graduated from George Washington University in 1951.

Through the intervention of a family friend, Jackie landed a job with the *Washington Times-Herald* as their $42.50-a-week "Inquiring Camera Girl."[75] Her job consisted of asking people for their reaction to various questions and taking their picture.

One of the people she interviewed for the column was Senator John F. Kennedy of Massachusetts. (She had met Kennedy previously at a dinner party, but had not realized the then Representative from Massachusetts was busy campaigning for the Senate.) Jacqueline considered Kennedy quixotic "because he had the temerity to state that he 'intended to become President.' "[76]

Kennedy called Jacqueline after the election and the couple began to date. Their courtship was sporadic and at times difficult for Jackie. Kennedy was not an overly affectionate man, and often would not contact her for a period of months. When they did spend time together, it was often passed with the extended Kennedy family at Hyannisport, Massachusetts. Eventually the relationship became serious, and in June of 1953, Jack and Jackie announced their engagement. The couple was married on September 12, 1953.

Following their honeymoon, the Kennedys set up housekeeping in Washington. Naive about the realities of political life, Jackie did not enjoy her role as the wife of the junior Senator from Massachusetts. She was uncomfortable with the politicians she was supposed to entertain, and was frankly bored with the endless discussions of strategy and legislation.

Their marriage was beginning to show signs of strain when Kennedy underwent double spinal-fusion surgery for recurring back problems (resulting from World War II injuries) in October 1954. The surgery was unsuccessful and he was not expected to live. He recovered but remained in constant pain. A second operation followed in February 1955; this surgery was successful, and Kennedy spent his convalescence at his father's home in Palm Beach, Florida.

During the long period of recuperation, Kennedy worked on a book about choices and bravery in politics. Aided by senatorial assistant Theodore Sorensen and Jackie, who helped to coordinate information, he produced *Profiles in Courage*, which later won the 1957 Pulitzer Prize for biography.

Eight months later, Kennedy returned to the capital and began his campaign for the Democratic vice presidential nomination in 1956. The Kennedy clan enthusiastically geared up for the coming fight, but Jackie recoiled at the idea of a national campaign. In fact, the family was uncertain how to present the cultured and aristocratic Jacqueline to the country.

They need not have worried, because Jackie became pregnant and was unable to participate in much of the campaign. When she was well enough to play any role at all, it was only a minor one.

Kennedy came close, but lost the vice presidential nomination by a narrow margin. Looking to a presidential race in 1960, he felt it necessary to demonstrate his popularity in Massachusetts to a potential national audience by being re-elected by a sizable margin in 1958. Jackie was shy and disliked politics, but she accompanied her husband everywhere during the campaign.[77]

There were two reasons for the Kennedys to celebrate in 1957. Jack was reelected to the Senate by the considerable margin he had hoped for, and, after two miscarriages, a child, Caroline, was born to the Kennedys on November 27.

On January 2, 1960, John F. Kennedy announced that he was a candidate for President of the United States. Though she would later be incapacitated by her fourth pregnancy, Mrs. Kennedy was active in the early part of her husband's primary campaign. Her mother-in-law Rose Kennedy expressed the family's surprise at discovering that Jackie was an unexpectedly good campaigner. Rose wrote: "She was not a natural born campaigner. But there she was travelling with Jack in motorcades, standing in lines, shaking hands along main streets, and even taking off on her own. . . . She was a wonder."[78]

Jackie campaigned for her husband in Wisconsin and West Virginia. Theodore Sorensen observed that Kennedy "spoke in every town and hamlet [in West Virginia], Jacqueline tirelessly at his side."[79] Jacqueline told an interviewer that she found campaigning tiring but exhilarating.[80] The combination of primary victories, a superbly organized campaign staff, and canny convention maneu-vering by campaign manager Robert Kennedy gave John F. Kennedy the nom-ination he sought on July 13, 1960.

By this time, Mrs. Kennedy was in the latter stages of pregnancy and had retired from all strenuous activity. One of her contributions to the presidential campaign was to write a short weekly newsletter entitled "Campaign Wife" that was distributed to Democratic Party workers.

On November 8, 1960, John F. Kennedy was elected President of the United States by the slimmest margin ever recorded in a general election: 114,673 votes.[81] At forty-three years of age, John Kennedy was the youngest man ever to be elected President. At thirty-one, Jacqueline was the third youngest First Lady, and the first to be born in the twentieth century.[82] Seventeen days after the election, a son, John Fitzgerald, Jr., was born to the Kennedys.

Various adjectives have been used to describe the Kennedy White House years. Words like vibrant, exhilarating, exciting, and exhausting are often em-ployed, while sentimentalists prefer to think of the administration as "Camelot." Many people, such as Mrs. Gerald Ford, feel that this time was "just fun."[83]

The Kennedys brought youth and style to the White House. Despite being reticent about meeting new people, growing ever contemptuous of intrusions by reporters, and dealing with a social schedule she did not always enjoy,

Jacqueline evidenced a positive change as First Lady. The Bouviers felt that Jacqueline "blossomed in the White House as never before. . . . [S]he could. . . be herself and get away with it."[84]

While her husband was concerned with the Bay of Pigs, Berlin, the Cuban Missile Crisis, inflation, and recession, Jacqueline Kennedy busied herself with restoring the White House and augmenting national interest in culture. The First Lady was not concerned with substantive issues, yet her way of accomplishing her goals, her presence at state dinners and parties, her trips abroad, and her flair, lent the Kennedy administration a sense of regalness.

In mid-November 1963, John F. Kennedy embarked on a short, pre–1964-campaign trip to Texas. Mrs. Kennedy accompanied him, her first public appearance since the death of the Kennedy's newborn son Patrick in August 1963. The usually reserved Mrs. Kennedy was particularly happy on the trip, telling the President, "I'll go anywhere with you this year."[85]

The happiness of that day—indeed all the glitter and promise of the Kennedy administration—was to end abruptly as the President of the United States was shot to death by a sniper as he rode through the streets of Dallas, Texas, on November 22, 1963.

Jacqueline Bouvier Kennedy left the White House with her children and lived briefly in Georgetown. Continuously annoyed by the press and curious onlookers, she then left Washington and moved to New York City. On October 20, 1968, Mrs. Kennedy was married to Greek shipping magnate Aristotle Onassis. She was widowed for a second time when Onassis died seven years later.

Jacqueline Kennedy Onassis currently resides in New York City. She is employed as an editor at Doubleday and Company, and remains one of the most popular women in the world.

Major Communication Activities of the First Lady

Following the 1960 election, Mrs. Kennedy was asked what she would do in the White House. She said, perhaps only half in jest, "I'll get pregnant and stay pregnant, it's the only way out."[86]

Various writers report that Mrs. Kennedy was almost despondent at the prospect of being First Lady.[87] She was thirty-one years old, had two very young children, found politics distasteful, and did not happily anticipate her White House duties. She was uncomfortable with the title of First Lady, and insisted that White House servants simply call her "Mrs. Kennedy."[88]

Mrs. Kennedy did not see her role as an advisor to the President or as a politician. She stated her feelings on the topic when she told a reporter that the most important role for the First Lady was to take care of her husband so that he could be the best possible President.[89] In another interview, Mrs. Kennedy explained that her official activities took her away from her family and, "if I were to add political duties, I would have practically no time with my children and they are my first responsibility."[90]

Though ambivalent, Jacqueline Kennedy engaged in some activities as public communicator. She hoped to refurbish the White House, and this project required publicity and national attention to succeed. The First Lady made a number of statements and gave press interviews about her project; later, she conducted a televised tour of the White House to display the results of her work. Mrs. Kennedy also used communication activities to dramatize her commitment to the arts and culture.

The First Lady begrudgingly took on some official duties while enthusiastically embracing others. Her penchant for style and drama made her one of the most popular First Ladies in history.

Advocacy. There is disagreement as to who was initially responsible for the idea of restoring the White House, but it seems that Mrs. Kennedy was planning the refurbishment well before she took up residence at 1600 Pennsylvania Avenue. With the help of Clark Clifford, Mrs. Kennedy set up the White House Historical Association. Later she enlisted the aid of John Walker, Director of the National Gallery of Art, and a variety of other people prominent in the art world to work on her newly established Committee of the Fine Arts Commission for the White House. The First Lady assisted in preparing "legislation designating the White House as a museum and enabling it to receive gifts."[91]

A campaign to secure private funding for the restoration was initiated. Money (including a $100,000 congressional appropriation), antiques, and paintings poured into the White House.[92] Mrs. Kennedy searched the White House basement and other government warehouses for authentic pieces. The First Lady also initiated and edited the first *White House Guidebook*, which identified all the important furnishings in the newly refurbished executive mansion. The guidebook, which went on sale to tourists for the price of one dollar, was a huge success, and according to J. B. West, former Chief Usher at the White House, it "entirely financed the restoration."[93] Finally, Mrs. Kennedy created the permanent position of White House Curator.[94]

On February 14, 1962, the American public was afforded the chance to observe the results of Mrs. Kennedy's highly publicized restoration. An estimated forty-six million people tuned into "Jacqueline Kennedy's Tour of the White House."[95] Mrs. Kennedy prepared the script for the tour with help from John Walker of the National Gallery and Lorraine Pearce, the White House Curator.[96] Viewer response was enthusiastic.[97]

The televised tour of the executive mansion, the first ever, reflected Mrs. Kennedy's careful work and helped to increase interest in the White House. In the same year, the number of visitors "was nearly two-thirds greater than in 1960."[98] Mrs. Kennedy's efforts were rewarded in another manner when she was awarded an Emmy for the televised tour.

The First Lady hoped to stimulate interest in the arts and all culture by inviting distinguished artists to perform at the White House. To this end, Pablo Casals, opera singer Grace Bumbry, Eugene Istomin, Isaac Stern, Igor Stravinsky, actor Frederic March, and the Metropolitan Opera entertained at State dinners and parties. Mrs. Kennedy sponsored and occasionally hosted a series of musical programs for young people at the White House.

Ceremonial Presence. Two changes that affected Washington social life occurred during Jacqueline Kennedy's White House tenure. First, she effectively ended the traditional social season. "The inauguration was quite enough," she told J. B. West.[99] Second, she altered the nature of White House entertaining. White-tie and six-course dinners were replaced by more informal but still dignified evenings at the executive mansion.

The Kennedy State dinners, frequently directed by the First Lady, were glittering and impressive.[100] Of particular note was the State dinner in honor of President Mohammed Ayub Kahn of Pakistan in July 1961. The evening, which consisted of transporting food, guests, workers, and musicians by boat to Mount Vernon, former home of George Washington, was one of the most glittering and memorable social achievements of the Kennedy administration. President Ayub was only one of sixty-six heads of state to be entertained by the Kennedys.

As First Lady, Mrs. Kennedy traveled a great deal in both an official and unofficial capacity. With the President she visited France, Canada, Mexico, Venezuela, Austria, Puerto Rico, and Columbia. On her own she toured Italy, Pakistan, India, and Greece. The First Lady traveled so much that a columnist once cracked "Goodnight Mrs. Kennedy, wherever you are."[101]

Mrs. Kennedy found some aspects of being First Lady to be tedious and boring, and her behavior occasionally provoked angry comments and embarrassed the Kennedy administration. In June 1962, Columbian President Guillermo Valencia and his wife were visiting the White House. Mrs. Kennedy sent word that she was ill and would not attend the scheduled dinner. Unfortunately, "the day that the dinner party was reported in the press, there was a picture of Mrs. Kennedy water skiing with John Glenn."[102] Mrs. Kennedy caused even more consternation in 1962 when she refused to see Mrs. Alejandrina Villeda-Morales, wife of the President of Honduras, who was visiting Peace Corps volunteer trainees before they were sent off to her country.[103]

Mrs. Kennedy's rudeness was not confined to international circles; she also upset people at home in the United States. She refused to attend political functions and ruled out participation in many of the "social concern" projects embraced by her predecessors. On at least one occasion, the President "stood in" for his wife when she announced herself to be "unavailable."[104]

Mrs. Kennedy was a participant in 166 events from January through November 1963.[105] She was assisted in her duties by social secretary Letitia "Tish" Baldridge and a large staff. The aggressive and efficient Miss Baldridge was later succeeded by Nancy Tuckerman.

Jacqueline Bouvier Kennedy was intelligent, elegant, and immensely popular, but at times she could also be petty and unpleasant, a liability to the Kennedy administration rather than the asset she sometimes was.

Approaches to Communication

During her White House years, Mrs. Kennedy made extended remarks on four occasions; on two of these occasions she spoke in a foreign language. The First Lady made more brief remarks when she thanked groups for visiting the White House and for aiding her in the White House restoration project. All her remarks were ceremonial in nature and were probably prepared by the First Lady herself.

Preparation for Speaking. Mrs. Kennedy's first exposure to audiences probably came in 1958, when her husband was running for reelection. She made brief remarks during the 1960 primary campaigns in Wisconsin and West Virginia, and she also delivered a short taped message that was broadcast just prior to Election Day, 1960, to urge voters to cast their ballots for the Kennedy-Johnson ticket.

Communication Style and Delivery. Mrs. Kennedy had always been a gifted linguist, and she was able to employ her talents when she visited foreign countries. When she visited Paris with the President in May 1961, the First Lady spoke to French President Charles de Gaulle and the French people in faultless French. When she and the President visited Mexico and Venezuela, she spoke in Spanish. In a 1964 interview, Mrs. Kennedy revealed that at least one reason for her discourses in French, Spanish, and Italian was that her husband had no facility with foreign languages.[106]

Mrs. Kennedy spoke softly in a whispery voice. A Kennedy family friend described it as a "sort of rather eager, breathless way of talking."[107]

Press Relations. Possibly because she had some understanding of press demands, having once been employed by the *Washington Times-Herald*, Mrs. Kennedy appointed the first full-time press secretary to her staff. The selection of twenty-three-year-old Pamela Turnure, who saw her job as helping to preserve Mrs. Kennedy's privacy and not create publicity, did not, however, please the press.[108] Helen Thomas said of Turnure that she "had about as much business being press secretary as I would have directing the space agency."[109]

Even though Turnure was Mrs. Kennedy's officially designated press secretary, the President's press secretary Pierre Salinger announced that he would release news of the First Lady. "Turnure," he said, "would serve as a liaison between himself, Social Secretary Letitia Baldrige and Mrs. Kennedy and she would provide reporters with lists of the First Lady's official appointments outside of the White House."[110] The arrangement did not work, and Salinger "threw all of the questions involving society . . . and millinery back to Pamela."[111]

Mrs. Kennedy could manipulate the press when she felt the need. Bonnie Angelo, White House correspondent for *Time* during the Kennedy years, said that the First Lady brought in the press when she "decided public opinion would help on her White House restoration project and pushed them aside on other stories which had wider reader interest."[112] Other reporters found that Mrs. Kennedy's attitude toward the press "seemed to run hot and cold."[113]

Occasionally the First Lady would write notes to reporters praising them for a particularly good story; at other times, she would try to have them barred from covering official events.[114] Helen Thomas writes that Mrs. Kennedy considered the press (especially Thomas and Francis Lewine of the Associated Press) to be "harpies" and intruders; with a regal attitude she ignored reporters.[115] Another newswoman commented that Mrs. Kennedy considered a few of the society reporters "repulsive."[116]

Mrs. Kennedy's personal feelings about reporters were made public when one of her private memoranda was published in 1969. The First Lady suggested "placing a few aides with bayonets near them [reporters]" through state dinners.[117]

Stories about the White House restoration and Mrs. Kennedy's travels were numerous and generally positive, but nonetheless the First Lady undoubtedly saw the press as an adversary. At best, Jacqueline Kennedy's press relations were strained.

Factors That Influenced the First Lady's Performance as Public Communicator

Relationship with Her Husband. The relationship of Jacqueline and John Kennedy has long been the subject of speculation in scores of sensational books and hundreds of newspaper and magazine articles. Evidence from serious authors tends to corroborate the widely held belief that Mr. Kennedy was engaged in extramarital affairs in both the pre–White House and White House period.[118]

The Kennedys had a stormy early marriage. Undoubtedly the requirements and demands of political life placed a strain on both partners. Despite stories of his infidelities and the aforementioned strain, Jacqueline Kennedy loved her husband and tried to aid him in his work when she could.

John Kennedy was not indifferent to his wife or her accomplishments. He told a friend, "you have no idea what a help Jackie is to me, and what she has meant to me."[119] He was proud of her achievements as First Lady and her popularity. In Paris in 1961 he commented on the tumultuous reception his wife had received when he quipped, "I am the man who accompanied Jacqueline Kennedy to Paris and I have enjoyed it."[120]

Ironically, the presidency may have strengthened the Kennedy's marriage. David Powers, a long-time friend and Special Assistant to the President, believes that the White House brought Jack and Jackie closer together. The President was able to spend more time with his wife and family because he lived and worked in the same place.[121] Another staff member adds: "His election to her [Jacqueline's] surprise, strengthened instead of strained their marriage. Those were their happiest years."[122]

Access to Presidential Decision Making. Jacqueline Kennedy had no interest in or desire to influence her husband's decision making. The President certainly did not involve his wife in any policy or political deliberations.

Occasionally the First Lady would ask McGeorge Bundy, Special Assistant to the President for National Security Affairs, to show her cables about whatever development was in the news, but this was her only connection with foreign affairs.[123] She was not the sort of presidential wife who would greet her husband with the query, "What's new in Laos?"[124]

The First Lady refused to be drawn into any discussion of substantive matters. During her tour of the White House, correspondent Charles Collingswood commented on the Kennedy administration's affinity for artists, musicians, writers, and poets. Then Collingswood asked, "Do you think there's a relationship between government and the arts?"[125] The First Lady replied: "That's so complicated. I don't know. I just think that everything in the White House should be the best."[126] Jacqueline Kennedy felt that her job was to provide a quiet home for her husband and children and not to advise on domestic or foreign problems.

The President's and First Lady's Perceptions of Women. In 1961, President Kennedy created the Commission on the Status of Women; Eleanor Roosevelt was appointed chair. The commission found evidence of widespread discrimination against women in professions and "discovered the peculiar professional handicaps of the married woman, the difficulties of balancing their home and work roles."[127]

Upon reading the report of the commission, the President created an interdepartmental bureau to review and oversee government hiring practices.[128] At the Chief Executive's urging, "Congress funded a model program to investigate local day care facilities. . . . The Equal Pay Act of 1963 and providing funds to state welfare agencies to expand their day care centers" were other administration accomplishments that directly benefitted women.[129]

Although his administration made some efforts to aid them, John Kennedy was not particularly sensitive to the problems of women.[130] A total of thirty women served in the Kennedy administration: fifteen women were appointed to high-level positions by the President and fifteen women continued to serve in positions to which they had been appointed by Kennedy's predecessors.[131] No woman was included in the major policy decisions of the Kennedy administration.

Jacqueline Kennedy did nothing to advance the cause of women. In her unique position of not just creating news but being news, she might have altered the perception of "woman as decoration" held by most Americans at the time (most notably her husband). Instead, she reinforced the view that women's predominant concerns were "taste, fashion, superficial culture and ceremony."[132]

Jacqueline Kennedy became a public communicator by necessity, not desire. She wanted to advance her White House projects, and this required public contact and media exposure. She gave no formal speeches, but delivered short statements and interviews, and chaired meetings that attracted attention. Her ceremonial activities also generated great interest.

Lou Hoover had utilized the new medium of radio to deliver nationally broadcast speeches in the early 1930s; her use of radio lent it a certain legitimacy. Jacqueline Kennedy did the same for television thirty years later. Her televised tour of the White House conferred credibility on the expanding medium.

Mrs. Kennedy did not attempt to achieve success in substantive areas while living in the White House. She did, however, give the Kennedy administration the style and mystique that made it memorable. Mrs. Kennedy's communication activities brought about tremendous national interest in the Kennedy family in general and Jacqueline in particular.

The public's appetite for information and pictures of the Kennedys seemed insatiable. There were books, films, and records about the First Family. Whatever the Kennedys' preference in food, sport, or fashion, it seemed to foster a national craze. The First Lady's pillbox hats and bouffant hairdo became overnight sensations. General circulation magazines could not print enough stories about the glamorous First Lady.

Mrs. Kennedy was personally popular and well-liked. The Gallup Poll found that Americans admired their First Lady, and for six years almost consistently rated her as the most admired woman in the world.[133]

Perhaps Jacqueline Kennedy's greatest achievement occurred during the terrible weekend of November 22, 1963. Standing erect and dry-eyed, and moving with great dignity, she helped a grieving nation mourn the loss of its leader. The memories of her foreign triumphs and White House tour might fade, but the image of Jacqueline Kennedy at Arlington Cemetary, and indeed throughout that weekend, would remain forever.

THELMA PATRICIA RYAN NIXON

Pat Nixon was an enigmatic public communicator as First Lady. From extensive experience in politics, she knew that if she hoped to draw attention to her projects and concerns she would have to be an active communicator. Mrs. Nixon rejected this course of action, and instead pursued a half-hearted attempt at publicizing her project, volunteerism.

Interestingly, Mrs. Nixon made numerous trips to publicize the work of those people who voluntarily devoted their time to hospitals, old-age homes, or community centers. Unfortunately she did not engage in other communication activities such as the speeches, press conferences or interviews, or radio and television broadcasts that would have dramatized and emphasized her commitment to the project. There was never any sense that Pat Nixon was dedicated to volunteerism or any other cause.

Pat Nixon never impressed her image on the consciousness of Americans. The consummate traditional political wife, she was a nondescript cypher, a woman who preferred to be neutral rather than committed. She was a woman who understood the enormous potential of her position and yet generally rejected it.

Route to the White House

Her father called his newborn daughter "St. Patrick's babe in the morn" because she just barely missed being born on St. Patrick's Day.[134] March 16, 1912, was the birthdate of Thelma Catherine Patricia "Pat" Ryan, daughter of William and Kate Ryan of Ely, Nevada.[135]

When Pat was a year old, the Ryans left Ely and the copper mines where William Ely had toiled for years. Their new home was Artesia, California, where they settled on a small truck farm. Pat remembers hard times but close family ties on the farm.[136] Her mother succumbed to cancer when Pat was twelve; five years later, William Ryan was dead of silicosis. At age seventeen, Pat was left to fend for herself.

"She was determined she said, 'to make something of myself.' "[137] She attended Fullerton Junior College for a year, paying her way by working at a bank. In 1930 she was offered a job chauffeuring an elderly couple from California to New York. She seized the opportunity to earn money and to see something of the world. Pat remained in New York for two years working as a secretary and as an X-ray technician at a hospital. She accumulated enough money to return to Los Angeles and enroll as a freshman merchandising major at the University of Southern California.

In order to maintain herself at the university, Pat took on a variety of jobs including paper-grader, salesgirl, and even movie extra. She graduated from the unversity with honors in 1937. She had intended a career in merchandising, and hoped to eventually become a department-store buyer, but when she was offered a job teaching business courses at Whittier High School for $190 a month, Pat signed a teaching contract.

Highschool teachers were encouraged to participate in local community activities, and Pat became involved in the amateur theatre group. It was there at casting tryouts for *The Dark Tower* that she met another amateur actor, lawyer Richard Nixon. Nixon writes of their meeting: "That night, a beautiful and vivacious young woman with titian hair appeared whom I had never seen before. I could not take my eyes away from her. . . . [F]or me it was a case of love at first sight."[138] Later that night, Nixon proposed to Pat.

Pat was less dazzled than Richard, and continued to see other men. Nixon, however, stopped dating other women. Whenever possible, he took Pat to football games, skating, and swimming. He "even drove her to meet other beaus in Los Angeles, waiting patiently to take her home at the end of the evening."[139] Nixon's persistence and patience finally paid off, and on June 21, 1940, he and Pat were married at the Mission Inn in Riverside, California.

After a honeymoon trip to Mexico, the Nixons began married life in Whittier. Pat returned to teaching and Dick continued practicing law. They did not remain long in Whittier, as Nixon accepted a position with the Office of Price Administration (OPA) in Washington, D.C., in December 1941. The stay at OPA was a brief one, too; Nixon enlisted in the Navy in August 1942.

While her husband saw combat in the South Pacific, Pat worked as a price analyst for the OPA in San Francisco. When Nixon returned from active duty, he was uncertain about what he should do in civilian life. He was approached by a local businessman who suggested that he run for Congress against Jerry Voorhis. Years later, Pat remembered that there had never been any talk about political life at all "either before or after their marriage."[140] When Nixon was offered the chance to run for Congress, she said: "I didn't feel strongly about it either way. . . . I felt that a man had to make up his mind what he wants to do, then after he made it up, the only thing I could do was to help him."[141] Just before Nixon won the Republican primary, Patricia "Tricia" Nixon was born on February 21, 1946.

Three weeks after Tricia's birth, Pat was on the campaign trail with her husband, typing press releases, mailing pamphlets, and keeping track of his schedule. Sometimes she would critique his performance.[142] Pat was very involved in the campaign, and "there were times when [she] wept with frustration, because they didn't have enough money to mail their political literature."[143] Their efforts paid off; in November, Nixon defeated Voorhis and went to Washington as the Congressman from California's twelfth congressional district. A second child, Julie, was born to the Nixons on July 5, 1948.

In 1950, Nixon campaigned for the U.S. Senate. Pat traveled with her husband and helped in any way possible. After a particularly sordid campaign that saw Nixon label his opponent Helen Gahagan Douglas as "the pink lady" and accuse her of Communist ties, Richard Nixon was elected.

In 1952, Dwight Eisenhower selected Nixon as his vice presidential running mate. Pat again joined her husband on the campaign trail, but this campaign was not like the others. On September 18, a story charging that Nixon had a secret fund of twenty thousand dollars appeared in the New York Post. Nixon maintained that the money, which had been raised privately for travel and Senate office expenses, was not illegal. His protestations of innocence were lost in a furor over the fund. Eisenhower was advised to drop Nixon from the ticket.

Nixon himself thought of leaving the ticket, but Pat opposed this move. According to Nixon, she said: "You can't think of resigning. If you do . . . you will destroy yourself. Your life will be marred forever and the same will be true of your family, and particularly your daughters."[144]

The vice presidential nominee decided to fight back with a nationally televised speech that he hoped would exonerate him and restore Eisenhower's trust. On September 23, Nixon stepped before the television cameras and delivered the "Checkers Speech." In the course of the address, Nixon discussed the purpose of the fund and gave an accounting of his personal finances. Pat played a role in the speech. Nixon told the audience that his wife had worked in his office for years without being placed on the government payroll. She was praised for being Irish and not being a quitter, and the audience learned that she owned a "respectable Republican cloth coat."[145]

Eisenhower decided to keep Nixon on the ticket. The American public supported him, and the entire gamble proved to be a huge success.[146] Years later, however, Nixon wrote that this experience caused Pat to lose her appetite for campaigning and politics. "From that time on, Pat was to go through campaign after campaign as a good trouper, but never quite with the same feeling toward political life. She had lost the zest for it."[147] On Election Day, voters indicated that they were not overly concerned with the fund scandal, and the Eisenhower-Nixon ticket was elected.

The Nixons traveled extensively during the vice presidential years, from 1953 to 1961. In 1957 Richard promised Pat that he would leave politics at the conclusion of his term in 1960.[148] The opportunity to run for the presidency proved to be too great, however, and Nixon broke his promise.

Nixon made a strong effort, campaigning in all fifty states, but he and Henry Cabot Lodge were narrowly defeated by John F. Kennedy and Lyndon Johnson. Pat, who had always been known for her strength and calm, saw her resolve crumble as her husband delivered his concession speech. " 'I felt bad inside' she explained 'because Dick had worked and tried so hard.' "[149]

After the 1960 election, Nixon joined a Los Angeles law firm. Still the titular head of the Republican Party, he began to consider a race for Governor of California in 1962. Pat opposed another campaign. According to Nixon, she was convinced that it would be a terrible mistake to run, but said that if he should decide to enter the race she would "be there campaigning with you as I always have."[150] Nixon did decide to run, and suffered a humiliating defeat. It was a low point in Nixon's life.

Affluence came late to the Nixon family, but it finally arrived when Richard left California and joined a Wall Street law firm as a senior partner. Those who saw Pat during the New York years when her husband was out of office said that she "appeared to be happier, more light-hearted, more relaxed than at any time in her years as an official wife."[151]

The respite from political life was short-lived. In February 1968, Nixon announced his candidacy for the Presidency. Pat was resigned; she had been happy in New York, but of course she would help.

He had been through numerous campaigns, but the 1968 campaign had to be the most satisfying and fulfilling for Richard Nixon. On November 5, 1968, he defeated Hubert Humphrey by 31,785,148 votes to 31,274,503.[152] Nixon had achieved the long-sought-after prize; he was President, and Pat was First Lady.

When Pat Nixon first entered the White House, she had no specific projects in mind. In mid–1969 she endorsed "volunteerism," encouraging people to help other people in hospitals, schools, and old-age homes. She traveled extensively with the President and by herself. In addition, she worked on the continuing White House restoration and entertained great numbers of people at the executive mansion.

The First Lady continued her activities after her husband's reelection in 1972. As disclosures of the Watergate scandal became more damaging, she tended to avoid the press and embarrassing questions. Always his strongest supporter, Mrs. Nixon advised her husband not to resign from office even as it became clear that he would be impeached.

Richard Nixon resigned the office of President of the United States on August 9, 1974. He and Pat returned to California. Mrs. Nixon suffered a stroke in 1976 but has made a successful recovery. The Nixons now reside in New Jersey.

Major Communication Activities of the First Lady

Pat Nixon engaged in a full spectrum of communication activities advocating a major project, campaigning, and faithfully fulfilling ceremonial obligations. However, she never fully established herself as a public communicator because her role in most of the aforementioned activities was limited.

Perhaps a major reason for her lack of impact was that the First Lady eschewed publicity. Helen Thomas said: "I don't think that she is the type who could go beat the bushes in her own behalf. Perhaps she expected others to just recognize how wonderful she was."[153] Julie Nixon Eisenhower observes: "She did so much. . . . She never tried to create an image for herself by . . . publicizing herself. She did so much quietly."[154]

Mrs. Nixon delivered no formal speeches as First Lady, but made extended remarks on ceremonial occasions. She made short remarks when she traveled around the country to support volunteerism, praising the people who were engaged in helping others. She also spoke briefly on trips to foreign countries and in press conferences.

Advocacy. Pat Nixon took many months to establish herself as First Lady. At a luncheon for cabinet wives and the Women's Press Corps in February 1969, she noted that everyone wanted to know what she was going to do. She said, "I'm going to be on the road soon, giving aid and support to the many projects I'm interested in."[155] Four months later, Mrs. Nixon had not endorsed any project or done any traveling. Late in June 1969, the First Lady embarked on a trip to Oregon and California, and proclaimed her support for her White House project, volunteerism. Mrs. Nixon explained that she had been a volunteer all her life and that "if more people would get involved, we could change things. . . . I feel that if each person would give only 20 minutes a day to lend a helping hand, the quality of life could be enriched, and that's my plea."[156]

On her initial venture, the First Lady spent three days visiting day-care centers, art centers, urban vegetable gardens, projects for the blind, and a volunteer service bureau.[157] Everywhere she went, she stressed the importance of people helping people. The trip generated enthusiasm and drew positive press notices; however, Mrs. Nixon did not leave the White House to endorse volunteerism again in 1969. One writer notes that Mrs. Nixon announced that she would become active in the Right to Read program, the environment, and improving the quality of life, but she evidenced no sustained commitment to any of these causes.[158]

The American public might have expected Mrs. Nixon to do more with volunteerism or other projects as she had promised. A reporter expressed this feeling in a retrospective article analyzing Pat Nixon's first year in the White House: "Early on and repeatedly she [Mrs. Nixon] has said 'I'm going to have lots of projects. I'm a doer.' " However, concluded the reporter, "She has since been hardly more specific" about other projects. [159]

Perhaps noting press criticism, Mrs. Nixon increased her pace, and from 1970 through 1972 made numerous trips to publicize her project. On the final day of a 1970 tour of college volunteer projects, the First Lady told a press conference that college volunteers "know an impersonal government can't change society. . . . There are good programs on the books, but it takes people to change society." [160] There was another feature of Mrs. Nixon's trips that was definitely unwanted and that she claimed to rarely see or hear—Vietnam War protesters. Wherever she traveled, the First Lady could always count on the presence of these people, who also picketed and demonstrated in front of the White House. [161]

Mrs. Nixon traveled to see volunteer projects less frequently after the 1972 election. Volunteerism never enjoyed the popularity of previous First Lady projects, but it still achieved some successes. Helen Thomas offered the opinion that Pat "did alot for volunteerism in the sense that she went to the places where she could put the spotlight on." [162]

Mrs. Nixon also continued the restoration of the White House begun almost seven years before by Jacqueline Kennedy. The First Lady hired Clement Conger as the new curator for the executive mansion, and with his help redecorated fourteen rooms. According to friends, "Jacqueline Kennedy's accomplishments, so much better known and more highly praised pale by comparison." [163] Conger concurs with this assessment, saying that Mrs. Nixon was much too modest and that she was responsible for transforming an " 'average' White House collection into the pre-eminent collection in the country.' " [164] Mrs. Nixon's efforts resulted in 500 paintings and antiques being donated to the White House. [165] She raised all the money for the restoration herself from private sources. [166]

Politics and Campaigning. In 1970 Mrs. Nixon was asked if the wives of public figures should express their own opinions. The First Lady responded: "It's a decision they have to make. They should know the facts before they speak out. . . . I don't speak on political issues because I don't have all the necessary background." [167] At the same time, she endorsed the belief that it was important for wives to campaign, and she said, "Unless you are willing to work for good government, then you won't have it." [168]

As mentioned earlier, the fund scandal of 1952 significantly diminished Mrs. Nixon's zest for politics, but this did not stop her from trudging through nine election campaigns with her husband. "I do or die," she said, "I never cancel out." [169]

During the nine campaigns of her public life, Mrs. Nixon was usually a presence by her husband's side, standing in receiving lines, attending teas and coffees, and participating in phonathons while expressing no views. Pat Nixon admittedly did not enjoy politics, but was a participant in the events of numerous campaigns. Her role was usually that of apolitical observer rather than advocate for her husband.

Ceremonial Presence. Mrs. Nixon was more widely traveled than any First Lady in history.[170] She visited twenty-four countries and covered 123,245 miles during her tenure in the White House. Her trips to Vietnam (August 1969), Peru (June 1970), and China (February 1972) deserve special mention.

The trip to Vietnam is notable because Mrs. Nixon became the first First Lady to visit a war zone since Eleanor Roosevelt visited American troops in the South Pacific in 1943.[171] While in Vietnam, the First Lady visited an orphanage and soldiers in a field hospital.

In June 1970 the First Lady escorted two planeloads of relief supplies to Huaras, Peru, the site of a devastating earthquake that had killed fifty thousand people.[172] After touring the disaster area and comforting earthquake victims, the First Lady conferred with national relief agency officials. A year later, Mrs. Nixon was decorated by the Peruvian government for the help she had rendered to the earthquake victims.[173]

Mrs. Nixon made a favorable impression on her Chinese hosts as she and the President toured that country in February 1972. While her husband engaged in dialogues with Premier Chou En-lai and Chairman Mao Tse-tung, the First Lady visited schools, hospitals, acupuncture clinics, communes, and stores. Mrs. Nixon's contribution to the trip was not trivial, she spread good will and helped to foster better U.S.-China relations.[174]

A gracious hostess, Pat Nixon was probably the most hospitable mistress of the executive mansion in the twentieth century up to the summer of 1974. There was no time when she was not giving teas, attending dedication ceremonies, or presenting awards. From January 1969 to August 1974 she participated in approximately 986 activities, the most for any First Lady since Eleanor Roosevelt.[175] Helen Thomas observed, "She was very, very hospitable, and she saw that as her role, to invite large groups and let them see the White House"[176]

Under the Nixons, official White House entertaining became more sedate and formal than during the Kennedy or Johnson administrations. White tie and tails, and gowns and long gloves were seen once again in the East Room.

Mrs. Nixon was responsible for planning some of the Nixon White House social functions, but unlike in any other administration, the President and the West Wing staff (the President's staff) were also intimately involved.[177]

In addition to being a gracious hostess, taking part in trips, and entertaining, Mrs. Nixon spent a significant amount of time on her mail. Usually the First Lady's correspondence section handles this chore, drafting replies and responding to the myriad queries addressed to the President's wife. However, Mrs. Nixon spent four to five hours a day reading her mail, reviewing and correcting replies, and personally signing thousands of letters.[178]

Press Relations. Pat Nixon's relations with the press were uneven. In approximately five and a half years in the White House, the First Lady had three press secretaries, women who were largely responsible for the varying levels of her success with reporters.

Gerry Van der Heuvel was the First Lady's first press secretary. The press was not pleased with the way in which she handled the press office by blocking access to Mrs. Nixon and herself. A disgruntled reporter wrote, "The attractive Mrs. Van der Heuvel may be the first press secretary in history who is unavailable to the press."[179] Van der Heuvel accepted another position and left the employ of the White House in October 1969.

Constance "Connie" Stuart was Van der Heuvel's successor. As soon as her appointment was announced, the new press secretary informed the press that there would be briefings twice a week, on Monday mornings and Thursday afternoons.[180] Stuart did her best to "sell" Pat Nixon and the First Family to the country. The First Lady gave Stuart some advice on handling the press: "Treat them with kid gloves and butter them up."[181]

Despite her instructions to her press secretary, Mrs. Nixon was well liked by the press. She had long-standing friendships with a number of reporters and admired the tenacity and competitiveness of those assigned to cover her activities.[182] The First Lady also understood the needs of a predominately female press contingent that still needed to legitimize its work. She had firm opinions and rarely said "no comment."[183] she continued press briefings, even when she felt the information was too trivial, because she "understood some of the pressures the journalists were under from their editors to get to the heart of every story."[184]

Stuart had considerable problems with the West Wing and White House Chief of Staff H. R. Haldeman. She made an honest effort to try and rectify them, but did not receive much support, and was eventually succeeded by another press representative.

In January 1973, Helen McCain Smith stepped into the job of press secretary. According to Helen Thomas, Mrs. Smith was an exceptional press secretary. Thomas said: "She was accessible 24 hours a day. She tried to help you. Always got you what you needed if it was at all possible."[185]

Mrs. Smith had the misfortune of working for Mrs. Nixon as the Watergate scandal worsened. Pat Nixon had always been friendly to reporters; but now she avoided the press and public appearances. At one point Thomas asked the First Lady to describe her feelings about Watergate. The question upset Mrs. Nixon terribly. Later "she told some of her staffers, 'How could Helen ask me such a question? I thought we were friends.' "[186]

Though she had always been wary, Mrs. Nixon had enjoyed a good rapport with the press. When Watergate began to bring down her husband's administration, she began to see reporters as enemies, as the President did.

Factors That Influenced The First Lady's Performance as Public Communicator

Relationship with Her Husband. The Nixon marriage has always had the appearance of a partnership, although at best it has been an unequal one. Pat

Nixon, though a dedicated wife and mother, devoted a major portion of her life to politics. However, she never influenced the style or substance of the politics in which she played a role.

Richard Nixon has always presented himself as a loving husband and has always depicted his family as being extremely close and supportive of his endeavors. In his memoirs and in newspaper articles, Nixon has said that Pat was his strength and that her faith in him made his political career possible.

Articles and books that have been published since the Nixons left Washington in disgrace present a different view. Two writers have advanced the opinion that "to the outside eye the Nixon's relationship never seemed to offer much emotional sustenance for Pat. Much of Richard Nixon's leisure was spent in recreation with his male friends."[187] Bob Woodward and Carl Bernstein report that the couple had not been close since the early 1960s, and that Mrs. Nixon had considered divorce in 1962.[188] To the public they appeared to be a loving couple, but this might have been a charade, especially toward the end of the Nixon administration. For example, the Nixons traveled in separate compartments on flights to speeches or campaign stops. When the plane landed, Mrs. Nixon was summoned "so that the Nixons could emerge together arm and arm."[189]

Richard Nixon might have benefited from sharing more of the burdens of the presidency with his wife. A more balanced partnership might have produced a different kind of First Lady and a somewhat different fate for the Nixon administration.

Access to Presidential Decision Making. In a 1971 interview, President Nixon said that he discussed issues with the First Lady, but "he did not ask her opinion on 'troop withdrawals.' "[190] A former aide corroborated the President's statement and said that Mr. Nixon never brought foreign affairs home to the dinner table. The aide commented, "I can't imagine Dick saying, 'An awful thing happened in Cambodia today, Pat.' "[191]

Earlier evidence seemed to indicate that Mrs. Nixon had neither the desire nor the ability to influence her husband's decision making. Lending credence to this belief was Mrs. Nixon's comment: "I don't claim to advise him. He's a pretty strong man."[192]

Julie Nixon Eisenhower suggests that her mother did influence decision making and that the First Lady urged the President to hold news conferences,[193] to appoint a woman to the Supreme Court,[194] and to fight impeachment proceedings.[195] Perhaps Mr. Nixon heeded his wife's advice about press conferences; he certainly did not follow her recommendations in the latter two matters.

While Mrs. Eisenhower offers interesting insights, it is unlikely that Pat Nixon wielded influence in any area. An aide to the President said that he had never heard the First Lady's name mentioned by the Chief Executive.[196] A 1978 article is even more definitive. "Intimates say that Nixon never discussed anything with his wife, and that she knew nothing about Watergate."[197] Mrs. Nixon seems to have had little if any impact upon decision making and was rarely consulted on any matter.

The President's and First Lady's Perceptions of Women. Julie Nixon Eisenhower writes that Pat Nixon "believed totally in the capabilities of women. It was something she never questioned. In her own life she had supported herself, obtained jobs, and accomplished what she set out to do."[198]

Her husband probably saw women as wives and mothers with no identity separate from that of their husbands. He may have held women in low esteem, but ever the politician, Richard Nixon saw the appointment of women to positions in his administration and certain legislation favorable to women as being politically expedient. Forty-two women were appointed to high-level positions within the Nixon administration. Seventeen women appointed to government positions by previous Presidents also served in the Nixon administration, bringing the total of women serving in high-level positions from 1969 through 1974 to fifty-nine.[199]

The administration's record on legislation favorable to women was mediocre. Nixon's Secretary of Labor, James Hodgson "announced in 1970 that federal contracts would henceforth contain a clause mandating the employment of a certain quota of women."[200] In addition to this, Attorney General John Mitchell "initiated federal suits . . . to end job discrimination against women . . . in large corporations."[201] In response to feminist pressure, the "Nixon Administration required 2,000 colleges and universities to turn over their personnel files so that it could determine whether females were victims of prejudice in hiring and wages."[202]

The First Lady may have felt that women were capable but she did not believe that discrimination against women existed. "And that's the President's opinion too," she said.[203] According to one historian, "President Nixon did not view women or minority groups as serious social problems."[204] The President reasserted his traditional view of females and their primary responsibility when he vetoed "the family assistance bill which would have provided federal funds for day-care centers."[205] His reasoning was that day care could undermine the structure of the family. Mrs. Nixon did nothing to further the cause of women and, overall, the Nixon administration had an unimpressive record in this area.

Pat Nixon was an indifferent public communicator. She was a gracious hostess, but she did not make speeches or engage in the activities that would have strengthened her White House refurbishment project or her own image as a truly concerned First Lady.

Volunteerism was a credible cause, and Mrs. Nixon seemed dedicated to it, but not passionately so. There were a few trips and a few statements, but nothing more. The project never gathered momentum, and was generally disregarded by the public. Liz Carpenter told the author that she could not understand why Mrs. Nixon's project had nothing to do with children. Because of her warmth and genuine affection for young children, the First Lady had seemed a natural for such an endeavor, said Carpenter.[206]

Pat Nixon did little to enlarge the scope of the First Lady's role. Indeed, her only wish was to go down in history as the wife of the President.[207] She saw her role as being supportive of but not separate from her husband, and that is the way she has been judged.

A number of characteristics bind Lou Hoover, Jacqueline Kennedy, and Pat Nixon together as emerging spokeswomen. All three women devoted some thought to the role of the First Lady as public communicator. Noting the potential power provided by the White House, all were involved in ongoing projects during their respective tenures. They used this national forum to draw attention to their concerns and interests. Consequently, there was a slight increase in rhetorical activity, some availability to the press, and limited use of different communications media including radio, television, magazines, and newspapers.

The emerging spokeswomen did not deal in substantive issues and causes. Their projects were all appropriately feminine in nature and acceptable to the public. None of the women had any impact on domestic or foreign policy.

Lou Hoover became an emerging spokeswoman principally because of the Depression and her relationship with her husband. The times were bleak and Mrs. Hoover may have felt that they warranted some response from the woman in the White House. Thus, she chose to give speeches, speak on the radio, and write magazine articles on women's role in the Depression.

Jacqueline Kennedy and Pat Nixon were emerging spokeswomen for considerably different reasons. As noted earlier, 1961 marked the beginning of a modern era for First Ladies. There were four major reasons for the change.

Beginning with the presidency of 1961, all First Ladies were born in the twentieth century. This meant that all occupants of the White House had been exposed to influences radically different than their predecessors. They had grown up with the vote, with changes in the role of women, and with a revolution in communications. Almost all post–1961 First Ladies had attended college or were college graduates.

All news media experienced growth after 1961, but none as great or dramatic as television. There had been a subtle shift in the 1950s as the printed word yielded to television, and now television, the instant communicator, took on great importance. The Kennedys were the first presidential family to take advantage of this medium.

The first press secretary to a First Lady was appointed by Jacqueline Kennedy. Previous First Ladies had not had to deal with the intense media coverage that was afforded Jacqueline Kennedy (and would be afforded others in the future). Gone were the days of the social secretary who released the First Lady's schedule to the press. Jacqueline Kennedy's primary goal in appointing a press secretary was to have someone shield her from reporters, but the fact that the appointment was made at all acknowledged the tremendous growth of the media. No future First Lady would be without a press secretary.

By 1961 the public's expectations of a First Lady were changing. It was expected that the mistress of the White House would have some cause or project to pursue. Every First Lady after 1961 was a political wife and a veteran of campaigns and public life. Then, too, came the realization that the First Lady could be a political asset, and that she might actually influence some voters.

Lou Hoover, Jacqueline Kennedy, and Pat Nixon consciously chose to play the roles of public communicator, advocate, and hostess. They were visible, expanding the ceremonial presence of the First Lady and taking part in increased and varied White House activities. If they did not receive unqualified support from their husbands, neither were they discouraged from taking on the attendant responsibilities.

This group of women enlarged the First Lady's role. Now the First Lady was not only a presence and party hostess, but could also be communicator, advocate, politician, and advisor. The political surrogates and independent advocates had a strong base from which to launch their own attempts to educate, to improve, and to influence.

NOTES

1. Biographical information has been culled from the following sources: Sol Barzman, *The First Ladies* (New York: Cowles, 1970), pp. 285–294; Margaret Bassett, *American Presidents and Their Wives* (Freeport, Maine: Bond Wheelwright, 1969), pp. 322–330; and Helen B. Pryor, *Lou Henry Hoover: Gallant First Lady* (New York: Dodd, Mead, 1969), pp. 1–162.

2. Barzman, *First Ladies*, p. 287.

3. Bassett, *American Presidents*, p. 322; Dorothy McGee, *Herbert Hoover: Engineer, Humanitarian, Statesman* (New York: Dodd, Mead, 1959), pp. 26–27; Pryor, *Lou Henry Hoover*, p. 23.

4. Barzman, *First Ladies*, p. 288.

5. Pryor, *Lou Henry Hoover*, p. 40.

6. Barzman, *First Ladies*, p. 289.

7. *De Re Mettallica* was not the Hoovers' only joint venture in publishing. They collaborated on *Principles of Mining*, a compilation of Herbert Hoover's lectures on the topic for university audiences. The resulting work became the definitive textbook for geology and mining engineering students for years: Pryor, *Lou Henry Hoover*, pp. 80–82.

8. William Henry Irwin, *Herbert Hoover: A Reminiscent Biography* (New York: Century, 1928), p. 126.

9. Only three hundred of the one and a half million dollars was not repaid: American Committee in London exhibit, Herbert Hoover Library, West Branch, Iowa (hereafter cited as HH Library).

10. Herbert C. Hoover, *The Memoirs of Herbert Hoover: Volume I: Years of Adventure 1874–1920* (New York: MacMillan, 1951), p. 144.

11. Letter, Herbert Hoover to Ambassador Walter Hines Page, undated: Lou Henry Hoover Papers, Subject File, American Committee in London Reports, 1914, HH Library (hereafter referred to as LHH Papers).

12. Eugene Lyons, *Herbert Hoover: A Biography* (Garden City, New York: Doubleday, 1964), p. 95.

13. Pryor, *Lou Henry Hoover*, p. 108.

14. Hoover, *Memoirs, Vol. I*, pp. 273–274.

15. President-elect Harding offered Hoover the position of Secretary of the Interior or Secretary of Commerce. Hoover chose Commerce, the seemingly less prestigious post, because he hoped to effect change in that department.

It is interesting to speculate how history might have been affected if Hoover had accepted the Interior post instead of Albert Fall, the man whose unscrupulous machinations led to the Teapot Dome Scandal: Hoover, *Memoirs, Vol. II*, p. 186; Lyons, *Herbert Hoover*, p. 144; Francis Russell, *The Shadow of Blooming Grove: Warren G. Harding in His Times*. (New York: McGraw-Hill, 1968), p. 425.

16. "Mrs. Hoover Names Sport Commission," *New York Times*, April 20, 1923, p. 14.

17. Joan Hoff-Wilson, *Herbert Hoover: Forgotten Progressive* (Boston: Little, Brown, 1975), p. 20.

18. Wilson, *Herbert Hoover*, p. 20.

19. "Mrs. Hoover Proving Big Help to G.O.P. during Westward Trek," *Christian Science Monitor*, undated, no page given: E. Pearl Stribling Scrapbooks, HH Library.

20. John L. Moore, (ed.), *Guide to U.S. Elections*, (Washington, D.C.: Congressional Quarterly, 1975), p. 288.

21. Lyons, *Herbert Hoover*, p. 236.

22. John D. Hicks, *Republican Ascendancy* (New York: Harper, 1960), p. 228.

23. Herbert Hoover, *The Memoirs of Herbert Hoover: Volume III, The Great Depression 1929–1941* (New York: MacMillan, 1952), p. 343.

24. Gertrude L. Bowman, interviewed by Raymond Henle, Washington, D.C., November 6 and 12, 1966, p. 16, Herbert Hoover Library Oral History Project (hereafter referred to as HHLOHP). HH Library.

25. "Mrs. Hoover Talks over Wide Hook-Up," *New York Times*, April 20, 1929, p. 3.

26. "Lou Hoover and the Girl Scouts," exhibit, HH Library, 1987.

27. Pryor, *Lou Henry Hoover*, p. 108.

28. Charlotte Kellogg, "Mrs. Herbert Hoover," *Outlook*, 149 (June 20, 1928), p. 318.

29. "Mrs. Hoover Holds Dish-Washing Housewife Has More Courage than the Big Game Hunter," p. 1.

30. "Efforts of Women during Economic Distress Praised," Clippings File, HH Library.

31. "Mrs. Hoover Calls for Relief Workers," *New York Times*, November 28, 1932, p. 3.

32. "Mrs. Hoover Calls for Relief Workers," *The New York Times*, November 28, 1932, p. 3.

33. For example, "Appeals Received during September 1931," LHH Papers, Subject File, Requests for Assistance, Field Investigations, Box 77, HH Library.

34. Thomas Thalkin, former Director of the Herbert Hoover Presidential Library, told me that some of the recipients of Mrs. Hoover's philanthropy discovered the identity of their benefactor. After Mrs. Hoover's death, Mr. Hoover was amazed to receive letters from people that Mrs. Hoover had aided asking, "Where's my check?": Thomas Thalkin, interviewed by the author, West Branch, Iowa, August 11, 1978.

35. Letter, Edith Harcourt to Bertha M. Daum, March 28, 1939, Mildred Hall Campbell Papers, HH Library.

36. Letter, Edith Harcourt to Bertha M. Daum, March 28, 1939.

37. Mrs. Hoover devoted a great deal of thought to the book, and solicited opinions about projected chapters from former First Ladies Edith Wilson and Grace Coolidge: Letter, Lou Hoover to Edith B. Wilson, May 26, 1932; letter, Lou Hoover to Grace Coolidge, July 11, 1932, LHH Papers, Personal Correspondence, 1929–1933, HH Library.

38. Letter, Thomas Thalkin to the author, January 22, 1982.

39. Herbert Hoover, *Memoirs, Vol. II*, p. 188.

40. Herbert Hoover, *Memoirs, Vol. II*, p. 323.

41. Thalkin interview.

42. "The White House Tea," *Mobile Press*, undated, no page number, LHH Papers, DePriest Incident, Clippings and Printed Matter, HH Library.

43. Untitled story, *Commercial Appeal*, Memphis, Tennessee, June 17, 1929, no page, LHH Papers, DePriest Incident, Clippings and Printed Matter, HH Library.

44. "What Do They Say?" *Birmingham Age-Herald*, Birmingham, Alabama, June 14, 1929, no page, LHH Papers, DePriest Incident, Clippings and Printed Matter, HH Library.

45. "House Deplores DePriest Incident," *Atlanta Constitution*, June 29, 1929, no page, LHH Papers, DePriest Incident, Clippings and Printed Matter, HHL.

46. Editorial, *The Nation*, 128 (June 26, 1929), p. 752.

47. Herbert Hoover, *Memoirs, Vol. II*, p. 324.

48. LHH Papers, Subject File, 1886–1943, Boxes 1–3, HH Library.

49. Thalkin interview.

50. Bess Furman, *Washington Bi-Line* (New York: Knopf, 1949), p. 8.

51. Furman, *Washington Bi-Line*, pp. 8–9.

52. LHH Papers, Subject File, "Clippings, 1928–Misrepresentations," Box 34, HH Library.

53. Letter, Lou Hoover to Edgar Rickard, October 4, 1928, LHH Papers, Subject File, Campaign of 1928, General, July–November, HH Library.

54. Delbert Clark, *Washington Dateline* (New York: Stokes, 1941), pp. 210–213.

55. Furman, *Washington Bi-Line*, p. 133.

56. Wilson, *Herbert Hoover*, p. 270.

57. Wilson, *Herbert Hoover*, p. 17.

58. Alonzo Fields, interviewed by Raymond Henle, Medford, Massachusetts, July 24, 1970, p. 23, HHLOHP.

59. Letter, Ruth Fesler Lipman to Margaret B. Klapthor, October 25, 1978, Oral History File, Ruth Fesler Lipman, HH Library.

60. Herbert Hoover, *Memoirs, Vol. II*, p. 324.

61. Letter, Thomas T. Thalken to the author, November 10, 1982.

62. Thalken interview.

63. Wilson, *Herbert Hoover*, p. 19.

64. Wilson, *Herbert Hoover*, p. 19.

65. Dr. Helen B. Pryor, interviewed by Raymond Henle, Stanford, California, November 2, 1971, p. 5, HHLOHP.

66. "Executive Order 5984, Amendment of Civil Service Rule VII, December 23, 1932," *Proclamations and Executive Orders of Herbert Hoover 1929–1932* (Washington, D.C.: Government Printing Office, 1977), p. 1389.

67. Letter, Thomas T. Thalken to the author, November 10, 1982.

68. Karen Keesling and Suzanne Cavanaugh, "Women Presidential Appointees Serving or Having Served in Full Time Positions Requiring Senate Confirmation, 1912–1977" (Congressional Research Service, March 23, 1978), pp. 23–24.

69. Mrs. Ellis R. Yost, "Informative Facts Concerning the President's Commissions" (Pamphlet), Publication of the Republican National Committee, April 1931, HH Library.

70. David Halberstam, *The Powers That Be* (New York: Dell, 1979) p. 443.

71. Biographical information has been culled from Barzman, *First Ladies*, pp. 328–337; Bassett, *American Presidents*, pp. 391–401; John H. Davis, *The Bouviers* (New York: Farrar, 1969); and Means, *Woman in the White House*, pp. 264–299.

72. Barzman, *First Ladies*, p. 329.

73. Barzman, *First Ladies*, p. 331.

74. Bassett, *American Presidents*, p. 393.

75. George Carpozi, Jr., *The Hidden Side of Jacqueline Kennedy* (New York: Pyramid, 1967), p. 14.

76. Barzman, *First Ladies*, p. 332.

77. David Powers, interviewed by the author, Waltham, Massachusetts, March 1, 1979.

78. Rose Fitzgerald Kennedy, *Times to Remember* (Garden City, N.Y.: Doubleday, 1974), p. 366.

79. Theodore C. Sorensen, *Kennedy* (New York: Bantam, 1965), p. 158.

80. "Kennedy's Wife Finds Campaign Exhilarating," *New York Times*, April 20, 1960, p. 29.

81. The final count showed Kennedy-Johnson having received 34,221,344 votes to 34,106,671 for Nixon-Lodge: John L. Moore (ed.), *Guide to U.S. Elections*, p. 296.

82. Frances Cleveland, the first White House bride, was the youngest First Lady at twenty-two years of age. Julia Tyler was second youngest at twenty-four years.

83. Mrs. Gerald R. Ford, interviewed by the author, Vail, Colorado, July 17, 1979.

84. Davis, *The Bouviers*, p. 409.

85. Kenneth P. O'Donnell and David F. Powers with Joe McCarthy, *Johnny, We Hardly Knew Ye* (New York: Pocket, 1973), p. 25.

86. Robert Curran, *The Kennedy Women* (New York: Lancer, 1964), p. 58.

87. Hugh Sidey, *John F. Kennedy, President* (New York: Atheneum, 1964), p. 81.

88. Arthur M. Schlesinger, Jr., *A Thousand Days: John F. Kennedy in the White House* (Boston: Houghton, Mifflin, 1965), p. 669.

89. Ruth Montgomery, *Hail to the Chiefs: My Life with Six Presidents* (New York: Coward-McCann, 1970), p. 224.

90. Helen Thomas, *Dateline: White House* (New York: Macmillan, 1975), p. 10.

91. Schlesinger, *A Thousand Days*, p. 670.

92. Stephen Birmingham, *Jacqueline Bouvier Kennedy Onassis* (New York: Grosset, 1978), p. 107; Mary Van Rensselaer Thayer, *Jacqueline Kennedy: The White House Years* (Boston: Little, Brown, 1967), p. 111.

93. J. B. West, *Upstairs at the White House* (New York: Warner, 1974), p. 277.

94. Sorensen, *Kennedy*, p. 432.

95. Benjamin C. Bradlee, *Conversations with Kennedy* (New York: Norton, 1975), p. 54.

96. Brenda Blaine, interviewed by the author, Waltham, Massachusetts, July 24, 1978.

97. "Memorandum for Mr. Salinger," February 15, 1962, PP5/Kennedy, Jacqueline,

January 1, 1962-March 10, 1962, Box 705, John F. Kennedy Library, Boston, Massachusetts (hereafter referred to as JFK Library).

98. Schlesinger, *Thousand Days*, pp. 670–671.

99. West, *Upstairs*, p. 286.

100. Anne H. Lincoln, *The Kennedy White House Parties* (New York: Viking, 1967).

101. Curran, *Kennedy Women*, p. 58.

102. Charles Burrows, interviewed by Dennis J. O'Brien, Washington, D.C., September 7, 1969, p. 21, John F. Kennedy Library Oral History Project (hereafter referred to as JFKLOHP). JFK Library.

103. Burrows interview, p. 20.

104. "Memorandum for Mr. O'Donnell, April 16, 1963," PP5/1 Kennedy, Jacqueline, December 11, 1962, JFK Library.

105. This figure is an approximation based on events listed in the *New York Times Index* and the Sanford Fox papers, JFK Library. (Mr. Fox served as Chief of the Social Entertainments Office during the Kennedy Administration.)

106. CBS News Special Interview, May 29, 1964, Audiovisual archives, JFK Library.

107. Dinah Bridge, interviewed by Joseph E. O'Connor, London, England, October 30, 1966, pp. 4–5, JFKLOHP.

108. Thayer, *Jacqueline Kennedy*, p. 32.

109. Winzola McLendon and Scottie Smith, *Don't Quote Me! Washington Newswomen and the Power Society* (New York: Dutton, 1970), p. 70.

110. Bess Furman, "First Lady, Art Experts Plan Decor," *New York Times*, January 25, 1961, p. 37.

111. Pierre Salinger, *With Kennedy* (Garden City, N.Y.: Doubleday, 1966), p. 119.

112. Bonnie Angelo, quoted in Norma Ruth Holly Foreman, "The First Lady as a Leader of Public Opinion: A Study of the Role and Press Relations of Lady Bird Johnson," (unpublished doctoral dissertation, the University of Texas at Austin 1971), p. 90.

113. McLendon and Smith, *Don't Quote Me!* p. 71.

114. McLendon and Smith, *Don't Quote Me!* p. 71.

115. Thomas, *Dateline*, p. 7.

116. Montgomery, *Hail to the Chiefs*, p. 244.

117. "Report on Mrs. Onassis Gives a New View of Her Role in the White House," *New York Times*, July 7, 1969, p. 20.

118. Birmingham, *Jacqueline Bouvier Kennedy Onassis*, p. 100; Maxine Cheshire, *Maxine Cheshire, Reporter* (Boston: Houghton-Mifflin, 1978), p. 54; McLendon and Smith, *Don't Quote Me!* p. 15.

119. Kay Halle interviewed by William M. McHugh, Washington, D.C., February 7, 1967, p. 10, JFKLOHP.

120. "Just an Escort, Kennedy Jokes as Wife's Charm Enchants Paris," *New York Times*, June 3, 1961, p. 7.

121. Powers interview.

122. Sorensen, *Kennedy*, p. 427; Schlesinger, *Thousand Days*, p. 671.

123. Schlesinger, *Thousand Days*, p. 666.

124. Schlesinger, *Thousand Days*, , p. 666.

125. "Excerpts from the Transcript of Mrs. Kennedy's T.V. Tour of the White House," *New York Times*, Feburary 15, 1962, p. 18.

126. "Excerpts from the Transcript of Mrs. Kennedy's T.V. Tour of the White House," p. 18.

127. Mary P. Ryan, *Womanhood in America* (New York: New Viewpoints, 1975), p. 417.

128. June Sochen, *Herstory: A Woman's View of American History* (New York: Alfred, 1974), p. 383.

129. Sochen, *Herstory*, p. 383.

130. Sochen, *Herstory*, p. 383.

131. Keesling and Cavanagh, "Women Presidential Appointees," pp. 36–38.

132. Sochen, *Herstory*, p. 384.

133. George Gallup, *The Gallup Poll Vol. III: 1959–1971* (New York: Random, 1972), pp. 1747, 1785, 1796, 1855, 1915, 1979, 2041.

134. Barzman, *First Ladies*, p. 349.

135. Biographical material had been culled from: Barzman, *First Ladies*, pp. 348–357; Madeleine Edmondson and Alden Duer Cohen, *The Women of Watergate*, (New York: Stein and Day, 1975), pp. 216–226; Julie Nixon Eisenhower, *Pat Nixon: The Untold Story* (New York: Simon, 1986); Richard M. Nixon, *The Memoirs of Richard Nixon: Vol. I* (New York: Warner, 1978), pp. 28–36; and Judith Viorst, "Pat Nixon Is the Ultimate Good Sport," *New York Times Magazine*, September 13, 1970, pp. 25–147.

136. Viorst, "Pat Nixon," p. 140.

137. Viorst, "Pat Nixon," p. 140.

138. Nixon, *Memoirs, Vol. I*, p. 28.

139. Viorst, "Pat Nixon," p. 142.

140. Earl Mazo and Stephen Hess, *Nixon: A Political Portrait* (New York: Harper, 1968), p. 34.

141. Mazo and Hess, *Nixon*, p. 34.

142. Nixon, *Memoirs, Vol. I.*, p. 43.

143. Henry D. Spaulding, *The Nixon Nobody Knows* (Middle Village, N.Y., 1972), p. 153.

144. Richard M. Nixon, *Six Crises* (New York: Pyramid, 1968), p. 92.

145. Richard M. Nixon, "My Side of the Story," *Vital Speeches*, 19 (October 15, 1952), pp. 11–15.

146. Clayton Knowles, "Messages Pour in Backing Nominee," *New York Times*, September 25, 1952, p. 1.

147. Nixon, *Six Crises*, p. 137.

148. There is some confusion as to when Richard Nixon promised Pat that he would retire from politics; it is possible that he made the promise more than once or even that he did not make it at all. Barzman, *First Ladies*, p. 354; Edmonson and Cohen, *Women of Watergate*, p. 221; Mazo and Hess, *Nixon*, p. 127; Spaulding, *Nixon Nobody Knows*, p. 396, Viorst, "Pat Nixon," p. 147; Bob Woodward and Carl Bernstein, *The Final Days* (New York: Simon, 1976), p. 165.

149. Viorst, "Pat Nixon," p. 26.

150. Nixon, *Memoirs, Vol. I*, pp. 296–297.

151. Viorst, "Pat Nixon," p. 147.

152. John L. Moore (ed.), *Guide to U.S. Elections*, p. 298.

153. Helen Thomas, interviewed by the author, Washington, D.C., June 6, 1979.

154. Lester David, *The Lonely Lady of San Clemente: The Story of Pat Nixon* (New York: Crowell, 1978), p. 128.

155. Charlotte Curtis, "President Crashes White House Party," *New York Times*, February 18, 1969, p. 44.

156. "Travelling with Pat Nixon: A Different Type of Tour," *U.S. News and World Report*, Vol. 66 (June 30, 1969), p. 9.

157. Lenore Hershey, "Compassion Power: On Tour with Mrs. Nixon," *Ladies Home Journal*, 86 (September 1969), pp. 86–88.

158. Betty Boyd Caroli, *First Ladies* (New York: Oxford University, 1987), p. 244.

159. Nan Robertson, "A Starring Role Is Not for Mrs. Nixon," *New York Times*, January 26, 1970, p. 16.

160. Nan Robertson, "Mrs. Nixon Describes Students as Idealists, 'Great Generation,' " *New York Times*, March 7, 1970, p. 21.

161. Eisenhower, *Pat Nixon*, pp. 265, 266, 272, 274, 277, 281, 282, 301, 316.

162. Thomas interview.

163. Edmondson and Cohen, *Women of Watergate*, p. 222.

164. Eisenhower, *Pat Nixon*, p. 263.

165. Julie Nixon Eisenhower, "My Mother," *Newsweek*, 87 (May 24, 1976), p. 13.

166. David, *Lonely Lady*, p. 128.

167. Eisenhower, *Pat Nixon*, p. 296.

168. Eisenhower, *Pat Nixon*, p. 296.

169. Caroli, *First Ladies*, p. 251.

170. David, *Lonely Lady*, p. 161.

171. "First Lady in the War Zone," *U.S. News and World Report*, 67 (August 11, 1969), p. 14.

172. Malcolm W. Browne, "The First Ladies of U.S. and Peru See Quake Area," *New York Times*, June 30, 1970, p. 5.

173. "Peru Decorates Mrs. Nixon for Quake Aid," *New York Times*, June 30, 1971, p. 37.

174. Members of the American Press Corps, *The President's Trip to China* (New York: Bantam, 1972), pp. 27–31.

175. This figure is an approximation based on events listed in *New York Times Index*.

176. Thomas interview.

177. Woodward and Bernstein, *Final Days*, p. 166; Thomas, *Dateline* p. 149.

178. Eisenhower, *Pat Nixon*, p. 322.

179. McLendon and Smith, *Don't Quote Me!* pp. 59–60.

180. Nan Robertson, "First Lady Names Woman, 31, as New Staff and Press Aide," *New York Times*, October 24, 1969, p. 24. Julie Nixon Eisenhower writes that her mother made the decision to hold press briefings: Eisenhower, *Pat Nixon*, p. 308.

181. Thomas, *Dateline*, p. 170.

182. Eisenhower, *Pat Nixon*, p. 311.

183. Thomas, *Dateline*, pp. 170–171.

184. Eisenhower, *Pat Nixon*, p. 311.

185. Thomas interview.

186. Thomas, *Dateline*, p. 203.

187. Edmondson and Cohen, *Women of Watergate*, p. 223.

188. Woodward and Bernstein, *Final Days*, p. 165.

189. Edmondson and Cohen, *Women of Watergate*, p. 224.

190. "Nixon Depicts His Wife as Strong and Sensitive," *New York Times*, March 14, 1971, p. 76.

191. Viorst, "Pat Nixon," p. 147.

192. Nan Robertson, "Starring Role," p. 16.

193. Eisenhower, *Pat Nixon*, p. 276.

194. Eisenhower, *Pat Nixon*, p. 321.

195. Eisenhower, *Pat Nixon*, pp. 399–430.

196. Flora Rheta Schreiber, "Pat Nixon Reveals for the First Time," *Good Housekeeping*, July 1986, p. 62.

197. *Harriet Van Horne, "The Painful Price Our First Ladies Pay," Ladies Home Journal*, 95 (July 1978), p. 138.

198. Eisenhower, *Pat Nixon*, p. 321.

199. Keesling and Cavanagh, "Women Presidential Appointees," pp. 8, 9, 10, 44–48.

200. William Chafe, *The American Woman* (London: Oxford University, 1972), p. 240.

201. Chafe, *American Woman*, pp. 240–241.

202. Chafe, *American Woman*, p. 241.

203. "Women's Rights à la Pat Nixon," *U.S. News and World Report*, 66 (May 19, 1969), p. 18.

204. Sochen, *Herstory*, p. 386.

205. Lois Banner, *Women in Modern America* (New York: Harcourt, 1974), p. 248.

206. Elizabeth Carpenter, interviewed by the author, Austin, Texas, February 1, 1979.

207. Robertson, "Starring Role," p. 16.

4

POLITICAL SURROGATES AND
INDEPENDENT ADVOCATES

Eleanor Roosevelt

Eleanor Roosevelt entered the White House at a time of national crisis. The Depression had reached its nadir, the economy was in shambles, the unemployed and homeless scrounged pathetically for food and shelter, and Americans seemed to have lost faith in their government.

Although Lou Hoover had tried to demonstrate to Americans through speeches and magazine articles that she and her husband were concerned about their welfare, the attempt had been largely unsuccessful. Mrs. Hoover made too few communication efforts too late, and the Hoovers had never been perceived as being particularly sympathetic.

Like her predecessor, Eleanor Roosevelt wanted to prove to discouraged Americans that Franklin D. Roosevelt cared about their well-being, but she also wanted to convey that she too was sympathetic to their plight. She took her campaign directly to the people, visiting poverty areas, jails, coal mines, farms, small towns, and major cities. She expressed her concern in continual speeches, lectures, radio broadcasts, press conferences, and books and magazine articles. Americans received the unmistakable impression that here was a vigorous administration dedicated to eradicating the effects of the Depression. They also learned that they had an ally in the White House, a woman who not only championed her husband's ideas but staunchly put forward her own. She was a force in her own right, an independent advocate, and the most committed and respected First Lady in history.

ROUTE TO THE WHITE HOUSE

The most patrician First Lady to ever live in the White House, Anna Eleanor Roosevelt was born in New York on October 11, 1884.[1] Her father, Elliot, was the younger brother of Theodore Roosevelt and a member of the Oyster Bay branch of the Roosevelt family. Her mother, Anna Ludlow Hall, was the daughter of an old, aristocratic Hudson River family. The Elliot Roosevelt family also included Eleanor's younger brothers Hall and Elliot Junior.

Wealthy and socially prominent, the Roosevelts enjoyed a life of ease. Eleanor had an upbringing befitting one born into that social milieu. She was tutored in French, toured Europe, and later attended the exclusive Mr. Roser's classes held at the mansions of the rich.

Young Eleanor was a solemn, unsmiling child. Her mother, a beautiful yet insensitive woman, looked critically at her young daughter and cruelly called her "Granny."[2] On one occasion Anna remarked; "Eleanor, I hardly know what's to happen to you. You're so plain that you have nothing to do but be good."[3]

Wealth and position could not insulate the Roosevelts from tragedy. Elliot Roosevelt was a sportsman, charming and good-looking; he was also an alcoholic. His drunken sprees progressed from being boisterous to being wild and violent. He tried to "take the cure" in Europe and the South, but to no avail.[4]

Anna and Elliot separated, and Elliot was only permitted to see his children occasionally, which was very difficult for the adoring Eleanor. In 1892 Anna died of diphtheria and the children were sent to live with her mother, Grandmother Hall. The following spring, Elliot Junior died of scarlet fever. In August 1894, Elliot Roosevelt died following a fall.

Her father's death confirmed Eleanor's feeling that she was an outsider. Her home life was grim. Grandmother Hall was well disposed and kindly but she was preoccupied with her own children; two of Eleanor's uncles were also alcoholics.[5]

In 1899 Eleanor was sent to Allenswood, a finishing school in England. Eleanor blossomed at Allenswood, she excelled at her studies, made friends, and came to appreciate art and theatre through regular trips to London. Perhaps the most important consequence of these years was her association with Allenwood's headmistress, Marie Sovestre.

Mademoiselle Souvestre was passionately concerned with public affairs and politics, and she imbued her young charges with a sense of social responsibility.[6] Mlle. Souvestre and Eleanor were drawn to each other. One historian believes that "Mlle. Souvestre laid the foundation for what Eleanor later in her life professed to be her social philosophy."[7] Her influence on Eleanor was profound.

Eleanor would have liked to remain at school, but she was summoned home by Grandmother Hall in 1902 to be presented to society. She disliked the tea parties and balls she attended, and though she had just been accepted into New York society, she set out to free herself of its dictates. She became active in the Junior League and worked with some of its members in settlement houses. She was also active in the Consumers League. At the same time, Eleanor became secretly engaged to her cousin, Franklin Delano Roosevelt.

Franklin was Eleanor's fifth cousin once removed, and two years her senior. The two had seen each other occasionally over the years, and they started to see each other regularly after Eleanor returned from Europe. Eleanor was not blind to the fact that Franklin was a popular, charming, and somewhat frivolous young man. According to one source, she wept when she became engaged, and lamented; "I shall never be able to hold him. He is so attractive."[8]

Franklin's mother, Sara Delano Roosevelt, adored her only child. She was not enamoured of her son's intended wife, and tried to dissuade Franklin from marrying Eleanor. Later Sara withdrew her opposition to the match, and on March 17, 1905, Eleanor (who was given in marriage by her uncle, President Theodore Roosevelt) and Franklin were married.

During the five years prior to her marriage, Eleanor had begun to emerge as an independent person. Now Franklin and Sara totally dominated her. Sara rented a house for them next door to her own, furnished it, and staffed it with servants. Her mother-in-law informed the new bride that she must abandon her work in settlement houses; such activities were not embraced by socially prominent matrons. Eleanor complied. When the Roosevelt's first child, Anna Eleanor, was born in May 1906, Sara insisted that they engage a nurse to care for the baby, and selected the nurse herself.

For the next ten years, Eleanor was occupied with childbearing. Five other children were born to the Roosevelts: James (1907), Franklin Junior (1909, died as an infant the same year), Elliott (1910), Franklin Junior (1914), and John (1916).

Franklin Roosevelt was engaged in advancing his career. After passing the New York bar exam, he had worked for a law firm, but like his cousin Ted, Franklin had always had a penchant for public service. Thus, when he became bored with legal practice, Franklin turned to politics over Sara's objections, and was unexpectedly elected to the New York State Senate.

The Roosevelts moved to Albany, and their home became a center of political activity. Eleanor, out of Sara's reach for the first time since her marriage, found the atmosphere invigorating.[9] Reporters were constantly in attendance, and one, Louis McHenry Howe, would become a friend and advisor to both Roosevelts.

In 1913 the Roosevelts moved again, to Washington this time, when Franklin, a supporter of President Woodrow Wilson, was appointed Assistant Secretary of the Navy. Eleanor turned her attention to "calling on" prominent people, and faithfully discharged her social duties as the wife of the Navy's number two man.

When war broke out in 1917, Eleanor became immersed in the work of the Red Cross. For the first time, her considerable abilities were utilized as she organized the Washington Red Cross canteen and the knitting that was done for soldiers.

Franklin's romance with Lucy Mercer, Eleanor's social secretary, is a factor that cannot be overlooked in assessing Eleanor's emergence as an independent person. Eleanor's suspicions of a relationship between her husband and the pretty Miss Mercer were confirmed when she inadvertently came across a cache of letters from Miss Mercer to her husband. Eleanor offered to divorce Franklin, but Sara Roosevelt is said to have threatened to cut her son off if he pursued that course of action. Then, too, Louis Howe probably told Franklin that such a move was political suicide. To compound matters, there were Franklin's five young children, who would be affected by his decision, and Lucy Mercer's Catholicism. Franklin agreed never to see Lucy again, but "Eleanor believed that the decisive factor with Franklin had been his realization that a divorce would end his political career."[10] An uneasy reconciliation was finally achieved.

In 1920, Franklin received the Democratic vice presidential nomination. Women had just become enfranchised, and in an effort to capture their votes, he decided to take Eleanor along on his campaign; she would only be a presence, but she would be seen by the female voters.

An important result of the campaign trip was Eleanor's friendship with Louis Howe. She had never liked Howe, but she had tolerated him. Years later, Mrs. Roosevelt wrote that she had learned that Howe had always liked her and thought she was worth educating, and that he had made an effort to get to know her on the campaign trip.[11] Slowly and patiently he began Eleanor's political education. He discussed Franklin's speeches with her. He explained how the press functioned and the role reporters played in a campaign. Eleanor came to like and admire Howe; the two were close friends until the latter's death in 1936.

Harding and Coolidge trounced Cox and Roosevelt.[12] The defeat, however, did not deter Franklin and Louis as they planned Franklin's bid for the governorship of New York in 1922. Eleanor joined the New York League of Women Voters.

In the summer of 1921, the Roosevelts were enjoying their usual sojourn at Campobello Island in Canada when Franklin was taken ill. The original diagnosis was a simple cold, but when Franklin's legs became paralyzed, the diagnosis was changed to infantile paralysis.

Sara Roosevelt insisted that her son return to Hyde Park, New York where he could spend his life as a country squire, albeit a crippled one. Eleanor, standing up to her mother-in-law for the first time, would not hear of it. She and Louis were determined that Franklin would return to politics. The two worked as a team to keep "Roosevelt's political urge alive. . . . [T]hey brought all kinds of people to see him and insisted on his keeping in touch with Democratic party leaders" all over the country.[13] Many historians believe that there was little chance that Roosevelt would have retired from politics. One writes, "If anything, his illness made him want to be more active, more involved."[14] Other writers, however, credit Eleanor with aiding in her husband's medical treatment and maintaining his interest in politics.[15]

While Franklin tried to recover the use of his legs, Eleanor became his surrogate with the Democratic Party. She kept his name before the public and increased her own participation in public affairs by becoming active in Dutchess County politics and joining the Women's Trade Union League.

Eleanor also became involved in two business ventures, the Val-Kill furniture factory, which produced reproductions of early American furniture, and the Todhunter School. Mrs. Roosevelt became a faculty member at Todhunter in 1927, teaching courses in American history, English, American literature, and current events.[16]

Eleanor was asked to head the women's division in Al Smith's campaign for President in 1928. She accepted this post and was so busy fulfilling her obligations that she devoted very little time to her husband's campaign for Governor of New York. Roosevelt was elected; Smith was not.

The First Lady of the state of New York was constantly busy, writing magazine articles, maintaining political contacts, teaching at Todhunter, and helping with Val-Kill. It was during the governorship years that Eleanor began to make inspection trips for her crippled husband. In this way she truly became Franklin's eyes and ears, going to the places he could not. In one especially memorable section of her autobiography, Mrs. Roosevelt recalls:

Walking was so difficult for him that he could not go inside an institution and get a real idea of how it was being run. . . . I was asked to take over this part of the inspection. . . . I learned to notice whether the beds were too close together. . . . I learned to watch the patient's attitude toward the staff, and before the end of our years in Albany, I had become a fairly expert reporter on state institutions.[17]

Roosevelt was reelected Governor by a landslide in 1930, and became a serious presidential prospect for 1932. Franklin never told Eleanor that he was planning to run for the presidency, but she knew that Louis Howe was planning the strategy necessary for a presidential bid.

When Roosevelt received the presidential nomination, Eleanor was surrounded by inquisitive reporters and photographers. Lorena Hickok, covering Franklin Roosevelt for the Associated Press, later reported that one of the female reporters gushed, "Mrs. Roosevelt, aren't you thrilled at the idea of being in the White House?" Mrs. Roosevelt's only reply, Hickok noted, was a look so unsmiling and forbidding that all further questions along that line ceased.[18] Later, Eleanor wrote that she did not want Franklin to be President. "It was pure selfishness on my part, and I never mentioned my feelings on the subject to him."[19]

Eleanor worked with the women's division of the Democratic National Committee during the 1932 election. It was considered inappropriate for her to campaign for Franklin, but she spoke all over New York state to support her friend Herbert Lehman for Governor.

Roosevelt swept into the presidency with 22,825,016 votes to Herbert Hoover's 15,758,397.[20] Eleanor was glad that Frankin had attained the prize he had sought, but she wept for her hard-fought independence, which she was certain would now have to be submerged, saying: "Now I will have no identity. I'll only be the wife of the President."[21]

She approached Franklin with the idea of being his "listening post" or perhaps handling his mail.[22] Franklin turned her down. Eleanor wrote, "I knew he was right . . . but it was a last effort to keep in close touch and to feel that I had a real job to do."[23] She was mistaken, of course, for in fact she would perform a very real job as the most active and involved First Lady in history.

It is unlikely that we shall see a First Lady like Eleanor Roosevelt again. She was First Lady for over twelve years, and was a prodigious worker. From March 4, 1933, to April 12, 1945, she authored countless magazine articles and book reviews, and wrote nine books. Beginning December 31, 1935, she wrote a four-hundred-word daily newspaper column entitled "My Day," that was syndicated in over one hundred newspapers.[24] She lectured for the W. Colston Leigh Agency, and spoke frequently over the radio on commercially sponsored broadcasts. She delivered well over one thousand speeches. At reporter Lorena Hickok's suggestion, she held regularly scheduled press conferences.[25] Her inspection tours for her husband became legion. Always curious and interested, the indefatigable Mrs. Roosevelt was apt to appear anywhere at any time. A now famous New Yorker cartoon shows two miners working in a mine shaft. One miner looks up and says, "For gosh sakes, here comes Mrs. Roosevelt." Perhaps former First Lady Grace Coolidge asked a question that was on the mind of all Americans when she wrote to Lou Hoover, "How does Mrs. Roosevelt have time for all she accomplishes?"[26]

More important than her lecturing, writing, and travel, was Mrs. Roosevelt's role in helping the American people. She was the defender of the downtrodden, taking up many groups' or individuals' requests with the appropriate government departments or officials. Often Mrs. Roosevelt would carry her campaign to the most powerful of all government officials, the President. Some observers believed that she nagged her husband; others preferred to believe that she lobbied with Franklin Roosevelt to obtain his aid and provide him with a more personal understanding of human misery.

Eleanor Roosevelt's White House career might be divided into two segments: the Depression years, 1933 through 1940, and the war years, 1941 through 1945. In the first period, the First Lady was concerned with the social welfare programs of the New Deal. Later she shifted her attention to the Office of Civilian Defense, in which she served as Deputy Director. During World War II, she improved morale and inspected conditions among American soldiers in Great Britain, the South Pacific, and the Caribbean.

Franklin Roosevelt died of a cerebral hemorrhage on April 12, 1945. Within twelve days, Eleanor Roosevelt had left the White House and Washington, and had moved to New York. A few days later, as she entered her apartment, she was approached by a reporter who asked her for a statement. "The story is over," Mrs. Roosevelt said quietly, and hurried on.[27]

Once again, Mrs. Roosevelt was mistaken. Ahead lay her service as a U.S. delegate to the fledgling United Nations and the chairmanship of that body's Human Rights Commission. There would be years of lecturing and travel. The former First Lady remained a political power in the Democratic Party, strongly advocating the candidacy of Adlai Stevenson in 1952, 1956, and 1960. In 1961, President John F. Kennedy appointed her to preside over the Commission on the Status of Women.

In 1960 Mrs. Roosevelt was diagnosed as having aplastic anemia, a fatal blood disease. She died on November 7, 1962, at the age of seventy-eight.

MAJOR COMMUNICATION ACTIVITIES OF THE FIRST LADY

More than any other First Lady, Eleanor Roosevelt understood the value of communication, and was in constant contact with the American people. She maintained this communication for a number of reasons. She believed that her husband's programs would benefit the country, and she wanted to demonstrate her support and encourage participation. She hoped to demonstrate that individual people were a priority in the Roosevelt administration (especially during the Depression). She also hoped to publicize her own projects and concerns.

To this end, there were countless trips, lectures, radio broadcasts, speeches, press conferences, books, magazine articles, and her daily newspaper column. Few people ever wondered about Eleanor Roosevelt's opinion on a given topic, as she expressed her feelings repeatedly.

Perhaps she was not as facile and smooth as her husband, but Eleanor Roosevelt was a masterful communicator, taking advantage of every opportunity to educate her audience as she discussed her program for a better America.

Advocacy

The Depression and World II were probably responsible in part for Mrs. Roosevelt's activism, but it is likely that her own sense of social justice and compassion would have galvanized her into action under any circumstances. The ubiquitous Mrs. Roosevelt was interested in any endeavor that could improve the human condition.

The First Lady became a clearinghouse for those who felt they had no other recourse but to write the President's wife, and to this end Mrs. Roosevelt carried on a voluminous correspondence with various government departments and agencies. The First Lady sought to redress grievances between citizens and the government, and she enjoyed a high rate of effectiveness.

Mrs. Roosevelt had no single project or cause; she was devoted to solving an infinite number of problems and publicizing or lending her support to many successful endeavors.

This volume will not attempt to describe the dozens of projects and causes that filled Eleanor Roosevelt's days. Instead, it will focus on three of the concerns to which Mrs. Roosevelt devoted the full measure of her communication efforts in both a quantitative and qualitative sense. The rights of blacks, subsistence farmsteads, and World War II (the inspection trip to the Southwest Pacific and the Office of Civilian Defense or OCD) found their way into Mrs. Roosevelt's speeches, radio broadcasts, magazine articles, press conferences, and "My Day" column more than any other topics.[28]

Eleanor Roosevelt was more persistently concerned with the rights of blacks than with any other issue.[29] The First Lady felt that discrimination was a moral issue, and she attempted to bring the plight of the blacks to the attention of her husband, his cabinet, and the American people.

Always more pro-black than her husband, hers was a lonely crusade.[30] Franklin Roosevelt was not insensitive or opposed to seeking more advantages for blacks, but it was never one of his priorities. Also, two of Roosevelt's top aides were Southerners and not overly sympathetic to the problem.

Mrs. Roosevelt utilized a number of strategies in attempting to further the black cause. Her initial attempts centered on the New Deal, which she felt should treat blacks on an equal basis with whites.[31] The First Lady sought and was successful in obtaining employment for blacks in the NYA (National Youth Administration), the FERA (Federal Emergency Relief Administration), and the WPA (Works Progress Administration).

Mrs. Roosevelt became friendly with Walter White of the NAACP and Mary McLeod Bethune, who directed the NYA's Division of Negro Affairs. Often the First Lady functioned as an intermediary, raising White and Bethune's concerns about legislation with the President. A particularly good example of this was a proposed federal antilynching bill in 1934. Blacks were almost exclusively the victims of lynchings and Walter White was a strong proponent of the antilynching measure. He tried to no avail to arrange a meeting with the President. In desperation he spoke with Mrs. Roosevelt, who was sympathetic to the bill and arranged the desired meeting. Roosevelt was not opposed to the bill, he explained to White, but he had to work with Congress and, as most of the major committees were chaired by Southerners, he had to be judicious in supporting certain controversial issues; he could not alienate these men.[32]

The President's lack of support did not end the efforts of White and Mrs. Roosevelt. The former continued to bombard the White House with letters, telegrams, and telephone calls urging presidential backing for the bill. White asked Mrs. Roosevelt to deliver a radio broadcast against lynching, but the First Lady could not comply. She told White that "the President felt it would raise unnecessary antagonism toward the measure and [had] asked that she wait until later."[33] She left memoranda for her husband and spoke to him about the legislation, but the best she could elicit from him was a tepid endorsement. The bill never came up for a vote.

Mrs. Roosevelt spoke extensively to both white and black audiences on the topics of discrimination and equality. The First Lady adopted two approaches in her speeches. She reproached white audiences and told them that they bore a moral responsibility for black problems. To blacks, "she stressed that the responsibility was as much theirs as the white man's."[34]

Mrs. Roosevelt's greatest contribution to blacks may have been "the example and leadership which she provided in her personal conduct as a citizen and First Lady."[35] In 1936 contralto Marian Anderson had been invited to the White House to sing for the President and Mrs. Roosevelt. Three years later, Miss Anderson was denied access to the Daughters of the American Revolution's (DAR's) Constitution Hall because she was black. The DAR's behavior enraged many people, including Eleanor Roosevelt, a DAR member, who declared in her February 28, 1939, newspaper column, "To remain as a member implies approval of that action, and therefore I am resigning."[36] Mrs. Roosevelt's action was almost universally applauded.

Franklin Roosevelt's record of appointing blacks to high office "exceeded those of all previous Presidents combined. Blacks scored significant gains throughout the 1930's which must be credited to the influence of the New Deal" and at least partly to the influence of Eleanor Roosevelt.[37]

Perhaps no area of the country felt the effects of the Depression as keenly as Appalachia. The mines had been closed for years, and poverty, disease, and misery were widespread. At the suggestion of the American Friends Service Committee, Mrs. Roosevelt visited the depressed mining villages in the vicinity of Morgantown, West Virginia, in the autumn of 1933. She saw adults and children living in squallor; she saw the faces of desperate, defeated people who had lost the hope of a decent life.

Appalled and distressed, the First Lady conveyed her impressions to the President, who felt that this area would be ideal for the first subsistence farmstead project. Franklin Roosevelt had long been interested in decentralization and agricultural planning, and had endorsed a bill to relocate destitute families to small farmsteads.[38] The newly created agency, the Subsistence Farmstead Division of the National Industrial Recovery Act "would buy the land, build the houses, acquire the livestock and farm machinery, bring in roads, water, and utilities, and then arrange to sell to the homesteaders over a period of thirty years,"[39] Arthurdale, near Reedsville, West Virginia, was selected as the site of the first farmstead.

Mrs. Roosevelt was intimately involved with Arthurdale from its inception. She was optimistic about its potential, served on the executive and population committees, and chaired the coommittee on admissions.[40]

Despite her enthusiasm and obvious concern, Mrs. Roosevelt committed a number of costly blunders. She had the cottages for the miners redesigned at two to three times the original cost because they were inadequate for West Virginia winters, and then insisted that the new houses have all the modern conveniences and be adequately furnished. Unfortunately the redesigned living units were self-defeating; the unemployed miners could not afford the upkeep of the expensive houses.

Secretary of the Interior Harold Ickes, who was responsible for the adminnistration of the subsistence farmstead division, complained to the President that Mrs. Roosevelt had no concept of cost-effectiveness. The President acknowledged his wife's lack of fiscal responsibility, and told the Secretary of the Interior, "My Missus, unlike most women, hasn't any sense about money at all."[41] Still, the President allowed Mrs. Roosevelt to continue her involvement with Arthurdale.

The criticism could not dampen her enthusiasm nor dim her high hopes for Arthurdale, and while there were many subsistence farmsteads, Arthurdale was always Mrs. Roosevelt's pet project. She donated her own money to the undertaking, and visited the relocated miners and their families for years. Unfortunately, poor planning, poor management, and the continued failure of Mrs. Roosevelt and the government to provide employment for the citizens of Arthurdale made the project a continuous drain on resources.

Arthurdale was liquidated in 1942 at an estimated loss of over two million dollars in federal funds.[42] Mrs. Roosevelt had always viewed Arthurdale in humanitarian terms, for she believed that the farmsteads could restore dignity and a source of self-worth to the destitute.[43] Years later she acknowledged that mistakes had been made, but still felt that people had been helped by the farmstead project.

All Mrs. Roosevelt's White House years were crowded with activity, and the war years, 1941 through 1945, were no exception. It was during this time that the First Lady rendered two services of note, serving as the Assistant Director of the Office of Civilian Defense (OCD), and visiting American combat troops stationed in the Southwest Pacific.

Her service in the Office of Civilian Defense represented two firsts for Eleanor Roosevelt. The job she accepted was the only government position she held during her husband's presidency. OCD also turned out to be Mrs. Roosevelt's only major failure as First Lady.

In May 1941, President Roosevelt established the Office of Civilian Defense and appointed Mayor Fiorello H. La Guardia of New York to head it. Mrs. Roosevelt was interested in the mobilization of volunteers and the use of women and young people in the defense effort, but she was wary of becoming involved with the new agency.[44] She feared that her involvement with OCD would provide an avenue for criticism of Franklin. Despite her misgivings, in September 1941 Mrs. Roosevelt was officially appointed Assistant Director of the OCD, in charge of volunteer participation and community organization.

The First Lady was appalled by the situation she found at OCD. There was little organization and Mayor La Guardia was "interested in whether there were good fire engines, but he was not interested in the other side of OCD morale building," she wrote.[45] With her customary efficiency, Mrs. Roosevelt began the process of setting up objectives and goals for OCD. There were to be nutrition, physical fitness, and child welfare programs to build up the home front.

Her speeches and newspaper column urged people to become active in the work of OCD. Her radio broadcasts during this period were devoted to discussions of morale and what people at home could do to aid the war effort.

The bombing of Pearl Harbor changed the tempo of OCD's work. In a radio message the evening of December 7, 1941, Mrs. Roosevelt exhorted her listeners: "We *must* go about our daily business more determined than ever to do the ordinary things. . . . [W]hen we find a way to do anything more in our communities to help others to build *morale,* to give a feeling of security, we do it."[46] OCD's pre–Pearl Harbor programs would continue, but now there were more pressing concerns. Cities and towns hurriedly assembled plans for dealing with bombings and evacuations.

Despite the seeming timeliness of its work, OCD was a failure. La Guardia had mismanaged the agency, but Mrs. Roosevelt was also to blame for many of its problems. She had a naive conception of defense, concentrating on its social-work aspects rather than the real work of community protection.[47] She had also made the mistake of appointing a number of her friends to positions within the organization for which they did not have the necessary background and experience.

Newspapers and members of Congress criticized Mrs. Roosevelt unmercifully, and in February 1942 she finally resigned because "she knew that she had lost her effectiveness."[48] Later, the First Lady wrote, "As long as I held a government position, even as a volunteer, I offered a way to get at the President and in war time it is not politically wise to attack the President."[49] OCD was Mrs. Roosevelt's most spectacular failure, but perhaps no one could have saved the organization; six months after she resigned, OCD was abandoned.

Mrs. Roosevelt wrote in *This I Remember* that the President was responsible for the idea of her traveling to the Pacific to visit American troops. Her husband, said the First Lady, was concerned about the lack of visitors to that part of the world.[50]

Mrs. Roosevelt had visited American troops stationed in Great Britain in 1942, but this trip would be longer in duration and would visit areas of recent combat. Carrying letters from Franklin to the Pacific commanders, the First Lady set out alone for the Pacific theatre. From Hawaii, Mrs. Roosevelt flew to Noumea to meet with Admiral William Halsey, Commander of the Pacific Fleet. Halsey was not glad to see her. "I think the trouble I give far outweighs the momentary interest it may give the boys to see me," she wrote to her husband.[51] She received a cool reception, but she had a job to do, and she began the task of inspecting hospitals, visiting service clubs, and talking to the men.

One can only imagine what wounded soldiers in hospitals felt when they opened their eyes and found Mrs. Roosevelt standing over them. An officer who escorted the First Lady through hospitals in Australia found her approach to be both motherly and kind. He wrote later, "Maybe it sounds funny, but she left behind her many a tough battletorn GI blowing his nose and swearing at the cold he had recently picked up."[52]

She walked down miles of hospital corridors, and her stoicism and strong resolve kept her from tears. That resolve almost failed her when she saw troops in full battle dress leaving for combat areas. Her voice quavered, but she recovered and she tried to wish each man good luck.[53] The unending hospital inspections were only part of her responsibilities. There were also speeches to the troops, radio broadcasts, and meetings with governments officials. Always she carried greetings from the President to the boys: "He [the President] asked me . . . to take his greetings to American men fighting everywhere and tell them how proud he is of their splendid spirit. May you get home safely, and may there be peace before many months go by.[54]

In Wellington, New Zealand, Mrs. Roosevelt praised the valor of fighting men, saying "by your fighting in the Pacific you have prevented us at home from discovering first hand what war means."[55] During her many stops from Rotorua in New Zealand to Guadalcanal, her routine was the same. She visited the hospitals and service clubs, ate chow with the boys, and conveyed greetings from the Commander in Chief. She looked at countless pictures of wives, girlfriends, mothers, and sisters, and she took scores of addresses of people in the United States whom she promised to contact for the soldiers when she returned home.

On her way back to Washington, Mrs. Roosevelt proclaimed her admiration for the young: "I've come back with an enormous respect for the ingenuity of the younger generation. We have heard that its members are soft. Golly, if that generation is soft I don't know what it is going to be when its gets tough."[56]

When she arrived home in Washington, Mrs. Roosevelt had covered 25,500 miles and still felt she had a job to do.[57] As promised, she contacted soldiers' families and friends; one startled young woman was sure Mrs. Roosevelt's telephone call was a prank.[58]

There were further radio broadcasts, speeches and descriptions of what she had seen in her "My Day" column in the months that followed. In 1944 Mrs. Roosevelt made a similar inspection trip to bases in the Carribbean. The First Lady "carried the colors" all over the world, and showed the troops that they were not forgotten by their President or by their friend his wife.

Politics and Campaigning

Franklin Roosevelt once told his wife that she would never be a good politician: she was too impatient.[59] Roosevelt was an accurage judge of people but he blundered in this assessment, for Eleanor Roosevelt was a shrewd, practical politician who disdained ideology. What could the Democratic party do for the people? she asked.

Her early upbringing never suggested that she would become such an active participant in the political process. She certainly evidenced no interest in politics during her first years of marriage to Franklin Roosevelt.

She may have lacked enthusiasm, but Eleanor Roosevelt was no political innocent. By 1920, the year of Franklin's campaign for the vice presidency, she had been the wife of a public official for ten years, and she had seen the entire spectrum of politics. Already she was capable of making discerning political judgments.

In 1921 Franklin's illness catapulted Eleanor into active political participation. To keep his name before the public and also to educate herself, she joined the League of Women Voters, the Women's City Club, and the Foreign Policy Association; chaired the Non-Partisan Legislative Committee; and served as a juror for the Bok Peace Award.[60] Her most significant action was joining the Women's Division of the New York State Democratic Committee. She began an active career as party fund-raiser and speaker, and also edited the *Women's Democratic News,* the new party organ.

Eleanor rose swiftly within the party ranks, and by 1928 she was being referred to as "one of our most authoritative and trustworthy spokesmen for the Democratic party."[61] She began to edit, prepare layouts, and solicit advertising for the *Democratic News,* a monthly publication of the Democratic National Committee.

In the same year Mrs. Roosevelt accepted the chairmanship of the Women's Division in Al Smith's presidential campaign. She acknowledged that this was a losing battle because of Smith's Roman Catholicism. Still, she continued to labor in Smith's behalf, planning strategy, organizing the office, handling mail, and greeting women visitors.[62]

She took to the stump and attempted to solicit popular support for Smith's presidential bid. In numerous speeches that fall, Mrs. Roosevelt attempted to tell audiences why Governor Smith would make a better Chief Executive than Republican candidate Herbert Hoover. She fought valiantly, but Smith was defeated by Hoover.

From 1928 through 1932, Eleanor, now the wife of the Governor of New York, was a less visible presence politically. However, she continued her association with the *Democratic News,* and she and an associate devised a program that brought thousands of women into the Democratic Party fold.[63]

When Franklin Roosevelt mounted his presidential campaign in 1932, Eleanor and her colleagues were prepared. Their network of workers was well-organized and these "grass trampers," as they were labeled by Louis Howe, went door-to-door nationwide in an effort to bring out the vote for Roosevelt. Mrs. Roosevelt also delivered nonpartisan speeches to labor, youth, and civic groups urging their members to vote.

During the White House years, Eleanor Roosevelt was theorist, strategist, conciliator, campaigner, and above all, a deadly serious politician. She was also a practical politician who understood well the vagaries of politics and government and yet was frequently impatient with bureaucratic machinery.

Mrs. Roosevelt herself became a campaign issue in 1936. Her conduct of the role of First Lady had been unprecedented, and the President's advisors feared that her stand on black rights, her frequent trips, and her constant presence before the public might cost Roosevelt dearly. Some politicians feared that the campaign might turn into a referendum on the First Lady herself.[64] These fears proved to be groundless, and Mrs. Roosevelt was popular on her husband's campaign train. Roosevelt and Garner were reelected by an overwhelming margin of 27,747,636 votes to 16,679,543 for Landon and Knox.[65]

The President and Mrs. Roosevelt had been perceived as a political duo for many years. In 1940 she was delegated by the President to travel to the Democratic National Convention to try and quell a revolt over Henry Wallace's nomination as Vice President.[66] One historian concludes that by 1940 Eleanor Roosevelt "had achieved a political stature sufficiently impressive that it mandated FDR's choice of her as his political emissary in a crucial situation."[67]

Eleanor Roosevelt was the most frankly political woman to ever live in the White House. With her extensive network of sources, she was able to keep her finger on the pulse of the American people and could shrewdly judge their enthusiasm or lack of it for her husband's initiatives. She was versatile and could perform the roles of campaigner, conciliator, or strategist with equal ease. Eleanor Roosevelt was an indispensable member of a classic political duo.

Ceremonial Presence

By 1933, when Mrs. Roosevelt entered the White House, society held little interest for her.[68] Her social secretary felt that Mrs. Roosevelt did not take the social side of the White House seriously enough. The First Lady believed that the world was unstable and to be concerned with purely social matters seemed frivolous and inappropriate.

Dogged in her determination to do the right thing, Mrs. Roosevelt discharged her ceremonial responsibilities fully. The social season still ran from the middle of December to the beginning of Lent, and the First Lady did not tamper with any of the traditional events.

The Roosevelt administration was less formal and more egalitarian than former administrations. The First Lady invited all types of people and groups to the White House. Her lack of discrimination greatly displeased Washington society, but the First Lady was indifferent to the criticism.

In *This I Remember*, Mrs. Roosevelt presents the reader with her social calendar for one week and comments, "I think you will see that a president's wife is not exactly idle."[69] This could be the ultimate understatement regarding Eleanor Roosevelt's ceremonial activity as the First Lady was the major participant in approximately 5,900 activities from March 4, 1933 through August 12, 1945.[70]

Mrs. Roosevelt could not understand the value of receiving thousands of people at teas and receptions at the White House. She discharged her obligations faithfully but felt she could do a great deal more than function as the chatelaine of the executive mansion.

Radio Broadcasts and Lectures

Mrs. Roosevelt had spoken over the radio prior to coming to the White House, but decided to abandon her broadcasts when her husband became President. In 1934, however, she decided to resume commercially sponsored radio broadcasts as a method of raising funds for her numerous projects, especially Arthurdale, the government resettlement project.

Her inaugural radio series was sponsored by the Johns Manville Company and, as expected, it caused a storm of controversy. Many people felt that she was commercializing and decreasing the dignity of the First Lady by accepting pay for her work. An enduring rumor charged that Mrs. Roosevelt received huge fees for her broadcasts and that she retained these monies for her personal use.[71] In fact, Mrs. Roosevelt received no fees for her services, as her salary (which eventually totalled almost seventy-five thousand dollars a year) was paid directly to the American Friends Service Committee.[72] Later, funds were disbursed at Mrs. Roosevelt's direction to many worthy causes. Criticism lessened somewhat but never entirely abated.

In her second broadcast series in 1934, Mrs. Roosevelt discussed, among other topics, "Relaxation and Rest," "Shall a Woman Be Herself?" and "When Will a Woman Become President of the United States?"[73] The topics were selected by Mrs. Roosevelt, but the radio scripts were prepared by a staff of writers. Similar series sponsored by a variety of corporate concerns followed.[74]

Perhaps the approach of war influenced Mrs. Roosevelt's topic selection in her final radio series, during 1941 through 1942. The subjects discussed in these programs were considerably more substantive and topical than those explored in previous broadcasts. The First Lady spoke out on democracy, German propaganda, and anti-Semitism, problems of national defense, national morale, and the war emergency.

Mrs. Roosevelt was an outstanding radio performer because she was always aware of her unseen audience. She seemed to know intuitively what to say, and could envision and identify with her listeners. She advanced her opinions with kindness and courtesy. In 1939 "she was dubbed the 'First Lady of Radio' by WNBC."[75]

From 1935 through 1941, Mrs. Roosevelt traveled the country as a paid lecturer for the W. Colston Leigh Bureau of Lectures and Entertainments. She undertook these lectures, wrote Mrs. Roosevelt, because they afforded her "a wonderful opportunity to visit all kinds of places and to see and get to know a good cross section of people."[76] For a fee of one thousand dollars, the First Lady would speak on any of five topics: "Relationship of the Individual to the Community," "Problems of Youth," "The Mail of a President's Wife," "Peace," and "A Typical Day at the White House." The lectures were delivered extemporaneously. They lasted one hour and were followed by a question-and-answer period.[77]

Mrs. Roosevelt's popularity as a lecturer never waned, and she undertook two long tours per year until late in 1941, when she ceased lecturing to devote her time to the Office of Civilian Defense. The author estimates that Mrs. Roosevelt gave 700 lectures over the six years that she worked for the Leigh Bureau.

Writings

In March 1933, Mrs. Roosevelt began a voluminous correspondence with Lorena Hickok. The First Lady would write chatty letters commenting on both her daily routine and news of the day. These letters might well have been the forerunner of "My Day," the column that Mrs. Roosevelt produced daily for over twenty-six years, from December 31, 1935 through September 11, 1962.

"My Day" was essentially a resume of Mrs. Roosevelt's daily activities and an occasional expression of her thoughts on current events.[78] Initially the column was not very good, even though the First Lady made a sincere attempt to describe her busy schedule, the people she encountered, and the books she read; one reader labeled it "amiable drivel."[79] Over the years, however, her writing improved, and the column became the syndicated voice of Eleanor Roosevelt commenting on the New Deal and expounding her social philosophy.

It was Mrs. Roosevelt's policy to avoid discussion of political topics, but occasionally "My Day" contained a few oblique references to issues under consideration by the President and members of his administration. In 1939 Arthur Krock of the *New York Times* commented that the First Lady's column was required political reading.[80]

"My Day" was not the First Lady's only venture in writing. She wrote monthly columns for *Women's Home Companion* (1933 through 1935), and *Ladies Home Journal* (1941 through 1949). She was also a frequent contributor of articles to numerous magazines.

Not everyone owned a radio, but most people could afford to buy a newspaper or magazine. Eleanor Roosevelt reached a vast audience and, using yet another communication outlet, shared her views on topics ranging from the mundane and trivial to the momentous.

APPROACHES TO COMMUNICATION

Preparation for Speaking

Shy and retiring, young Eleanor Roosevelt could not conceive of ever facing an audience. With Louis Howe's help, however, she began to develop as a speaker. He encouraged her to speak on different topics to different audiences.

By the time she arrived in the White House, Mrs. Roosevelt was a seasoned speech-writer and a passable speaker. Her vocal tone had improved, but frequently she experienced lapses when she could not control her voice, and the resulting sound could be grating. In fact, her cousin Alice Roosevelt Longworth became the star of many Washington parties because she could mimic Eleanor's high-pitched squeal so accurately.

In 1938 Elizabeth von Hesse, a speech teacher, began to work with Mrs. Roosevelt. With coaching and vocal exercises, von Hesse helped improve the First Lady's resonance, tone production, and projection.

The work bore dividends and, within a few months, Mrs. Roosevelt was being congratulated on her improvement. The First Lady continued to study with von Hesse for many years.[81]

Preparation of Texts

The volume of Mrs. Roosevelt's spoken discourse was astonishing. The author estimates that the First Lady delivered approximately fourteen hundred speeches, lectures, and radio broadcasts, and innumerable short statements from 1933 through 1945. Even more astonishing were the facts that Mrs. Roosevelt did not utilize the services of a speech-writer and that she usually spoke extemporaneously, preferring to refer to notes rather than a prepared manuscript.

The First Lady employed no ghostwriters to help her draft her many addresses. Indeed, she told a 1935 press conference, "I dictate, or sometimes write in long hand, every article or speech which I make."[82] However, the demands on Mrs. Roosevelt's time were great, and occasionally she sought information and statistics for inclusion in her speeches from research organizations and government departments.

Communication Style and Delivery

Mrs. Roosevelt once told an audience of prospective speakers: "Never make a speech unless you feel you have something really worthwhile to say; then say it, and having said it, stop talking. Nothing is more important than to know how and when to stop."[83] This statement emphasizes Mrs. Roosevelt's belief in simplicity and brevity in one's speaking style.

The First Lady did not always follow her own advice. Often her speeches lacked logical organization and were simply too long. Though not formally educated, Mrs. Roosevelt possessed an "educated" vocabulary. She was judicious, however, in word selection, taking great care not to use words or phrases that would be misunderstood by her audiences.

Mrs. Roosevelt rarely quoted from outside sources. She was a gifted storyteller, especially when relating personal anecdotes. She also knew how to appeal to an audience's emotions. The First Lady used clichés and platitudes, and made an occasional grammatical error. Her failings, however, augmented her credibility. One observer wrote, "Because she's just not smooth they [audiences] trust her motives and believe in her sincerity."[84]

Mrs. Roosevelt strove to be conciliatory toward audiences, believing that an antagonistic stance only encouraged listeners to disagree with the speaker regardless of what was said.[85] Eleanor Roosevelt's kindness and consideration for audiences contributed to her successful speaking, and led one critic to observe that the First Lady's shortcomings as a speaker "were frequently more than offset by 'the warmth, sincerity and earnestness prevalent in her voice.' "[86]

Press Relations

Eleanor Roosevelt's press relations were one of her most remarkable achievements as First Lady. Historically, reporters had had extremely limited access to the President's wife, and the result was often a one-dimensional or unsympathetic portrait of the First Lady. Louis Howe had taught Mrs. Roosevelt to respect and understand the press, and she arrived "at the White House with a fully developed knowledge of newspaper needs."[87] When Lorena Hickok suggested that the new First Lady hold press conferences,[88] Mrs. Roosevelt, with Franklin and Louis's blessings, agreed.[89]

Male reporters scoffed at the idea of a First Lady meeting the press. Byron Price, Manager of the Associated Press, told a reporter that the conferences would not last long.[90] Most newsmen eventually revised their opinions of Mrs. Roosevelt's conferences, but some remained adamant, arguing that only occasionally did genuine news emerge in the weekly sessions.[91] It was not Mrs. Roosevelt's intention to "break" major stories; rather, she sought to shed light on other important and often neglected topics.

Eleanor Roosevelt's first press conference, and the first ever held by a First Lady, took place on March 6, 1933. Thirty-five newspaperwomen met the new First Lady (who was armed with a box of candied fruit which she passed around) in the Red Room of the White House.[92] Mrs. Roosevelt spoke about her husband's inaugural address, the economic crisis, and settling in at the White House. Although the initial press meeting did not generate much news, the efforts of "God's gift to newspaper women," as she was later called, were genuinely appreciated.[93]

For the next twelve years, one month, and six days, press conferences were held every Monday morning that Mrs. Roosevelt was in Washington.[94] The First Lady informed reporters that she would not discuss political topics, but she felt free to express her opinions on issues of the day. The 353 press conferences,[95] which were never well organized, touched on hundreds of subjects.[96] The First Lady usually spoke about her greatest concerns or those that were most pressing. Contrasting Franklin's and Eleanor's press conferences, Bess Furman wrote, "At the President's press conferences, all the world's a stage; at Mrs. Roosevelt's all the world's a school."[97] Mrs. Roosevelt used her press conferences to educate reporters and their readers about government projects or current events, and often would introduce an expert to provide more technical information about a given area.

She did not fear the controversy created by any of her press conference statements, said Mrs. Roosevelt. Indeed, she felt her pronouncements could have positive consequences. Still, reporters sought to protect the First Lady when she made a statement that might elicit unfavorable comment. On one occasion Mrs. Roosevelt responded, "What you don't understand is that perhaps I am making these statements on purpose to arouse controversy and thereby get the topics talked about and so get people to thinking about them."[98] Reporters and the American public never knew when Mrs. Roosevelt was representing her own opinion or the President's on a topic.

Another extraordinary facet of her press relations was the access that Mrs. Roosevelt permitted newswomen. An astonished Bess Furman noted that Mrs. Roosevelt befriended reporters, inviting them to lunch at the White House and to travel with her in a White House limousine.[99] The First Lady invited reporters to accompany her on some of her travels and "telephoned them when she was in inaccessible spots so that they could get their stories on the wire."[100] Perhaps most extraordinary of all, reporters could telephone Mrs. Roosevelt at the White House to solicit her views.[101]

Eleanor Roosevelt's press relations stand as a watermark in the history of press relations between a First Lady and the fourth estate. Characterized by candor and total access, the relationship benefitted both parties. Mrs. Roosevelt aired her views, and newspaperwomen were afforded a chance to further legitimize their work by covering a controversial and newsworthy public figure.

FACTORS THAT INFLUENCED THE FIRST LADY'S PERFORMANCE AS PUBLIC COMMUNICATOR

Their relationship was responsible in large measure for Eleanor Roosevelt's becoming an active communicator. To serve Franklin and her own needs, she had to have a visible public presence. She was called on to express the President's pride in a successful New Deal project or his disappointment at a failed legislative initiative. Franklin encouraged her in this enterprise, and Eleanor traveled the country as his eyes, his ears, and sometimes his voice. To a lesser but still important extent, Mrs. Roosevelt's input into presidential decision making contributed to her assuming an active public role.

Relationship With Her Husband

Mrs. Roosevelt wrote that she and Franklin were young and inexperienced when they decided to marry. "I was sure I was really in love . . . and yet I know now that it was years before I understood what being in love was or what loving really meant."[102]

The Roosevelt marriage survived the disclosure of Franklin's infidelity, but it underwent dramatic changes. Elliott Roosevelt comments that after this episode, his mother "was willing to have him [Franklin] as a partner in public life, not ever again as a husband."[103] Eleanor became an independent woman with a life of her own. The marriage became a partnership in the truest sense of the word, for Franklin encouraged Eleanor to share his activities and public life.

In the White House, Mrs. Roosevelt's primary motivation was to help those who could not help themselves. Sometimes, however, she was unrelenting in pressuring her husband for ideas or for legislative or financial remedies for a problem. A number of people who knew her felt that Eleanor had a propensity to nag and lacked a sense of humor.[104] Anna Roosevelt Boettinger noted her mother cross-examining the President during a White House dinner, and said jokingly (but with some truth), "Mother, can't you see you are giving Father indigestion?"[105]

After Franklin's death, Eleanor offered this assessment of the role she had played in her husband's life: "I think I sometimes acted as a spur, even though the spurring was not always wanted or welcome. I was one of those who served his purposes."[106]

Access to Presidential Decision Making

The Roosevelts were such a well-known political team that by the time they entered the White House, the phrase " 'Eleanor and I' was known over the entire country."[107]

Mrs. Roosevelt always denied that she had any influence with the President beyond that of a regular petitioner, and protested "that a President's wife does not see him enough to tell him what to do."[108] This was simply untrue. The First Lady wielded considerable influence with her husband, and her opinions and beliefs were reflected in New Deal programs, legislation and government appointments. The First Lady "was generally credited with responsibility for the creation of the NYA, the surplus food program for relief clients, the arts and crafts section of WPA and resettlement and community projects such as Arthurdale."[109]

Occasionally Mrs. Roosevelt revealed her hand. A good example of this occurred in the summer of 1938. On August 8, the President was holding a news conference which the First Lady attended. At times he seemed lost for words, and Mrs. Roosevelt prompted him with a word or phrase.[110] The following day, Mrs. Roosevelt's column "My Day" contained some of the identical figures of speech and ideas used by the President in his press conference. Writing in the *New York Times*, Arthur Krock pointed out that Mrs. Roosevelt had always been scrupulously fair in giving credit for borrowed ideas and expressions, yet gave none here.[111] "The inference he drew was that she gave no credit [in her column] because none was due"; the thoughts were her own.[112] It was clear that the First Lady had access to presidential decision making.

In later years Mrs. Roosevelt admitted that she had discussed many issues with her husband, and she remarked, "Well, you don't just sit at meals and look at each other."[113] Despite having access, the First Lady was often frustrated by the President's sense of political necessity. Rarely if ever could she make

Franklin move faster than he wished on any issue. Grace Tully recalls hearing the President tell Mrs. Roosevelt many times, "I'm just not ready to talk about that yet, darling."[114] Mrs. Roosevelt herself recalled the President saying, "First things come first, and I can't alienate certain votes I need for measures that are more important at the moment by pushing any measure that would entail a fight."[115]

Though he might become annoyed with her eternal prodding, the President relied on his wife's opinions and reports from her many inspection trips. Secretary of Labor Frances Perkins recalled the President saying in cabinet meetings, "You know my Missus gets around a lot or my Missus says that they have typhoid fever in that district."[116] Grace Tully said that it was not unusual to hear Mrs. Roosevelt "predicate an entire line of questioning upon a statement that 'My Missus told me so and so' "[117]

The President never attempted to silence or restrain the First Lady, even when she said things that placed him in a tenuous position. Once she asked him if he minded that she planned to express a certain opinion. Franklin responded; "No, certainly not. You can say anything you want. I can always say, 'Well, that is my wife; I can't do anything about her!' "[118]

Eleanor Roosevelt had greater access to presidential decision making than any First Lady in history up to that time. She made herself part of her husband's administration, and often operated as his conscience in regard to the social welfare measures of the New Deal.

The President's and First Lady's Perceptions of Women

Mrs. Roosevelt had a long history as an advocate of women. Just after she arrived at the White House, she published a book entitled *It's up to the Women.* The volume set forth her philosophy on a variety of topics of concern to women.

Capable women must help in combating the Depression, she wrote in her book, but the First Lady was also concerned with unemployed and destitute women. To help these women, Mrs. Roosevelt convened the White House Conference on the Emergency Needs of Women, "for the purpose of defining their problems and needs and suggesting possibilities for their constructive employment."[119] With the help of Harry Hopkins, Administrator of the Federal Emergency Relief Administration, approximately 100,000 women were hired by the Civil Works Administration (CWA) by the end of 1933.[120]

The First Lady prevailed on the President to appoint women to high office. Though she denied that she alone was responsible for female appointments, it is likely that many female Roosevelt appointees owed some debt to Eleanor Roosevelt's advocacy. While Mrs. Roosevelt tried to promote the idea of women serving in important positions, she would not lend her support to an office-seeker just because she was a woman. The First Lady felt that any office-seeker had to be qualified for the job in question.

President Roosevelt appointed twenty-eight women to high-level positions

within his administration, and a total of thirty-seven served in high-level positions (nine having been appointed to their positions by Roosevelt's predecessors).[121] Mrs. Roosevelt's influence on her husband's appointment of women to
high office within his administration was considerable.

Mrs. Roosevelt did not support the Equal Rights Amendment (ERA) endorsed
by the National Women's Party. Her opposition was almost exclusively based
on labor considerations. In a 1933 press conference, she said that the women's
party represented the views of "a very limited high type group of women who
[were] able to defend themselves. The mass of laboring women . . . still needed
the protection of maximum hour and minimum wage laws."[122] Mrs. Roosevelt
continued to oppose ERA during her entire White House tenure, and did not
become a convert until just prior to her death.[123]

Women had to vote and join political parties if they ever hoped to affect
public policy, preached Mrs. Roosevelt. She believed that women had a unique
contribution to make to politics. "I think emotion is the contribution which
women have to make. They can at times be objective and analytical, but they
can also feel things in a way that is rarely given to men to feel."[124]

Mrs. Roosevelt's proselytizing and Franklin Roosevelt's own experience with
women while Governor of New York contributed to his perception of women
when he entered the White House. Like his wife, the President felt that women
were capable, and he depended on them for advice and opinions. The most
visible woman in the Roosevelt administration was Eleanor Roosevelt. She was
part of the President's inner circle and one of his most trusted advisors.

The status of women began to improve during the Roosevelt years. For both
Roosevelts, women were not a minority to be ignored but rather valuable,
responsible citizens who could make important contributions to government
decision making and aid in enriching the life of the nation.

In a recent essay about Eleanor Roosevelt, a writer notes that when discussing
First Ladies, many comments are prefaced with the words "since Eleanor Roosevelt" or "of course, Eleanor Roosevelt"[125] The First Lady set the standard by
which all previous and future presidential wives are judged, and she established
a political surrogate–independent advocate model.

Eleanor Roosevelt was the first First Lady to establish an identity as a communicator entirely separate from that of her husband. This was a significant
achievement, for Franklin Roosevelt was a powerful communicator with superior
skill in utilizing radio.

More than any other First Lady, Eleanor Roosevelt understood what she could
and could not accomplish through media exposure. She knew that her ideas
would be carried to millions if she used the national podium afforded her. At
the same time, she knew that she would attract unwanted attention and was
bound to be criticized for her actions. Criticism had never troubled her and she
felt many causes were worth the risk; however, she was always sensitive to
comments that reflected on the President.

For twelve years she fulfilled her obligations with dignity and selflessness.

Without doubt, Eleanor Roosevelt expanded the concept of what a President's wife could do, and made it possible for her successors to embrace any number of activities and roles. Some First Ladies might still see their role as that of party-giver, and some might embrace only a single concern and publicize it. To Eleanor Roosevelt, however, the White House offered unending possibilities for usefulness, and from 1933 through 1945 she accomplished all that was humanly possible to help her country.

Perhaps her most enduring legacy was the life of her own that she built on the foundation of her White House experiences.[126] The woman who wept that she would have no identity save that of the President's wife emerged not as Mrs. Franklin D. Roosevelt, but as Eleanor Roosevelt, a respected world figure.[127]

NOTES

1. Biographical information has been culled from the following sources: Tamara K. Hareven, *Eleanor Roosevelt: An American Conscience* (Chicago: Quadrangle, 1968); Joseph P. Lash, *Eleanor and Franklin* (New York: Norton, 1971); Alfred A. Rollins, Jr., *Roosevelt and Howe* (New York: Knopf, 1962); Eleanor Roosevelt, *This Is My Story* (New York: Garden, 1937); Eleanor Roosevelt, *This I Remember* (New York: Harper, 1949); Eleanor Roosevelt, *The Autobiography of Eleanor Roosevelt* (New York: Harper, 1961); Elliot Roosevelt and James Brough, *The Roosevelts of Hyde Park: An Untold Story* (New York: Putnam's, 1973); and Joan Hoff-Wilson and Marjorie Lightman, eds., *Without Precedent: The Life and Career of Eleanor Roosevelt* (Bloomington: Indiana University, 1984).

2. Eleanor Roosevelt, *Autobiography*, p. 9.

3. Joseph Alsop, *FDR: A Centenary Remembrance* (New York: Viking, 1982), p. 39.

4. For an interesting discussion of Elliott Roosevelt, see Michael Teague, *Mrs. L.: Conversations with Alice Roosevelt Longworth* (New York: Doubleday, 1981), pp. 151–152.

5. Carol Felsenthal, *Alice Roosevelt Longworth* (New York: Putnam, 1988), p. 49.

6. Lash, *Eleanor and Franklin*, p. 81.

7. Hareven, *Eleanor Roosevelt*, p. 7.

8. Felsenthal, *Alice Roosevelt Longworth*, p. 138.

9. Lash, *Eleanor and Franklin*, p. 171.

10. Lash, *Eleanor and Franklin*, p. 227.

11. Eleanor Roosevelt, *Autobiography*, p. 109.

12. John L. Moore (ed.), *Guide to U.S. Elections* (Washington, D.C.: Congressional Quarterly, 1975), p. 286.

13. Samuel I. Rosenman, *Working with Roosevelt* (New York: Harper, 1952), p. 37.

14. James MacGregor Burns, *Roosevelt: The Lion and the Fox* (New York: Harcourt, 19565), p. 90.

15. Sol Barzman, *The First Ladies* (New York: Cowles, 1970), pp. 301–302; Frances Perkins, *The Roosevelt I Knew* (New York: Viking, 1946), p. 34; Rollins, *Roosevelt and Howe*, pp. 184–185; Rosenman, *Working with Roosevelt*, p. 37.

16. Eleanor Roosevelt, *Autobiography*, p. 146.

17. Eleanor Roosevelt, *Autobiography*, pp. 154–155.

18. Doris Faber, *The Life of Lorena Hickok* (New York: Morrow, 1980), p. 87.

19. Eleanor Roosevelt, *This I Remember*, p. 69.

20. John L. Moore (ed.), *Guide to U.S. Elections*, p. 289.

21. Felsenthal, *Alice Roosevelt Longworth*, p. 180.

22. Lash, *Eleanor and Franklin*, pp. 357–358.

23. Eleanor Roosevelt, *This I Remember*, p. 76.

24. Index to "My Day," Franklin D. Roosevelt Library, Hyde Park, New York (hereafter referred to as FDR Library).

25. Eleanor Roosevelt, *This I Remember*, p. 102.

26. Letter from Grace Coolidge to Lou Hoover, June 24, 1933, Lou Hoover Papers, Personal File, Herbert Hoover Library, West Branch, Iowa.

27. Joseph P. Lash, *Eleanor: The Years Alone* (New York: Norton, 1972), p. 15.

28. Mrs. Roosevelt employed the term "Negro" to refer to black Americans. It was not used in a derogatory sense but rather reflected the historical period.

29. Hareven, *Eleanor Roosevelt*, p. 112.

30. Jonathan Daniels, interviewed by Emily Williams, Hilton Head Island, South Carolina, November 16, 1979, pp. 5–6, Eleanor Roosevelt Oral History Project (hereafter referred to as EROHP) FDR Library.

31. Hareven, *Eleanor Roosevelt*, pp. 115–116.

32. Lash, *Eleanor and Franklin*, p. 516.

33. Robert L. Zangrando, *The NAACP Crusade Against Lynching, 1909–1950* (Philadelphia: Temple University Press, 1980), p. 113.

34. Hareven, *Eleanor Roosevelt*, pp. 113–114.

35. Hareven, *Eleanor Roosevelt*, p 117.

36. Eleanor Roosevelt, "My Day," February 28, 1939.

37. Nathan Miller, *F.D.R.: An Intimate History* (New York: Doubleday, 1983), p. 389.

38. Hareven, *Eleanor Roosevelt*, p. 92.

39. Arthur M. Schlesinger, Jr., *The Age of Roosevelt. Volumn II: The Coming of the New Deal* (Boston: Houghton Mifflin, 1957), p. 365.

40. Rollins, *Roosevelt and Howe*, p. 407.

41. Harold L. Ickes, *The Secret Diary of Harold L. Ickes: The First Thousand Days, 1933–1936* (New York: Simon, 1954), p. 218.

42. Hareven, *Eleanor Roosevelt*, p. 109.

43. Hareven, *Eleanor Roosevelt*, p. 92.

44. Lash, *Love, Eleanor*, p. 354.

45. Hareven, *Eleanor Roosevelt*, p. 176.

46. Pan American Coffee Bureau Broadcast Transcripts, December 7, 1941, Eleanor Roosevelt Papers, FDR Library (hereafter referred to as ER Papers).

47. Hareven, *Eleanor Roosevelt*, p. 178.

48. Daniels interview, p. 10.

49. Eleanor Roosevelt, *This I Remember*, p. 250.

50. Eleanor Roosevelt, *This I Remember*, p. 295.

51. Lash, *Eleanor and Franklin*, p. 685.

52. Robert M. White, quoted in Lash, *Eleanor and Franklin*, p. 687.

53. Untitled story, *New York Times*, September 13, 1943, p. 21.

54. "First Lady Views Canberra Parade," *New York Times*, September 5, 1943, p. 21.

55. "First Lady Praises Valor of Wounded," *New York Times*, August 30, 1943, p. 8.

56. "First Lady Found Worries in Pacific," *New York Times*, September 24, 1943, p. 15.

57. "First Lady 'Proud' of Pacific Troops," *New York Times,* September 30, 1943, p. 5.

58. " 'White House Call' Real," *New York Times,* September 30, 1943, p. 24.

59. Frank B. Freidel, *Franklin D. Roosevelt* (Boston: Little, Brown, 1952), p. 500.

60. James R. Kearney, *Anna Eleanor Roosevelt: The Evolution of a Reformer* (Boston: Houghton Mifflin, 1968), p. 101.

61. Kearney, *Anna Eleanor Roosevelt,* p. 106.

62. Eleanor Roosevelt, *This I Remember,* p. 41.

63. May Thompson Evans, interviewed by Thomas F. Soapes, Alexandria, Virginia, January 30, 1978, pp. 16–17, EROHP. FDR Library.

64. Lash, *Eleanor and Franklin,* p. 445.

65. John L. Moore (ed.), *Guide to U.S. Elections,* p. 290.

66. Rosenman, *Working with Roosevelt,* p. 203.

67. Kearney, *Anna Eleanor Roosevelt,* p. 141.

68. Lash, *Eleanor and Franklin,* p. 376.

69. Eleanor Roosevelt, *This I Remember,* pp. 94–95.

70. The author's estimate is based on events reported in *New York Times Index* and "My Day."

71. Letter, Malvina Thompson to Congressman Fred Biermann, July 25, 1934, PPF 2/Eleanor Roosevelt, 1934, FDR Library.

72. Barzman, *First Ladies,* p. 303.

73. Simmons Broadcasts, July 9-September 25, 1934. Speech and Article File, 1933–1934, Box 3027, ER Papers, FDR Library.

74. Among Mrs. Roosevelt's sponsors were the Typewriters Education Bureau, the Selby Shoe Company, Ponds, and Sweetheart Soap.

75. Lash, *Eleanor and Franklin,* p. 419.

76. Eleanor Roosevelt, *This I Remember,* p. 152.

77. Lash, *Eleanor and Franklin,* p. 421.

78. Franklin D. Roosevelt Library Finding Aid to the Eleanor Roosevelt Papers, FDR Library.

79. Felsenthal, *Alice Roosevelt Longworth,* p. 178.

80. "My Day," *The Saturday Evening Post,* 212 (September 19, 1939), p. 24.

81. Eleanor Roosevelt, "My Day," January 28, 1938.

82. "Radio Broadcast, Press Conference, March 22, 1935," Speech and Article File, 1935, Box 3030, ER papers, FDR Library.

83. "Rules for Speaking Given by First Lady," *New York Times,* January 12, 1940, p. 19.

84. Virginia Pasley, "First Lady to the Common Man," *American Mercury,* 58 (March 1944), p. 279.

85. "Rules for Speaking Given by First Lady," p. 19.

86. Kearney, *Anna Eleanor Roosevelt,* p. 235.

87. Ishbel Ross, *Ladies of the Press,* (New York: Harper, 1936), p. 310.

88. Eleanor Roosevelt, *This I Remember,* p. 102.

89. Lash, *Eleanor and Franklin,* p. 361

90. Bess Furman, *Washington Bi-Line: The Personal History of a Newspaper Woman* (New York: Knopf, 1949), p. 153.

91. Delbert Clark, *Washington Dateline* (New York: Stokes, 1941), p. 153.

92. "All Alike in Crisis Says Mrs. Roosevelt," *New York Times*, March 17, 1933, p. 5. Male reporters were not invited to Mrs. Roosevelt's press conferences.

93. Ruby Black, *Eleanor Roosevelt: A Biography* (New York: Duell, 1940), p. 155.

94. Furman, *Washington Bi-Line*, p. 153.

95. Maurine H. Beasley, ed., *The White House Press Conferences of Eleanor Roosevelt* (New York: Garland, 1983), p. 5.

96. Black, *Eleanor Roosevelt: A Biography*, p. 158.

97. Furman, *Washington Bi-Line*, p. 194.

98. Lash, *Eleanor and Franklin*, p. 363.

99. Furman, *Washington Bi-Line*, p. 153.

100. Ross, *Ladies of the Press*, p. 311.

101. Ross, *Ladies of the Press*, p. 311.

102. Eleanor Roosevelt, *This Is My Story*, p. 111.

103. Roosevelt and Brough, *Roosevelts of Hyde Park*, p. 96.

104. Daniels interview, pp. 5–6; Teague, *Mrs. L.*, p. 151.

105. Grace Tully, *F.D.R., My Boss* (New York: Scribners, 1949), p. 110.

106. Eleanor Roosevelt, *This I Remember*, p. 349.

107. Barzman, *First Ladies*, p. 302.

108. "First Lady not the Boss," *New York Times*, March 13, 1939, p. 19.

109. Pasley, "First Lady," p. 283.

110. "Mrs. Roosevelt Joins In," *New York Times*, August 9, 1939, p. 4.

111. "My Day," *Saturday Evening Post*, 212 (September 9, 1939), p. 24.

112. "My Day," *Saturday Evening Post*, September 9, 1939, p. 24.

113. Kearney, *Anna Eleanor Roosevelt*, p. 138.

114. Tully, *F.D.R., My Boss*, p. 110.

115. Eleanor Roosevelt, *This I Remember*, p. 162.

116. Kearney, *Anna Eleanor Roosevelt*, p. 131.

117. Kearney, *Anna Eleanor Roosevelt*, p. 131.

118. Hareven, *Eleanor Roosevelt*, p. 123.

119. Hareven, *Eleanor Roosevelt*, p. 64.

120. Lash, *Eleanor and Franklin*, p. 389.

121. Karen Keesling and Suzanne Cavanagh, "Women Presidential Appointees Serving or Having Served in Full Time Positions Requiring Senate Confirmation 1912–1977" (Congressional Research Service, Library of Congress, March 23, 1978), pp. 1, 13, 15, 16, 25–27. Historian Susan Wolfe Ware writes that the President

was only willing to go so far in entrusting major responsibilities to women. When Daisy Harriman was mentioned for a diplomatic post in 1937, Roosevelt replied that the foreign situation was so complicated that he could not put a woman in charge anywhere except a country unlikely to get involved in European hostilities.

In Susan Wolfe Ware, "Political Sisterhood in the New Deal: Women in Politics and Government, 1933–1940" (unpublished doctoral dissertation, Harvard University, 1978), p. 74.

122. "Woman's Party Hit by Mrs. Roosevelt," *New York Times*, July 7, 1933, p. 19.

123. Lash, *Years Alone*, p. 317.

124. "Trialog on Office Holders," *Independent Woman*, 18 (June 1938), p. 18.

125. Abigail Q. McCarthy, "E.R. as First Lady," in Hoff-Wilson and Lightman *Without Precedent,* p. 216.

126. McCarthy, "E.R. as First Lady," p. 224.

127. June Sochen, *Movers and Shakers: American Women Thinkers and Activists, 1900–1970* (New York: Quadrangle, 1973) p. 151.

5
POLITICAL SURROGATES AND
INDEPENDENT ADVOCATES

Lady Bird Johnson

Lady Bird Johnson was an active public communicator in the White House. A journalism major at the University of Texas, she understood the value of speeches, statements, and effective press coverage to the achievement of both her husband's objectives and her own. She selected national beautification as her primary White House project, and for her entire tenure as First Lady she devoted her energies to publicizing this endeavor. She took trips, planted trees, addressed conservation groups, and held meetings to support her effort. The "saleswoman" for the Great Society did not limit herself to a single project, she also devoted her time to championing her husband's poverty program and Project Head Start.

The First Lady was an astute politician and enthusiastic campaigner. In October 1964 she embarked on a memorable forty-seven speech whistle stop train trip through the South to sell Lyndon Johnson, the man who had passsed the Civil Rights Act, to his enraged countrymen. No First Lady had ever campaigned without her husband, and Mrs. Johnson thus broke a long-standing tradition.

Lyndon Johnson encouraged his wife to be an activist, to air her opinions, and to take an active role in his presidency. A remarkable woman, Lady Bird Johnson took up her husband's challenge and became involved in almost every facet of Lyndon Johnson's stewardship, both public and private, for over five years. She was unafraid to express her opinions, and she influenced those of her husband.

Lady Bird Johnson was a whirlwind of activity who enjoyed her time as First Lady and used it productively to share her concerns for the environment and other projects with the nation.

ROUTE TO THE WHITE HOUSE

On December 22, 1912, a daughter, Claudia Alta, was born to Minnie Patillo Taylor and Thomas Taylor of Karnack, Texas.[1] At the age of two Claudia acquired the nickname that would become familiar to the world when her nursemaid, Alice Tittle, described her as being "purty [sic] as a lady bird."[2]

Lady Bird's mother was the daughter of an aristocratic Alabama family. Cultured, well-read, and well ahead of her time, Minnie Taylor supported woman suffrage and integration.[3] Her husband, Thomas, was a prosperous landowner and shopkeeper.

Minnie Taylor died when Lady Bird was five years old. Her sister Effie Patillo moved from Alabama to Texas to care for the little girl. Lady Bird attended elementary school in a one-room schoolhouse. Following her highschool graduation she attended a junior college and then enrolled at the University of Texas in Austin. She earned a B.A. and was graduated with honors in 1933 but decided to remain at the university another year to pursue a degree in journalism.

A few months after graduation, Lady Bird was introduced to a young congressional secretary named Lyndon B. Johnson. The future Mrs. Johnson commented on their first meeting: "It was just like finding yourself in the middle of a whirlwind. . . . I wasn't sure I wanted to get caught up in it as a matter of self-preservation."[4]

Lady Bird was startled when Lyndon Johnson proposed marriage to her the day after their first meeting. She turned down his proposal, but agreed to meet his family and his employer, Congressman Richard Kleberg. Thomas Taylor enthusiastically approved of Johnson, telling his daughter: "You've been bringing home a lot of boys. This time you've brought home a man."[5]

Lady Bird Taylor was one of the first recipients of what would later become known as the "Johnson Treatment." From Washington, Lyndon deluged her with telephone calls, telegrams, and mail, exhorting her to be his bride. After two months he returned to Texas to argue his case in person. Lady Bird was still unsure, but her father told her, "some of the best deals are made in a hurry."[6] Lady Bird finally said yes, and the couple was married in St. Mark's Episcopal Church in San Antonio on November 17, 1934.

Following a honeymoon in Mexico, the Johnsons set up housekeeping in Washington, D.C. The new bride had to learn how to run a home, but perhaps even more important, her political indoctrination was beginning. Mrs. Johnson told an interviewer that her husband requested that she learn about the economy of the counties that Congressman Kleberg represented. She was also to familiarize herself with the names of men in each county who were able to accomplish things.[7] In February 1937, Johnson announced his candidacy for the congressional seat from Texas's tenth congressional district. No source discusses Lady Bird's feelings about her husband's initial political campaign. If she was not entirely enthusiastic, she gave another important endorsement when she provided Lyndon with ten thousand dollars from her inheritance to help defray campaign costs. Lady Bird played no public role in the campaign, being too shy to face audiences. That was not the only reason for her lack of participation, and she told an interviewer "In 1937, it [women campaigning] wasn't done in Texas."[8] She kept busy licking envelopes, calling people, and driving voters to the polls on Election Day.[9]

Johnson ran unopposed for reelection to Congress in 1938 and 1940. In 1941 he ran for the Senate, and lost the only race of his political career. Still a member of the House, he returned to Washington to continue his legislative work. On December 7, 1941, the Japanese bombed Pearl Harbor; three days later Johnson turned over the operation of his congressional office to Lady Bird and began a period of active service as a lieutenant commander in the U.S. Navy.

Lady Bird took over the operation of Lyndon's congressional office (without salary) because she cared about her husband's work and his constituents. The experience was a positive one for Lady Bird because it helped her to better understand Lyndon Johnson and it convinced her that she was competent, able to earn a living and learn new things.[10] In addition, the experience stimulated her interest in politics, and she commented, "I have always been more interested in politics since then."[11]

Johnson returned to Washington in July 1942. In January 1943, Lady Bird purchased debt-ridden radio station KTBC in Austin. Not only did she literally clean up KTBC with a mop and pail; she was involved in every facet of the operation. Friends were especially impressed with her business acumen, and KTBC flourished under Mrs. Johnson's close scrutiny. In the early 1950s, KTBC expanded to include KTBC-TV. The success of the television station greatly augmented the Johnson family fortune.[12]

The Johnsons had hoped for a family, and after numerous miscarriages and great disappointment, Lady Bird gave birth to Lynda Bird on March 9, 1944. Lucy Baines was born on July 2, 1947.

Johnson ran for and was elected to the Senate in 1948 by a margin of eighty-seven votes. His rise in the Senate was swift and spectacular. Two years after entering the Senate, fellow Democrats elected him their Whip. Two years later he was elected to the prestigious and influential office of Senate Majority Leader.

Following his recuperation from a heart attack in 1955, Johnson busily began to lay the groundwork for a presidential bid in 1960. Lady Bird was also preparing for such a race. Though she loved meeting people, she was frightened of delivering formal speeches and knew she would occasionally be expected to do so. To deal with her apprehensiveness she took a public speaking course at the Capitol Speakers Club.[13]

Nineteen-sixty was not, however, Lyndon Johnson's year for the presidency and he lost the nomination to Senator John F. Kennedy. After a good deal of discussion and argument with Lady Bird, who was "somewhere between negative and neutral," Johnson accepted Kennedy's offer of the second spot on the Democratic ticket.[14]

Lady Bird played an active role in the 1960 campaign. Her speech training stood her in good stead as she traveled extensively, speaking at numerous political events across the country.

The Kennedy-Johnson ticket was victorious, and Lady Bird found herself as "second lady." During the vice presidential years, Mrs. Johnson covered 120,000 miles and visited thirty-three countries with her husband.[15] She entertained frequently, and "stood in" for First Lady Jacqueline Kennedy a number of times.

"It all began so beautifully," writes Mrs. Johnson of the trip to Dallas on Friday, November 22, 1963.[16] Before the day was over, Lyndon B. Johnson was President of the United States and Lady Bird Johnson was First Lady. Told by her friend and Executive Assistant to the Vice President Elizabeth Carpenter that she should have something to say to the press when she returned to Washington from Dallas, Mrs. Johnson said: "I have no statement. . . . The way I feel it has all been a dreadful nightmare and somehow we must find the strength to go on . . . "[17] Carpenter told her to repeat those words as her statement.

As the shock and horror of the assassination began to dissipate, the realities of being the President's wife became apparent to Mrs. Johnson, and she told a friend, "I feel like I am suddenly on stage for a part I never rehearsed."[18] Later, as the Johnson family moved into the White House, Mrs. Johnson said, "I will try to be balm, sustainer and sometimes critic for my husband. . . . [F]or my own self, my role must emerge in deeds, not words."[19] Mrs. Johnson told the author that she did not consciously decide to model herself after any previous First Lady.[20] She understood the potential for achievement inherent within her position, and determined to be an active, working First Lady.

The new First Lady endorsed national beautification, Project Head Start and the poverty program. She entertained extensively at the White House and campaigned for her husband and other Democratic Party office-seekers. Mrs. Johnson's swing through the South in the fall of 1964 attempted to hold recalcitrant Southern states for the President in the wake of the 1964 Civil Rights Act. The President swept to victory, soundly defeating Republican Barry Goldwater by a popular vote of 43,126,584 to 27,177,838 votes.[21]

The years of 1964 and 1965 were a period of accomplishment for the Johnson administration, and Lady Bird Johnson found enthusiastic audiences wherever she traveled to endorse a project. By 1966, however, Vietnam War protesters greeted her at almost every engagement. Despite their chanting and picketing, she continued to travel and support her projects.

Mrs. Johnson opposed her husband running for another term as President in 1968. Subtly and gently she urged him to make up his own mind.[22] Lyndon Johnson announced on March 31, 1968, that he would not seek another term as President, and in January 1969 he retired from elective public office after a political career that had spanned almost four decades.

Lyndon Baines Johnson died following a heart attack on January 22, 1973.

Lady Bird Johnson remains active and involved in the National Wildflower Research Center (which she founded), the board of National Geographic, and a variety of business enterprises.

MAJOR COMMUNICATION ACTIVITIES OF THE FIRST LADY

Lady Bird was an active, involved public communicator. During her White House tenure she delivered 164 speeches, took part in press briefings, wrote magazine articles, made statements, and used both radio and television to share her ideas with the nation.

Mrs. Johnson always maintained that she was simply highlighting her husband's programs. This was true; however, through her communication activities she also began to emerge as an independent person with ideas and passions of her own.

Advocacy

Mrs. Johnson was interested in many things, but she knew that she could not support every cause, no matter how worthy. She decided to channel her energies into one major project, the preservation of the natural American landscape. The project became known as beautification.[23]

The First Lady had always loved the land, and had always been an environmentalist. That she would be drawn to a cause that would work for the maintenance and preservation of the environment was natural. Mrs. Johnson mentioned that she selected beautification (a name she never liked as it sounded too institutional and clinical)[24] because it was a project "that made my heart sing."[25]

The beautification program came into existence in December 1964. Mrs. Johnson's initial idea was to endorse conservation in the city of Washington, D.C. Later, encouraged by an enthusiastic response and with growing confidence, she enlarged her vision to include the entire country.

Mrs. Johnson told an audience that "beautification means our total concern for the physical and human quality of the world we pass on to our children."[26] The First Lady's concept of beautification did not merely include planting flowers; indeed, she viewed the program encompassing the design of aesthetically pleasing living space, the clean-up and revitalization of urban areas, lighting, designation of certain areas as national parks or recreation facilities, and the preservation of historic sites.

Mrs. Johnson enjoyed the support of another person greatly interested in beautification, the President of the United States. In his 1965 State of the Union address, Lyndon Johnson spoke of the necessity of preserving the natural beauty of America. He publicly advocated many of his wife's ideas: landscaping highways, planning more aesthetically pleasing cities, and enforcing strong controls for air and water pollution.[27] The President promised legislative support; Lady Bird Johnson would take the issue to the people.

On February 5, 1965, the beautification program was kicked off with a luncheon at the White House hosted by Mrs. Johnson. Among the luncheon guests were women who possessed expertise in various aspects of conservation. The main speaker was Mrs. Albert (Mary) Lasker, a New York philanthropist who had been interested in and supported conservation for over twenty years. "Plant masses of flowers where the masses pass," preached Mrs. Lasker.[28] She and the First Lady also urged planting trees and improving lighting in cities.

On February 8 the President sent a special message on natural beauty to Congress. In an interview a few days later, Mrs. Johnson echoed and amplified many of the ideas expressed by her husband in the natural beauty message. She especially criticized profusions of billboards along highways and the eyesore created by automobile junkyards.[29] She told interviewers, "the things worth remembering in a lifetime are often—with me—associated with beauty."[30]

The Committee for a More Beautiful Capitol met for the first time at the White House on Feburary 11, 1965. Mrs. Johnson told a group, which consisted of Mrs. Lasker, Secretary of the Interior Stewart Udall, and fourteen others, that much could be done to beautify the capitol city.

The beautification committee met each month, and suggestions about future projects and donations of varying amounts were received. Interest burgeoned, and Mrs. Johnson was overwhelmed with hundreds of requests to address garden clubs, city and state beauty councils, and conservation groups. The First Lady herself gave approximately sixty speeches on the topic. To assist in the beautification effort, Mrs. Johnson formed a speaker's bureau of Cabinet and Senate wives and staff to help in filling requests.[31]

In May 1965 Mrs. Johnson opened the White House Conference on Natural Beauty. In her remarks the First Lady decried ugliness and the loss of an attractive environment: "Our peace of mind, our emotions, our spirits—even our souls— are conditioned by what we see. Ugliness is bitterness."[32]

Highest on Mrs. Johnson's list of annoyances were billboards, which she felt obscured roadside plantings and cluttered views of the surrounding countryside. Surely it was not fortuitous that the President referred the Highway Beautification Act to Congress. The bill if passed would require that billboards be located 660 feet beyond right-of-ways and that junkyards be screened.[33]

Although the First Lady was not the author of the legislation, she was involved in it from its inception. The proposed legislation met with formidable opposition from small businessmen and civic associations who felt their livelihood would be threatened if the billboards were removed. Mrs. Johnson spearheaded a multifaceted effort to promote passage of the measure. She and a working group "met with the President to determine specific lobbying assignments."[34]

The First Lady telephoned Congressmen and had members of her staff write to architects, park executives, and garden club members.[35] Press secretary Liz Carpenter visited members of the Texas congressional delegation, "coordinated lobbying through conservation groups and elicited favorable newspaper editorials as the vote neared."[36] The vote on S–2084 (the Highway Beautification Act) was 245–138 in favor of the "Lady Bird Bill." President Johnson signed the bill into law on October 22, 1965.

The First Lady used television to help persuade Americans that her crusade was important. In an hour-long documentary entitled "A Visit to Washington with Mrs. Lyndon B. Johnson on Behalf of a More Beautiful Capitol," and telecast on November 25, 1965, the President's wife attempted the most extensive and persuasive grass-roots effort of her project. The film contrasted the ugliness of the slums with the grandeur and majesty of the famous edifices of Washington. Mrs. Johnson stressed that Americans could help improve their surroundings. She advised planting trees and flowers and cultivating an interest in the design of public buildings.

Mrs. Johnson knew that her project was just beginning to gain national acceptance. To continue the momentum, she put on gardening gloves, took shovel in hand, and planted flowers and trees all over the country. Liz Carpenter noted that the White House actually lost count of how many trees Mrs. Johnson planted.[37]

Trips also played an integral part in Mrs. Johnson's strategy. They not only permitted her to discourse on beautification, but provided the added bonus of drawing extensive press attention to whatever she was doing. Occasionally the object of a trip was to dedicate a new outdoor recreational area such as the Roosevelt Campobello International Park, Big Sur Scenic Highway in California, and Padre Island off the coast of Texas. The First Lady's efforts in this area were particularly successful. Carpenter noted that attendance increased at almost every park or historical site that Mrs. Johnson visited.[38]

Without question Mrs. Johnson raised the country's consciousness about beautification. Though not directly responsible, her continued emphasis on this issue resulted in impressive legislative accomplishments by the Johnson administration. In addition to the landmark Highway Beautification Act of 1965–1966, the Clean Rivers Restoration Act (1966), the Air Quality Act (1967), the National Trail Systems Act (1968), and the Wild and Scenic Rivers Act (1968) were passed. At the very least Mrs. Johnson helped to create the climate that made passage of such legislation possible. Lyndon Johnson wrote of his wife: "I believe that Lady Bird Johnson touched a fundamental chord in the American people with her quiet crusade to beautify our country. She enriched the lives of all Americans."[39] Mrs. Johnson sincerely loved her work, and told Americans that the environment was topic they simply could not afford to ignore.

In spite of the great amount of time she devoted to beautification, Mrs. Johnson also demonstrated a continuing interest in and commitment to Operation Headstart, the Poverty program, and the restoration of the White House.

Operation Headstart was aimed at helping to prepare young disadvantaged children for school. Mrs. Johnson told an interviewer that the children of Head Start had been stranded on "an island of nothingness. . . . Some don't know even a hundred words because they have not heard a hundred words. . . . Some have never seen a book or held a flower."[40] The First Lady traveled to Head Start Centers all over the United States and delivered approximately a dozen speeches on the topic. She also visited poverty areas to observe how the President's "War on Poverty" was succeeding.

The final phases of the White House restoration remained to be completed when the Johnsons entered the White House. The First Lady worked long hours familiarizing herself with all the new White House furnishings acquired by Jacqueline Kennedy and entered enthusiastically into the process of selecting additional paintings and pieces of furniture.[41] Later Mrs. Johnson collaborated with Lonelle Aikman of National Geographic on The Living White House, a guide to the history of the executive mansion. Mrs. Johnson probably also persuaded the President to sign Executive Order 11145 which provided a permanent curator for the White House and established a permanent Committee for the Preservation of the White House.[42]

Mrs. Johnson also initiated "Women Doer Luncheons," an attempt to gather distinguished women activists from various fields and solicit their opinions on the nation's pressing problems. Crime, education, and pollution were among the topics discussed at the sixteen luncheon meetings.

Politics and Campaigning

When she entered the White House in November 1963, the New York Times wrote, "Mrs. Lyndon B. Johnson is the most politically minded woman to enter the White House as First Lady since Mrs. Franklin D. Roosevelt."[43]

Lady Bird Johnson enjoyed politics and campaigning. Beginning in 1941, she accompanied her husband on his numerous trips to win votes; in the late 1950s she began to campaign by herself. She told an interviewer, "Campaigning . . . is the greatest adventure anyone can have."[44]

Members of President Johnson's staff understood that the First Lady was a valuable political asset. Just prior to the 1964 presidential campaign, Special Assistant to the President Douglass Cater wrote that the First Lady would be more sought after than the vice presidential candidate.[45] Secretary of the Interior Stewart Udall urged that the First Lady be used to cover crucial states "where Presidential campaigning will be limited or non-existent."[46]

Previously Mrs. Johnson had spoken on behalf of her husband and other Democratic candidates, but no task she undertook was more important or impressive than her whistle-stop train trip through the South, October 6 through 9, 1964. Evidence suggests that Mrs. Johnson was also responsible for the idea of the whistle-stop.[47] The Johnsons had successfully utilized a whistle-stop in the 1960 campaign and Mrs. Johnson hoped for positive results in 1964. The Civil Rights Act of 1964 had alienated much of the South, and the President, though he was expected to win the general election, was not expected to carry that section of the country. Meeting with staff members prior to the trip, Mrs.

Johnson requested that the campaign train visit the "difficult" towns. "Anyone can get into Atlanta—it's the new modern South. Let me take the tough ones," she told her staff.[48]

The First Lady was counseled to avoid the trip, but she was adamant, saying: "We must go. . . . [W]e must let them know that we love the South. We respect them. We have not turned our backs on them."[49]

The routine followed by the "Lady Bird Special" was similar to that utilized by President Harry S Truman in 1948. When the *Lady Bird Special* pulled into a depot, Mrs. Johnson, Luci or Lynda, and local and state officials, would appear on the rear platform of the final car of the train. Mrs. Johnson would be introduced by the state's Governor or Senator (if that official was aboard), and then the First Lady would step forward and deliver her remarks.

In Car Three of the train, campaign officials would try to persuade uncommitted local and state politicians to support the Johnson-Humphrey ticket. Mrs. Johnson occasionally joined in the political talk, but "if there was threatening to be done in campaigning, the male campaigners did it."[50]

A great deal of care was expended in writing Mrs. Johnson's whistle-stop speeches. The First Lady's staff took advantage of President Johnson's observations on trying to win the South over to accepting civil rights or a civil rights presidential candidate. One way, said Johnson, was to support civil rights firmly; another was to dwell on the Southerners' love of the Constitution. Finally, the South's economic and social gains, achieved under a Democratic administration and more important than "holding down the Negro," needed to be stressed. These suggestions were incorporated into the First Lady's discourses.

The first speech of the forty-seven given on the whistle-stop tour was the most carefully written of the entire trip.[51] At Alexandria, Virginia, Mrs. Johnson set the tone for the four-day, forty-seven-stop, 1,682-mile journey to New Orleans when she said,[52] "I know that many of you do not agree with the Civil Rights Bill or with the President's support of it, but . . . I believe that . . . it would be bottomless tragedy for our country to be racially divided."[53]

The First Lady continually stressed the link between the prosperity being enjoyed in the South and the Democratic administration. She told an audience in Richmond that Virginians were currently earning $205 more per year than they did in 1960, and added "I would be remiss if I did not point out that these were Democratic years."[54] In addition to Alexandria, Fredericksburg, and Richmond, the *Lady Bird Special* stopped at Ashland, Petersburg, Suffolk, and Norfolk, Virginia.

In speeches later that day at Charlotte, Wilson, and Selma, North Carolina, the First Lady spoke about her husband as Chief Executive: "You can tell what sort of President he will make because you have lived through these ten months with us."[55] As the train traveled south through Burlington, High Point, Lexington, and Salisbury, North Carolina, the welcomes grew warmer. Crowds were sizable, and "Negroes in large numbers appeared at all the stops."[56]

The train wended its way into South Carolina: Rock Hill, Wilmington,

Chester, and Winnsboro. Mrs. Johnson spoke "of her Southern birth, kinfolk and memories and of White House support" for the South.[57] In Columbia, South Carolina the warm audience responses abruptly ceased and the campaign train encountered trouble. Just as Mrs. Johnson was preparing to speak, hecklers began to boo and shout: "We want Barry [Goldwater, the Republican candidate for President]! We want Barry!" Retaining her composure, the First Lady said: "My friends, this is a country of many viewpoints. I respect your right to your viewpoints. Now it's my time to express mine."[58] The heckling subsided.

The men on the train were greatly offended by the hecklers and rose to defend the First Lady, but she told them: "Look . . . I know you're chivalrous and they make you mad, but I didn't expect this would be an easy assignment. I'll handle it."[59] Mrs. Johnson needed that strong resolve, for she was heckled throughout the rest of South Carolina and much of the remainder of her trip.

After Charleston and Orangeburg, South Carolina, the train crossed over into Georgia. As the whistle-stop visited Valdosta, Savannah, Waycross, and Thomasville, Mrs. Johnson spoke of her husband's vision for America: "The President has brought with him to the White House many lessons of the past. It is this more than anything else that lies behind the programs he has fought for, what he calls the requirements of the Great Society."[60]

The First Lady intertwined the space program and a reference to the Civil Rights Act in her speech at Tallahasee, Florida, when she said, "Surely a nation and a state which masters all the intricacies of Saturn V can also master the engineering of human relationships."[61] After other stops in the state, the train went on to Alabama and then Mississippi.

Finally the train reached New Orleans and Mrs. Johnson delivered her last address, a declaration of support for the Civil Rights Act. In her remarks, the First Lady said, "We are testing as a nation whether we shall move forward with understanding of each other and of each other's needs or whether we shall move backward toward a denial of each other's needs, towards a national climate of fear and dislike."[62]

Lady Bird Johnson's whistle-stop tour through the South accomplished at least two major objectives. President Johnson carried three of the states (Virginia, North Carolina, and Florida) visited by the First Lady, and the trip opened the way for reconciliation of a recalcitrant "South with the National Democratic Party after the election."[63]

In 1964 Mrs. Johnson served in the capacity of campaign strategist, Presidential helpmate, and independent campaigner.[64] She filled these roles in varying degrees during all the years of the Johnson administration. The First Lady was not an observer of the political process, but rather an active, vocal participant.

Ceremonial Presence

During her White House tenure, Mrs. Johnson was a participant in 718 different ceremonial activities and estimated that she spent 75 percent or more of her time on official duties.[65] Unlike other First Ladies, the time expended did not trouble or annoy Mrs. Johnson, and she commented, "I knew a unique page out of a long life and interesting official duties."[66]

APPROACHES TO COMMUNICATION

Preparation for Speaking

Mrs. Johnson characterized her early political speaking as "brief, scared, personal, on the Lyndon I knew—not on issues."[67] Shy and nervous before audiences, Mrs. Johnson spoke rapidly, her vocal pitch rising, "and the words . . . rolling out one after the other."[68]

In an attempt to improve her oral skills, Mrs. Johnson began studying with a speech teacher. She learned to relax and "how to organize material and how to sit and stand on the speaker's platform."[69]

Preparation of Texts

According to her staff director and press secretary Liz Carpenter, the writing of Mrs. Johnson's speeches was occasionally a cooperative effort, but most often the result of a collaboration between herself and the First Lady.[70]

In planning a speech, Mrs. Johnson would ask Carpenter to analyze her prospective audience. "Who am I looking at?" she would ask. The First Lady wanted to know three or four things about her listeners.

Mrs. Johnson would read background material and briefing papers, or would just think about her topic, and then she and Carpenter would discuss the speech. Carpenter would jot down certain phrases used by Mrs. Johnson as they spoke.

Later, Carpenter would "marry phrases" and weave together a speech. Mrs. Johnson would edit the draft and make additions, corrections, and deletions. Mrs. Johnson characterized this phase of preparation as "all very hard work."[71]

Occasionally Carpenter would consult experts in various government agencies to provide facts and figures. Sometimes these agencies would send the First Lady "suggested remarks" she could give on a topic or even drafts of entire speeches. Presidential speechwriters occasionally contributed ideas and drafts for speeches. Sharon Francis, a member of the First Lady's staff, wrote many of Mrs. Johnson's speeches on beautification.[72] Liz Carpenter, however, was the First Lady's primary ghostwriter.

Communication Style and Delivery

Lady Bird Johnson's speeches were not inspirational or moving, but were well-reasoned, carefully worded attempts to educate. The First Lady became known for her descriptive style. Carpenter said that one of Mrs. Johnson's English teachers was responsible for this trait in the First Lady's oral and written discourse. The teacher advised the young Lady Bird never to use the same word or phrase twice within a speech, and to utilize descriptive adjectives whenever possible. According to Carpenter, this training made Mrs. Johnson a wordsmith, and she favored the use of metaphors, "non-trite" words, and active verbs. Mrs. Johnson devoted a great deal of practice time to every speech, "whether . . . five minutes or thirty minutes."[73]

Press Relations

A journalism major, Lady Bird Johnson understood the needs of the working press. According to Carpenter, "She knew the language of the trade, the difference between an A.M. and P.M. deadline, that it was better to be accessible than evasive."[74] Moreover, Mrs. Johnson genuinely liked the newswomen who covered her activities.

The First Lady appointed her old friend, the former Executive Assistant to the Vice President, Elizabeth S. ("Liz") Carpenter to the position of Staff Director and Press Secretary to the First Lady. Carpenter's appointment was historic in that she was the first professional newswoman to direct a First Lady's East Wing press operation.

Experienced and knowledgeable, Mrs. Carpenter assured the First Lady efficient press relations. The new press secretary solicited advice on running the press office from former press colleagues. Their advice essentially consisted of three suggestions: "Never lie. Tell us that you can't tell us, but don't lie. Return our phone calls. Don't resent our intrusion. It's our job to know where the First Lady is and what she is doing."[75] Carpenter never saw her role as shielding the First Lady from the press, but rather saw herself as "a person hired to accommodate the representatives of public curiosity."[76]

Mrs. Johnson did not hold press conferences. Carpenter felt that they put the First Lady on guard and made her say things that sounded unnatural.[77] Instead, Carpenter held occasional press briefings; there were always briefings prior to one of the First Lady's trips, and reporters knew that Carpenter would call them if a story came up.[78] Marie Smith of the *Washington Post* said, "We know Liz will call us if there is a story and if she calls us, there *is* a story."[79] In addition, Carpenter arranged interviews and distributed press releases, schedules, and texts of the First Lady's speeches. Always accessible, she averaged 150 telephone calls per day from the press.[80]

The press gave the First Lady uniformly excellent reviews. Nan Robertson of the *New York Times* wrote: "The First Lady . . . has an instinctive sense of public relations polished during nearly 28 years in public life. . . . [S]he is sympathetic to reporters' problems and needs."[81] Mrs. Johnson's relationship with reporters was cordial, and she enjoyed efficient and productive press relations.

FACTORS THAT INFLUENCED THE FIRST LADY'S PERFORMANCE AS PUBLIC COMMUNICATOR

An examination of the private Lady Bird Johnson—wife, helpmate, and woman—provides a better understanding of the activist Mrs. Johnson. Lyndon Johnson respected his wife's judgment and encouraged her to actively share in his endeavors. Their relationship, his willingness to listen to her opinions, and his perception of women as capable people made this possible.

Relationship with Her Husband

Lyndon Johnson said of his wife: "She is a warm, understanding person who is patient and enduring and always genuinely just. . . . She has great character. She is the first to tell me about any mistakes."[82]

The Johnson marriage was loving and was truly a partnership. For thirty-eight years, thirty-five in public life, Lyndon and Lady Bird Johnson shared equally in each other's joys and disappointments. They expected total loyalty of each other and they depended on each other; they were never disappointed.

Of course, Lyndon Johnson expected twenty-four-hour-a-day devotion from his wife. A friend commented that Lyndon adored Lady Bird but that "he worked her to death!"[83] Historian Doris Kearns-Goodwin, who assisted the President in organizing his memoirs, writes that Lyndon would tell Lady Bird what to wear and what to avoid, and expected her not only to run their home but also "to manage him."[84] Even motherhood became a luxury, for often Lady Bird had to choose between staying with Lynda and Luci or being with Lyndon. Lyndon usually won out.[85]

For all her devotion, Mrs. Johnson was not blind to her husband's faults. One observer noted, "She soothed friends he had rode roughshod over and shielded him when he was boorish."[86] Sometimes Mrs. Johnson was the target of her husband's wrath or crudity. White House Usher J. B. West was upset by the fact that the President was abusive to his wife, shouting at her "as he shouted at everybody else."[87]

Lady Bird, however, survived the demands of a dominating and occasionally overbearing husband quite well. Though she may have subordinated some of her wishes to her husband's, the First Lady remained her own person. She felt free to criticize her husband and to speak her mind. Indeed, "she was the only one who could tell him, 'You're wrong . . . and please shut up.' "[88] Lyndon Johnson, the President of the United States, listened to Lady Bird.

Both Johnsons benefitted from their union. Lyndon Johnson, for all his occasional callousness and insensitivity, understood that he would not have succeeded in politics or in life without the devotion and forbearance of his wife. Kearns-Goodwin concludes, "She was quite simply a figure central to his life."[89]

Access to Presidential Decision Making

Mrs. Johnson has consistently hedged on the question of access to presidential decision making. Shortly after the Kennedy assassination, she told *Time* magazine that she gave her husband advice freely and that he often utilized her suggestions. "I see some of my ideas put into practice. I'm not sure Lyndon remembers where he got them, she said.[90]

In later statements and interviews, the First Lady tended to downplay the importance of her counsel. In 1967 she told a writer that her value to the President resided in the fact that she reacted like litmus paper; her reaction to a presidential initiative would be the same as that of millions of Americans.[91] When the writer suggested that she was being too modest and was able to influence the President in regard to politics, Mrs. Johnson replied firmly: "I think perhaps you think I've entered into it [politics] more substantively than I have. . . . [N]o . . . I don't think of myself as deeply versed."[92]

Despite her protestations and denials, Mrs. Johnson did influence the President in substantive areas. She reviewed speech drafts,[93] and she read critical mail "so that she could tell the President what people were bothered about."[94] She urged her husband to run for President in 1964,[95] and not to seek reelection in 1968.[96] She acknowledged that the President most often discussed conservation and education matters with her.[97] The First Lady was not directly consulted on matters of foreign policy, but certainly she was aware of all developments.

The President also seems to have valued his wife's opinion in regard to appointments. In an August 1968 letter to Katie Louchheim (at the time serving as a deputy secretary of state), Mrs. Johnson writes, "Katie, I think you would be excellent for the appointment to UNESCO [United Nations Educational, Social and Cultural Organization] and I will talk to the President about it."[98] Three months later, Mrs. Louchheim's appointment to UNESCO was announced in the *New York Times*.[99] While it is impossible to prove that the First Lady advocated Mrs. Louchheim's appointment, the evidence suggests that she wielded influence in the area of personnel.

Possibly the reason she was influential and effective had to do with the manner in which the First Lady advanced her suggestions. Hers was never a frontal attack, but rather was subtle and gradual; "I infiltrate," she said.[100] The President and First Lady would discuss options in a given situation, and "sooner or later we would come around to the same way of thinking," said Mrs. Johnson.[101]

In early 1987 Mrs. Johnson finally acknowledged, "If he asked me, I sure didn't mind expressing my feelings."[102] Lady Bird Johnson had always shared in her husband's decision making, and was a welcome, objective voice in his deliberations.

The President's and First Lady's Perceptions of Women

Both Johnsons displayed a positive commitment to women's rights while in the White House.[103] A historian points out that "Despite their Southern backgrounds, both [Johnsons] believed that women should participate actively in all areas of life."[104] Mrs. Johnson's view of women, which undoubtedly influenced her husband, was that women were competent and capable of being successful wives, mothers, and career women. A mild but definite feminism runs through the First Lady's speeches about women.

The First Lady felt that her activities in the White House were not affected by the Women's Movement,[105] but she was concerned with the policies of her husband's administration and the part that women played in them.[106] She was also aware of and concerned about the difficulties encountered by women moving in and out of the labor market as they took time off to raise their families.[107]

As President, Lyndon Johnson sought to recruit greater numbers of women for high-level decision-making positions. In January 1964 he initiated a program to recruit competent women for government posts. He told his cabinet, "The day is over when top jobs are reserved for men."[108]

The President appointed twenty-seven women to high-level positions within his administration.[109] Twenty-five other women appointed by Johnson's predecessors and serving in various capacities brought to fifty-two the number of women serving in the Johnson administration. An additional sixty-five women were appointed to administration positions that did not require confirmation by the Senate.[110]

Johnson boosted the salaries of thousands of woman civil servants and helped to eliminate job discrimination through the passage of the Civil Rights Act of 1964 and the signing of Executive Order 11246 in September 1965.

The former piece of legislation prohibited "employment discrimination on the basis of race, color, sex or national origin."[111] Further, the Civil Rights Act established the Equal Employment Opportunity Commission to oversee the employment provisions of the act. Executive Order 11246 required "federal contractors and subcontractors to eliminate discrimination based on race, color, religion, national origin or sex."[112]

Late in his life Lyndon Johnson lamented that his administration had not done enough for women, yet he did help them to achieve great strides in the twentieth century.[113]

Unlike Eleanor Roosevelt, the woman with whom she is most frequently compared, Lady Bird Johnson was not an innovator. From her first days in the White House she had said that she would lend support to her husband's programs, not initiate new endeavors.[114] She felt her primary function as First Lady was to provide Lyndon Johnson with a serene and healthy home environment in which to work.[115]

She did not become involved in the more substantive issues of public policy. Some find it curious and unfortunate that Mrs. Johnson never made a statement about the most critical issue of her husband's presidency, the Vietnam War.[116] Mrs. Johnson embraced beautification, Project Head Start, and the Poverty program, all important programs but essentially women's concerns and therefore considered safe. The First Lady's actions rarely sparked criticism or controversy.

However, even though she did advocate projects that were safe, and was not an initiator, these criticisms are tempered by all that she did accomplish. Without question, Lady Bird Johnson informed the American people that beautification was a national priority. Moreover, she helped to ease the way for Betty Ford, Rosalynn Carter, and future activists who would build on her fine example of responsible and enlightened concern.

NOTES

1. Biographical material has been culled from the following sources: Sol Barzman, *The First Ladies* (New York: Cowles, 1970), pp. 338–347; Pauline Frederick, *Ten First Ladies of the World* (New York: Meredith, 1967), pp. 19–37; Merle Miller, *Lyndon: An Oral Biography* (New York: Putnam, 1980); Ruth Montgomery, *Mrs. L.B.J.* (New York: Holt, 1964); and "Lady Bird Johnson," Charles Moritz, ed., *Current Biography Yearbook, 1964* (New York: Wilson, 1964), pp. 212–215.

2. Moritz. *Current Biography*, p. 213.

3. Moritz. *Current Biography*, p. 213.

4. Miller, *Lyndon*, p. 44.

5. Montgomery, *Mrs. L.B.J.*, pp. 19–20.

6. Frederick, *Ten First Ladies*, pp. 24–25; Miller, *Lyndon*, p. 52.

7. Henry Brandon, "A Talk with the First Lady," *New York Times*, September 10, 1967, VI, p. 158.

8. Frederick, *Ten First Ladies*, p. 26.

9. Eric F. Goldman, *The Tragedy of Lyndon Johnson* (New York: Knopf, 1969), p. 350.

10. Miller, *Lyndon*, p. 93.

11. Montgomery, *Mrs. L.B.J.*, p. 30.

12. "The Story of the Johnson Family Fortune," *U.S. News and World Report*, 56 (May 4, 1964), p. 38.

13. "New First Lady Has Many Roles," *New York Times*, November 23, 1963, p. 16.

14. Miller, *Lyndon*, p. 260.

15. Anne Morrow Lindbergh, "As I See Our First Lady," *Look*, 28 (May 19, 1964), p. 106.

16. Lady Bird Johnson, *A White House Diary* (New York: Holt, 1970), p. 3.

17. Michael Amrine, *This Awesome Challenge* (New York: Putnam, 1964), p. 22.

18. Johnson, *White House Diary*, p. 16.

19. "Johnsons Move to White House," *New York Times*, December 8, 1963, p. 66.

20. Mrs. Lyndon B. Johnson, interviewed by the author, Austin, Texas, February 2, 1979.

21. John L. Moore (ed.), *Guide to U.S. Elections* (Washington, D.C.: Congressional Quarterly, 1975), p. 297.

22. Johnson, *White House Diary*, pp. 518, 549–550, 566–567, 570, 573, 612, 617.

23. For the most comprehensive research and discussion on the issue of beautification, see Lewis L. Gould, *Lady Bird Johnson and the Environment: A First Lady's Commitment* (Lawrence, Kans.: University Press, 1988).

24. Johnson, *White House Diary*, p. 522.

25. Johnson interview.

26. "Address of Mrs. Lyndon B. Johnson at Yale Political Union, New Haven,

Connecticut, October 9, 1967," Mrs. Johnson's Releases, 1967, Lyndon B. Johnson Library, Austin, Texas (hereafter referred to as LBJ Library).

27. "Transcript of the President's Message to Congress on the State of the Union," *New York Times,* January 5, 1965, p. 16.

28. "First Lady Praises Aim of Mrs. Lasker to Beautify the City," *New York Times,* February 6, 1965, p. 13.

29. "Ways to Beautify America," *U.S. News and World Report,* 58 (February 22, 1965), pp. 72–78.

30. "Ways to Beautify America," p. 74.

31. Sharon Francis helped to coordinate the speaker's bureau. The First Lady received beautification speaking requests at the rate of twenty-five per week: Memo from Sharon Francis to Liz Carpenter, December 2, 1965, WHSF/"Beautification Speaker's Bureau," LBJ Library.

32. "Remarks by Mrs. Lyndon B. Johnson, White House Conference on Natural Beauty," May 24, 1965, Mrs. Johnson's Releases, 1965, LBJ Library.

33. See Lewis L. Gould, "First Lady as Catalyst: Lady Bird Johnson and Highway Beautification in the 1960's," *Environmental Review,* 10 (Summer 1987), pp. 72–92.

34. Gould, "First Lady as Catalyst," p. 84.

35. Gould, "First Lady as Catalyst," p. 85.

36. Gould, "First Lady as Catalyst," p. 85. Head counts, copies of telegrams to wavering legislators, and correspondence for and against the Highway Beautification Act provide a sense of the enormity of the lobbying effort in securing passage of this legislation: WHSF/Beautification Files, "Screening Junkyards," Box 14, "Highway Beautification Act of 1965–1966," LBJ Library.

37. Liz Carpenter, *Ruffles and Flourishes* (New York: Pocket, 1971), p. 183.

38. Liz Carpenter, interviewed by the author, Austin, Texas, February 1, 1979.

39. Lyndon Baines Johnson, *The Vantage Point: Perspectives of the Presidency 1963–1969* (New York: Holt, 1971), pp. 336–337.

40. Margaret Mead, "Mrs. Lyndon B. Johnson: A New Kind of First Lady?" *Redbook,* 125 (July 1965), p. 14.

41. Mrs. Johnson told an interviewer that Mrs. Kennedy prepared a long memorandum on the White House refurbishment for the new First Lady: Nancy Kegan Smith, "On Being First Lady: An Interview with Lady Bird Johnson," *Prologue,* Vol. 19, (Summer 1987), pp. 136–137.

42. J. B. West, *Upstairs at the White House* (New York: Warner, 1973), p. 332.

43. "New First Lady Has Many Roles," p. 16.

44. Marjorie Hunter, "Public Servant without Pay: The First Lady," *New York Times,* December 15, 1963, VI, p. 72.

45. Memo from Douglass Cater to the President, August 18, 1964, Ex pp/5 Johnson, L.B. July 15, 1964–October 1, 1964, LBJ Library.

46. Memo from Stewart Udall to the President, August 19, 1964, Ex pp/5 Johnson, L.B. July 15, 1964–October 1, 1964, LBJ Library.

47. Carpenter told the author that she was not sure who in fact was responsible for the idea of the "Lady Bird Special," but "it seems like Lady Bird was": Carpenter interview.

48. Carpenter, *Ruffles and Flourishes,* p. 115.

49. Carpenter, *Ruffles and Flourishes,* p. 115.

50. Norma Ruth Holly Foreman, "The First Lady as a Leader of Public Opinion: A

Study of the Role and Press Relations of Lady Bird Johnson" (unpublished doctoral dissertation, University of Texas at Austin, 1971), p. 172.

51. Carpenter interview.

52. Carpenter, *Ruffles and Flourishes*, p. 124.

53. "Remarks by Mrs. Lyndon B. Johnson, Alexandria, Virginia," October 6, 1964, Mrs. Johnson's Releases, 1964, LBJ Library.

54. Remarks by Mrs. Lyndon B. Johnson, Richmond, Virginia," October 6, 1964, Mrs. Johnson's Releases, 1964, LBJ Library.

55. "Remarks by Mrs. Lyndon B. Johnson, Charlotte, North Carolina," October 7, 1964, Mrs. Johnson's Releases, 1964, LBJ Library.

56. Nan Robertson, "First Lady's Tour Cheered in South," *New York Times*, October 7, 1964, p. 33.

57. Nan Robertson, "First Lady Booed in South Carolina," *New York Times*, October 8, 1964, p. 32.

58. Robertson, First Lady Booed, p. 32.

59. Goldman, *Tragedy*, p. 360.

60. "Remarks by Mrs. Lyndon B. Johnson, Valdosta, Georgia," October 8, 1964, Mrs. Johnson's Releases, 1964, LBJ Library.

61. "Remarks by Mrs. Lyndon B. Johnson, Tallahassee, Florida," October 8, 1964, Mrs. Johnson's Releases, 1964, LBJ Library.

62. "Remarks of the President, Mrs. Lyndon B. Johnson, and Miss Luci Johnson upon Arrival of the 'Lady Bird Special' at Union Station, New Orleans, Louisiana," October 9, 1964, Mrs. Johnson's Releases, 1964, LBJ Library.

63. Helen Fuller, "The Powerful Persuaders: Lady Bird's Trip through the South," *New Republic*, 151 (October 24, 1964), p. 11.

64. Foreman, "First Lady," p. 183.

65. The estimates of the number of activities and time expended were offered by two sources. The former source was the Lyndon B. Johnson Library; the latter was Mrs. Lyndon B. Johnson: letter from Nancy Smith to the author, January 27, 1982.

66. Mrs. Lyndon B. Johnson quoted in a letter, Nancy Smith to the author, January 27, 1982.

67. Mrs. Lyndon B. Johnson's written answers to questions submitted by the author, February 1, 1979.

68. Marie Smith, *The President's Lady* (New York: Random House, 1964), p. 187.

69. Alfred Steinberg, *Sam Johnson's Boy* (New York: MacMillan, 1968), p. 511.

70. Unless noted otherwise, all information in this section is from the Carpenter interview.

71. Mrs. Lyndon B. Johnson's written answers to the author.

72. Foreman, "First Lady," p. 137.

73. Mrs. John (Ashton) Gonella interviewed by Dorothy Pierce McSweeney, Washington, D.C.; February 19, 1969, p. 22, University of Texas Oral History Project. LBJ Library.

74. Carpenter, *Ruffles and Flourishes*, p. 91.

75. Carpenter, *Ruffles and Flourishes*, p. 91.

76. Nan Robertson, "First Lady's Lady Boswell," *New York Times*, April 11, 1965, VI, p. 131.

77. Carpenter interview.

78. Foreman, "First Lady," p. 134.

79. Marie Smith, quoted in Foreman, "First Lady," p. 134.

80. Carpenter, *Ruffles and Flourishes*, p. 97.

81. Robertson, "First Lady's Lady Boswell," p. 135.

82. Montgomery, *Mrs. L.B.J.*, pp. 197–198.

83. Miller, *Lyndon*, p. 353.

84. Doris Kearns-Goodwin, *Lyndon Johnson and the American Dream* (New York: Harper, 1976), p. 83.

85. Luci Johnson Turpin at the conference "Modern First Ladies: Private Lives and Public Duties," Ford Museum, Grand Rapids, Michigan, April 18–20, 1984.

86. Helen Thomas, *Dateline: White House* (New York: MacMillan, 1975), p. 93.

87. West, *Upstairs*, pp. 329–330.

88. Harriet Van Horne, "The Painful Price Our First Ladies Pay," *Ladies Home Journal*, 95 (July 1978), p. 138.

89. Kearns-Goodwin *Lyndon Johnson*, p. 84.

90. "The New First Lady," *Time*, 82 (November 29, 1963), p. 33.

91. Brandon, "Talk," p. 163.

92. Brandon, "Talk," p. 163.

93. Gonella Oral History, p. 32; Montgomery, *Mrs. L.B.J.*, p. 70.

94. Katie S. Louchheim, *By the Political Sea* (Garden City, N.Y.: Doubleday, 1970), p. 223.

95. Mrs. Lyndon B. Johnson's written answers to the author.

96. Johnson, *White House Diary*, pp. 518, 549–550, 566–567, 570, 573, 612, 617, 642–647.

97. Brandon, "Talk," p. 175.

98. Letter from Lady Bird Johnson to Katie Louchheim, August 15, 1968, LBJ Library.

99. "Mrs. Louchheim Gets Title," *New York Times*, November 28, 1968, p. 28.

100. Goldman, *Tragedy*, p. 357.

101. Thomas *Dateline*, p. 109.

102. Smith, "On Being First Lady," p. 139.

103. June Sochen, *Herstory: A Woman's View of American History* (New York: Alfred, 1974), p. 384.

104. Sochen, *Herstory*, p. 384.

105. Mrs. Lyndon B. Johnson's written answers to the author.

106. "With Lady Bird in the White House," *U.S. News and World Report*, 58 (February 1, 1965), p. 33.

107. Lindbergh, "As I See Our First Lady," p. 108.

108. Miller, *Lyndon*, p. 447.

109. Karen Keesling and Suzanne Cavanagh, "Women Presidential Appointees Serving or Having Served in Full-Time Positions Requiring Senate Confirmation 1912–1977" (Congressional Research Service, March 23, 1978), p. 41.

110. "Executive Appointments of Women Since January 1, 1966," LBJ Library.

111. U.S. Commission on Civil Rights, *Civil Rights Directory, 1981* (Washington, D.C.: Clearinghouse Publications, 1981), p. 3.

112. U.S. Commission on Civil Rights, *Civil Rights Directory, 1981*, p. 3.

113. Miller, *Lyndon*, p. 444.

114. Mrs. Lyndon B. Johnson interview.

115. Mrs. Lyndon B. Johnson's written answers to questions submitted by the author.

116. Even though she did not discuss it in public, Mrs. Johnson was not insensitive to the agonies of the Vietnam War. She told an interviewer: "It was a long war, it was an undeclared war. . . . If we ever got, heaven help us, into anything else . . . it had sure better be preceded by an Alamo or a Pearl Harbor so that there is a clear cut declaration and coalescing of the American people": Smith, "On Being First Lady," p. 141.

1. **FLORENCE HARDING** Well-liked by the public, Florence Harding opened the White House to visitors and advised the President on substantive matters. Courtesy of the Library of Congress.

2. **GRACE COOLIDGE** Gregarious and outgoing, Grace Coolidge had little contact with Americans because of her husband's "no interview, no quote" policy. Courtesy of the Library of Congress.

3. **LOU HOOVER** The first First Lady to speak over the radio, Lou Hoover discussed the effects of the Depression with a national audience. Courtesy of the Library of Congress.

4. ELEANOR ROOSEVELT "The First Lady of the World," Eleanor Roosevelt became the voice of the common man during the Depression and war years. Courtesy of the Library of Congress.

5. **BESS TRUMAN** The least active First Lady of the twentieth century, Bess
Truman preferred the calm and quiet of her home in Independence, Missouri.
Courtesy of the Harry S Truman Library.

6. **MAMIE EISENHOWER** A military wife, Mamie Eisenhower had moved over
twenty times before entering the White House in 1953. Courtesy of the Library of
Congress.

7. **JACQUELINE KENNEDY** Jacqueline Kennedy strikes a pensive pose in the executive mansion that she refurbished. Courtesy of the John F. Kennedy Library.

8. **LADY BIRD JOHNSON** Lady Bird Johnson takes spade in hand and plants a tree as part of her program to beautify America. Courtesy of the Lyndon B. Johnson Library.

9. **PAT NIXON** A gracious hostess and political professional, Pat Nixon urged Americans to become involved in their communities through her volunteerism program. Courtesy of the Library of Congress.

10. **BETTY FORD** A strong and vocal advocate of the Equal Rights Amendment, Betty Ford addresses the International Women's Year Congress in 1975. Courtesy of the Gerald R. Ford Library.

11. **ROSALYNN CARTER** Rosalynn Carter proudly presents the report of the President's Commission on Mental Health to the Chief Executive. Courtesy of the Jimmy Carter Library.

12. **NANCY REAGAN** "Say No to Drugs" became synonymous with Nancy Reagan's national anti-drug campaign. Courtesy of the Library of Congress.

POLITICAL SURROGATES AND INDEPENDENT ADVOCATES

Betty Ford

Betty Ford is probably more sharply defined in the minds of Americans than most First Ladies. She entered the White House at a time of national uncertainty and disillusionment. Candid, warm, and spontaneous, she seemed to be the antithesis of her predecessor Pat Nixon.

An active, able communicator, Mrs. Ford told the country her position on many issues in speeches, radio and television broadcasts, and press conferences. Americans did not always agree with her opinions, but by virtue of her many communication activities they knew exactly how she felt about issues of the day.

ROUTE TO THE WHITE HOUSE

Elizabeth Anne Bloomer, the third child and only daughter of William and Hortense Bloomer, was born in Chicago, Illinois, on April 8, 1918.[1] The Bloomers moved to Grand Rapids, Michigan, when Betty was three years old. William Bloomer, a traveling salesman, was able to provide his family with a modest but comfortable lifestyle: The family lived in a fashionable section of Grand Rapids and summers were passed at a cottage on Whitefish Lake in Michigan.

Mrs. Ford describes her girlhood years as sunny and wonderful.[2] A lifelong love of the dance was born when Betty took her first dance lesson at the age of eight.[3] She studied all forms of dance but was particularly fascinated by modern dance, favoring the freedom of movement it permitted.[4] By the time she reached fourteen, Betty was teaching dance herself and modeling.[5]

Betty persuaded her mother to let her attend the Bennington School of Dance at Bennington College in Vermont. During the summers of 1936 and 1937 she studied with noted dance teachers José Limón, Anna Sokolow, and Louis Horst.[6] No one, however, would influence the young Betty Bloomer more than Martha Graham. Mrs. Ford greatly admired Miss Graham, and wrote: "She was a tough disciplinarian . . . but . . . I admired that strictness. You can't be a dancer without it; not only your body but your mind must be disciplined."[7]

In 1939 Betty went to New York to study with Martha Graham on a full-time basis. Miss Graham told her that she had a future in dance but that she would have to give up everything, including a lively social life, to have a successful career.

Hortense Bloomer, who had never been enamored of her daughter's career, persuaded Betty to come back to Grand Rapids for six months. At home, Betty found a job as an assistant fashion coordinator and later fashion director at a Grand Rapids department store. In her spare time she taught modern dance; her professional dance career came to an end.

In 1942 Betty was married to William C. Warren, an insurance agent. The marriage was not successful and ended in divorce on the grounds of incompatibility five years later.

In the fall of 1947 Betty began to date Jerry Ford, a young lawyer also from Grand Rapids. Betty and Jerry saw each other frequently but not steadily. Then, in February 1948, Jerry Ford proposed, saying, "I'd like to marry you . . . but we can't be married until next fall and I can't tell you why."[8] In the spring Ford explained to his fiancée that he was running for Congress and would be busy campaigning until a Republican primary was held in September; their wedding would have to wait.

The future Mrs. Ford had no idea what running for Congress or being a political wife entailed. She enthusiastically joined in the primary campaign and aided her fiancé's effort by stuffing envelopes with Ford literature.

Ford won the primary, and Betty's life as a political helpmate had begun. She was warned about her future spouse's new responsibilities by Jerry Ford's sister-in-law Janet, who told her: "You won't have to worry about other women . . . Jerry's work will be the other woman."[9]

Gerald Ford was elected to Congress and the couple moved to Washington, D.C. Betty attended House sessions, escorted visiting constituents around the federal city, and joined the Congressional Club. The Ford's family began to grow: Michael was born in 1950, and was followed by John (1952), Steven (1956), and Susan (1957).

During the next few years, Betty Ford was busy raising her children. In addition, she taught Sunday school, served as a den mother for a Cub Scout troop, and was involved with the Cancer Fund Drive. Betty did not receive much help from her husband, who was often away from home giving speeches on behalf of other Republicans. In his autobiography Gerald Ford commented, "Even as a junior member of the House, I was on the road constantly, and it was difficult to establish a patterned presence at home."[10]

Gerald Ford was continually returned to Congress. In 1965 he was elected

House Minority Leader. His responsibilities increased; he was away as many as 258 days a year attending meetings and giving speeches.[11] Betty Ford's responsibilities increased as well; now she was almost solely responsible for running the Ford home and raising four active children.

The burden of being both mother and father and the strain of fulfilling the obligations of a political wife aggravated an injury that Mrs. Ford had incurred years before.[12] The pinched nerve and osteoarthritis that later developed in her neck kept her in constant pain. In an attempt to ease her physical and emotional pain, Mrs. Ford began seeing a psychiatrist. She said: "I was really giving too much of myself and not taking any time out for Betty. It was all going to the children and my husband and consequently I was a little beaten down and he built up my ego."[13] The psychiatry helped Mrs. Ford to rediscover a sense of self-worth, and she eventually ceased seeing her doctor.

Gerald Ford had always aspired to be Speaker of the House, but by 1973 he felt that his dream would never become a reality. He and Betty agreed that he would run for reelection to the House one more time in 1974 and then announce his retirement from public life.[14] The retirement plans changed abruptly, however, when Richard Nixon nominated Gerald Ford to succeed the disgraced Spiro Agnew as Vice President.

The new Vice President's wife decided that art and dance would be her special projects.[15] She would also decorate Admiralty House, the new residence of the Vice President. Legions of curious reporters queried Mrs. Ford about her views, and one interviewer wrote: "Unlike some wives of famous men in Washington, Mrs. Ford will tell you what she thinks. . . . She considers herself a feminist, a supporter of the Equal Rights Amendment and a believer in federal assistance to day care centers."[16] Impressed with Betty Ford's forthrightness, United Press International's Helen Thomas paid Mrs. Ford the ultimate compliment when she said, "She's down to earth and very approachable."[17]

Although she knew President Nixon's Watergate problems were increasing—among other less-than-subtle indications she noticed a picket outside the White House that read "Pick Out Your Curtains, Betty"—Betty Ford refused to believe that Gerald Ford might succeed to the presidency.[18] On August 9, 1974, Richard Nixon resigned from office and Gerald Ford did indeed become President.

In her first news conference, the first full-fledged White House news conference held by a President's wife since 1952, Mrs. Ford told reporters that she intended to be an active First Lady. She said that she would work for the ratification of the Equal Rights Amendment, declared her support for abortion, and endorsed participation of women in politics.[19]

The new First Lady was just warming to her job when it was discovered that she had breast cancer; a radical mastectomy was performed on September 28, 1974. Betty Ford made a conscious decision to discuss her mastectomy publicly. She said, "I felt that if I had it, many other women had it . . . and I thought . . . if I don't make this public, then their lives will be gone."[20] Public sympathy and support were tremendous, and Mrs. Ford's forthright approach to her disease achieved her desired goal: There was a great increase in requests for information about breast cancer and for breast examinations. The *New York Times* noted that thousands of women were scheduling appointments at free breast-cancer detection centers because of the publicity generated by Mrs. Ford's surgery.[21] Months afterward, a reporter wrote, "If she achieved nothing else during her husband's administration, the light her trouble has shed on a dark subject would be contribution enough."[22]

Her cancer operation gave Mrs. Ford new insight into the power and role of the First Lady. She wrote: "Lying in the hospital, thinking of all those women going for cancer checkups because of me, I'd come to recognize more clearly the power of the woman in the White House. Not my power, but the power of the position, a power which could be used to help."[23] Years later, Mrs. Ford would write that being an occupant of the White House "is no breeze. You have no private life, the demands on your time are constant, you are under terrible pressure."[24] In spite of pressure and stress, Betty Ford used her influence to support the Equal Rights Amendment, to discuss cancer, to champion the arts, and to focus attention on the problems of the handicapped and retarded citizens.

Betty Ford was always candid and honest, which enraged some but endeared her to many people. In the course of her now famous "60 Minutes" television show interview in August 1975, Mrs. Ford took a strong pro-abortion stand, said that her children had probably smoked marijuana, and also said that she wouldn't be surprised if daughter Susan had an affair.

Mrs. Ford was terrified by the furor that arose over "60 Minutes." She feared that she had become a political liability to her husband.[25] Gerald Ford might have had good reason to be concerned; editorials criticizing his wife for being too candid (and for having opinions judged to be too liberal by some people) abounded. However, the President reacted to the controversy with calm and good humor. He told a Minneapolis audience, "When I first heard it [the "60 Minutes" interview] I thought I'd lost 10 million votes. . . . When I read it in the paper the next morning, I raised it to 20 million."[26]

Initial reaction to the interview was negative, but a Harris poll conducted two months after the "60 Minutes" interview, however, showed a shift in opinion. Not only did a majority of Americans support Mrs. Ford, but she had become a solid asset to her husband and one of the most popular First Ladies in the twentieth century.[27]

Mrs. Ford released her husband from his pledge to retire from politics in 1977, and he declared his intention to seek a full term as President. The entire Ford family campaigned vigorously in 1976, but Gerald Ford was defeated by former Georgia Governor Jimmy Carter by 39,146,006 to 40,829,046 votes.[28]

The Fords retired to Rancho Mirage, California. In April 1978 Mrs. Ford was admitted to the Alcohol and Drug Program at Long Beach Naval Hospital. Years of pain killers for her neck pain, tranquillizers for her emotional pain and alcohol had taken their toll. The drowsiness and slow, slurred speech noted by friends and White House staff were indications of drug and alcohol dependence.[29]

Once again Mrs. Ford publicly explained a troubling personal problem. Her statement that she was addicted to pain medication and alcohol was featured prominently in the print and electronic media. With the help of the professional staff at Long Beach and the emotional support of her family, Betty Ford conquered her twin addictions.

Mrs. Ford was so grateful for the help she had received at Long Beach that she decided to aid others with drug and alcohol problems. In 1983 the Betty Ford Center for the treatment of chemical abuse opened its doors. Mrs. Ford is President and takes an active role in both fund-raising and counseling. Betty and Gerald Ford, busy and involved in a variety of activities, continue to reside in California.

MAJOR COMMUNICATION ACTIVITIES OF THE FIRST LADY

Betty Ford blossomed into an active public communicator in the White House. She became an independent advocate for women's rights and a number of other politically charged and unpopular issues. She also served as Gerald Ford's political surrogate, making appearances and campaigning for her husband.

Like Eleanor Roosevelt and Lady Bird Johnson, Betty Ford understood the importance of sharing her ideas and concerns with a national audience. She traveled the country giving almost one hundred speeches, speaking to the press, and using television appearances to dramatize her support for various causes.

Her attempts to communicate were generally successful, and Mrs. Gerald P. Ford was perceived as Betty Ford, an independent person, an advocate of many measures.

Advocacy

Mrs. Ford wrote that when she first arrived at the White House, she was asked "What is your program going to be?"[30] Betty Ford did not confine her support to the traditional First Lady concerns such as the Girl Scouts or the Heart Association. Neither did she embrace sustained formal projects or programs such as subsistence farmsteads or national beautification. Instead, Mrs. Ford endorsed several causes in which she became personally involved and took strong stands on a number of political issues. Ratification of the Equal Rights Amendment and women's concerns were her major focus. In addition, she was enthusiastic about raising the country's consciousness about cancer. However, the new First Lady also spoke out on abortion, marijuana legalization, and other emotionally charged issues.

Mrs. Ford's opinions on women's rights had been formulated during many years. She expressed a middle-of-the-road philosophy, arguing that women who wanted to remain at home should be permitted to do so. She noted that being a housewife and mother was a responsible job. She also supported women's right to work if that was their choice. Regardless of what they chose, she felt "women ought to have equal rights, equal social security, equal opportunities for education, an equal chance to establish credit."[31]

Mrs. Ford told the author that her interest in ERA and women's issues predated her husband's presidency.[32] Ron Nessen, Gerald Ford's press secretary, wrote that her support was genuine, and not an act to create a chic media image by selecting an issue that was timely; Sheila Weidenfeld, Mrs. Ford's press secretary, concurs in this opinion.[33] The First Lady left no doubt that she strongly supported ERA when she told her first White House news conference that she would campaign for passage of the measure.[34]

Early in 1975, Mrs. Ford began telephoning legislators in states where ERA had come up for a vote (Illinois, Missouri, North Dakota, Georgia, Nevada, and Arizona) to demonstrate her support and to bolster their stand on the proposed amendment. Her actions met with almost immediate criticism from the more conservative sections of the country. Mrs. Ford was unperturbed, and vowed to continue her lobbying efforts.[35]

The First Lady's mail expressed strong opposition to her stand, running three to one against her support of ERA.[36] Mrs. Ford was undeterred and noted, "It's those who are against [ERA] who are doing the writing. Those who are for it sit back and say 'Good for her—push on.' "[37] By the end of February, her mail began to turn around, and Mrs. Ford seemed to be at least partly vindicated.

Mrs. Ford used other strategies in encouraging support of ERA. She continued to telephone state legislators, sent telegrams of encouragement to organizations supporting the amendment, and appeared on national television to proclaim her views. In her "60 Minutes" interview she said: "I feel that the E.R.A. ought to pass in our bicentennial year. . . . [W]hat could be greater than that?"[38]

On October 25, 1975, the First Lady addressed the International Women's Year Congress. The speech she delivered was her major policy address on ERA and women's issues. Mrs. Ford felt that this was the most important speech of her White House tenure.[39] She commented, "It was important because I was not only speaking to the more activist as far as the liberated woman is concerned, but I was also speaking to the homemakers and I had to prepare very carefully to make sure that it balanced out."[40] The speech represented an effort to unite ideologically militant and less militant women. In her remarks Mrs. Ford said: "The Equal Rights Amendment when ratified will not be an instant solution to women's problems. It will help knock down those restrictions that have locked women into old stereotypes of behavior and opportunity. It will help open up more options for women. But it is only a beginning."[41]

She was grateful, said Mrs. Ford, that women now had the option to leave their homes and seek employment in the marketplace. Many women, however, were required or elected to remain at home, and their contributions to American life should not be denigrated: "We have to take the 'just' out of 'just a housewife' and show our pride in having made the home and family our life's work."[42]

Mrs. Ford's support for equal rights was not solely of a rhetorical nature. The

First Lady was a vocal advocate of women in government, and prevailed upon her husband to appoint qualified women to positions within his administration.

Betty Ford was a strong advocate of ERA during the Ford administration; she continued to send telegrams, make telephone calls, and support women whenever possible. Much to her chagrin, ERA was not ratified during her tenure as First Lady, but even after leaving the White House she remained active and committed to its passage. In November 1981 Mrs. Ford expressed disappointment that Nancy Reagan opposed ERA.[43] Later that year, Betty Ford served as Honorary National Chairman of the ERA Countdown Committee.

Mrs. Ford gave a number of speeches on cancer, and on several occasions presented American Cancer Society awards. In her discourses on the disease, Mrs. Ford urged Americans to have regular medical checkups and to take advantage of available cancer detection tests. Lending credibility and emotion to her cancer-related speeches, the First Lady referred to her own experiences. Receiving the American Cancer Society's Communicator of Hope Award, she said: "Breast cancer is such a personal and emotional experience for any woman. . . . Fortunately, I had the advantage of being married to a very fine man and having our lovely children. They helped me through the difficulties I had to face in life."[44]

Mrs. Ford might have done more than give speeches to raise the country's consciousness about cancer, but she chose not to. Perhaps she did not want to be too strongly identified with cancer, or possibly her experience had made her reluctant because it caused her to confront her own mortality. Sheila Weidenfeld recalled a conversation during 1976 when Mrs. Ford told her angrily: "I'm sick of the cancer thing. . . . I hate the thought that every time people look at me they clutch their bosoms."[45] Another Ford staff member speculates that the First Lady shied away from more cancer-related activities "because she didn't want to be reminded of her close call."[46]

It is interesting to note that Mrs. Ford is strongly identified with ERA and cancer, yet she only devoted a total of ten speeches, less than 10 percent of her total discourse, to these two topics. One may assume that her pronouncements were dramatic and made an impression on the public, and that her other communication activities (in the case of ERA, telephone calls, telegrams, and other shorter statements) sustained this perception.

Mrs. Ford also expressed her support for the arts, opera, drama, and especially dance during the Ford administration. A warm and motherly woman, Mrs. Ford voiced concern for mentally retarded Americans and children, especially those receiving treatment at Washington's Hospital for Sick Children. Mrs. Ford did not initiate any program to bolster these potential projects, but rather gave a single speech or made a short statement on each.

Mrs. Ford shared her opinions on emotionally charged issues with the American people. The Supreme Court decision on abortion was "a great, great decision," according to Mrs. Ford. It would move abortion from the backwoods to hospitals where it belonged.[47] She favored lighter sentences for marijuana users, especially first-time offenders,[48] and amnesty for Vietnam draft evaders, suggesting that they settle their obligations by working for their communities.[49] She opposed busing,[50] and supported handgun registration.[51]

Politics and Campaigning

Gerald Ford wrote of his wife, "Although she'd never enjoyed politics, she had a good ear and remarkable sensitivity for the nuances of what was happening."[52]

Mrs. Ford may not have enjoyed congressional politics, but campaigning was more to her liking. She found meeting the voters of Michigan's fifth congressional district to be a pleasant duty. She said: "We love to campaign, we've been doing it all our lives. . . . [E]very time he ran for office . . . I was usually in our district in Michigan helping, whether it was at a church social or polkaing at the Polish hall . . . or just listening to him [give] so many speeches."[53]

The Fords were spared the rigors of a national election campaign when Gerald Ford was appointed Vice President and later succeeded to the presidency. However, by the spring of 1975 it was apparent that if Ford wanted to remain President he would have to face not only a fight against a Democratic opponent but also a serious primary challenge from Ronald Reagan.

The Ford team headed north to New Hampshire and an initial testing of the political waters. Mrs. Ford visited the handicapped and elderly, and made phone calls to people to urge them to vote for Gerald Ford for President.[54] Both the press and the citizens of New Hampshire seemed to love Betty Ford. One newspaper commented: "Betty Ford is the clear favorite in the White House. Her husband is running neck and neck with Ronald Reagan in the Republican primary, but she's out front with both parties, with young and old, with liberated and unliberated alike."[55]

After the success of her short stint in New Hampshire, the President Ford Committee (PFC), which was charged with overseeing the election of the president, suggested that Mrs. Ford take a more prominent role in the presidential campaign. The PFC had discovered that Betty Ford had her own, diverse constituency. Her popularity seemed to cut across ethnic, religious, age, and interest groups. Campaign buttons reading "Betty's Husband for President in '76,"[56] and "Betty not Jerry in '76," began to appear all over the country.[57]

Mrs. Ford visited sixteen states in pursuit of primary victories. She spoke to voters and encouraged them to vote for her favorite candidate, Gerald Ford. Just prior to the Republican National Convention, a Harris Poll found that Mrs. Ford was one of her husband's strongest assets, and that she received a high 71 percent positive rating on the job she had done as First Lady.[58]

Gerald Ford won the Republican nomination for President after a bitter struggle against Ronald Reagan. Mrs. Ford was disappointed that her husband had had to fight for every delegate and, displaying her publicly repressed political acumen, told a reporter: "I don't know who's to blame—maybe the President himself. But they [the primary organizations] were not organized early enough and were not good enough. In some states, we had nothing at all."[59]

The challenger was now Democrat Jimmy Carter, and Mrs. Ford again took to the hustings. Her schedule was much the same as it had been in the primary campaign—short speeches, meeting crowds and shaking hands, phone banks, and fund-raising events. Occasionally she was forced to limit her activities because of osteoarthritis.

The First Lady avoided substantive issues because she felt that they should be addressed by her husband. Instead, her strategy was to function as an enthusiastic admirer, determined to get out the vote. She used the same simple and personal approach that had been utilized successfully in the primaries. Opening the campaign in Lansing, Michigan, in September 1976, Mrs. Ford told prospective voters: "Jerry Ford—is a man to count on. . . . I know that in everything he does he is a man of deep integrity. I believe the American people want to trust their president to keep his word. That's why—with your help—President Ford will be elected."[60]

The President was the man who had made the difficult decisions since coming to the White House, said Mrs. Ford. "He has made some tough decisions that have saved billions of your tax dollars. With your vote and support, he will keep fighting for you and your concerns."[61] Over and over again, Mrs. Ford told audiences about her husband's honesty, leadership, and concern for the future of America.[62]

Betty Ford fought hard for victory, but Gerald Ford lost the 1976 election to Jimmy Carter. Reviewing the loss, Betty's press secretary Sheila Weidenfeld said that she felt Mrs. Ford's effectiveness as a campaign asset had been diminished by her husband's election committee. The former press secretary said that Mrs. Ford had been effective initially because she was perceived as being apolitical. The PFC, said Weidenfeld, overexposed the President's wife, using her too often and involving her "in the hackneyed rituals of campaigning."[63]

Weidenfeld's assessment would appear to be partially correct. The PFC did overexpose Mrs. Ford, and the appearances that they chose for her were occasionally ill-advised. Mrs. Ford, however, was never apolitical. She was her husband's political surrogate and campaigner; she willingly accepted both roles.

Ceremonial Presence

Mrs. Ford has expressed the view that "a good bit" of the First Lady's job is still ceremonial.[64] Archivists at the Gerald Ford Library estimate that Mrs. Ford was the major participant in over 600 activities during her two and a half years in the White House.

Two events that took place in 1976 and provoked responses by Mrs. Ford deserve description because they say much about Betty Ford as a First Lady and as a person. On June 22, 1976, Mrs. Ford was about to be presented with a bible by Dr. Maurice Sage at a dinner of the Jewish National Fund when Dr.

Sage suffered a heart attack. The First Lady's Secret Service agents and others attempted to revive Dr. Sage. The audience of twenty-five hundred people was becoming restive when Mrs. Ford moved to the microphone and said: "Can we all bow our heads for a moment for Rabbi Sage. He is going to the hospital and needs our prayers. Would you rise and bow your heads."[65] Then Mrs. Ford led the audience in a prayer.

Mrs. Ford commented: "I was very fond of Dr. Sage, I felt that something had to be done and at that point nobody was doing anything. . . . I did go to the microphone and ask everybody to say a prayer for him. . . . I certainly didn't plan it, it was something that happened."[66] Mrs. Ford understood the mood of the audience and the need for words of solace. Her rhetorical initiative restored calm and rational judgment to the audience.

A second unusual occurrence took place the day after the 1976 presidential election. Post-election protocol dictates that the loser in a presidential race send the President-elect a telegram of congratulations. Part of this ritual includes the loser reading the contents of his concession statement over national radio and television.

On the morning of November 3, 1976, the tradition was altered when Betty Ford stepped before a battery of microphones and cameras to deliver her husband's concession statement. In a strong, clear voice, and with great dignity, the First Lady thanked President Ford's campaign workers and extended congratulations to President-elect Carter.

In their respective autobiographies, both Fords write that Mrs. Ford's action arose from necessity; Gerald Ford was physically unable to speak. He had lost his voice during the last weeks of campaigning.[67] Helen Thomas has suggested that President Ford was overcome with emotion and could not admit defeat in the hard-fought race. Thomas said: "When he was defeated, he couldn't read the concession, she [Betty] did. . . . [S]he's the one who went around. . . . [S]he pulled everyone together."[68] Betty Ford again showed herself to be a strong personality and a competent communicator as she successfully carried out a difficult assignment.

APPROACHES TO COMMUNICATION

Preparation for Speaking

Mrs. Ford had taken a public speaking course in high school. Her only other formal speech training occurred about 1950, when she and twelve other Republican women hired a public-speaking teacher to teach them the fundamentals of speaking. "That was the limit, mine was on-the-job training," said Mrs. Ford.[69]

As a congressional wife she held the positions of program chair and president of a number of organizations, which necessitated making introductions to guest speakers. Mrs. Ford did little speaking during her husband's brief tenure as Vice President.

Communication Style and Delivery

Betty Ford's speeches differ from those of her predecessors; her talk is characterized by informality, warmth, and folksiness. Her discourses were not stylistically complex. She did not quote from outside sources frequently. Phrasing was simple; the First Lady said what was on her mind without equivocation or guile. Frances "Kay" Pullen served as her primary speech-writer.

Mrs. Ford enjoyed speaking, though she admitted to stage fright and a preference for having a speech text in front of her "in case I go blind, deaf and dumb and I can read it. I know it's like a security blanket."[70] In time the First Lady became a good extemporaneous speaker and was able to speak from "talking points," topic outlines for speeches.

The First Lady was especially sensitive to the mood of her listeners, and said, "I think being able to detect the reaction of your audience as to whether you ought to continue . . . maybe delete something then jump to something else or add a little something is important."[71] Weidenfeld added, "She's a great ad-libber."[72]

Press Relations

Betty Ford made a conscious decision to be more accessible to the press than her predecessor, Pat Nixon. Mrs. Ford said: "I did [decide to be more accessible to reporters] because . . . many stories had been written about Mrs. Nixon . . . referring to her as 'Pat, the unavailable.' They were unkind stories . . . and naturally, I was going to try and benefit from those criticisms of her."[73]

Initially, Helen McCain Smith, Mrs. Nixon's press liaison, performed Mrs. Ford's press chores. In October 1974, Mrs. Ford appointed Sheila Rabb Weidenfeld, a television producer, to be her new press secretary. Weidenfeld felt that it was the job of the First Lady's press secretary "to communicate the human side of the First Lady and the First Family."[74]

Weidenfeld explained that she did not have Mrs. Ford hold regularly scheduled press conferences because she did not want to overexpose the First Lady, and because Mrs. Ford "got too nervous. . . . She would not have done that well."[75] Still, Mrs. Ford saw reporters and answered their questions at various ceremonial or political events on a regular basis, and her press secretary attempted to answer additional press queries if possible.

Reporters sincerely liked Mrs. Ford, and enjoyed her "shoot from the hip" style. Helen Thomas commented, "She enchanted reporters from the outset with her frankness and strong stands on controversial issues."[76] Another Ford staff member noted that reporters loved the First Lady "because she was always good for a colorful quote."[77]

Mrs. Ford enjoyed the company of reporters, and described her press relations as being effective and pleasant. She commented: "I enjoyed the press. . . . We kidded a lot back and forth. . . . I was willing to accept a certain amount of criticism. . . . [T]hey . . . were surprised . . . to have me not beat around the bush and come right out and answer their questions."[78]

Betty Ford saw the press as an ally to help her publicize her causes. She liked and respected reporters, and in turn she enjoyed exceptionally good press notices.

FACTORS THAT INFLUENCED THE FIRST LADY'S PERFORMANCE AS PUBLIC COMMUNICATOR

Relationship with Her Husband

By all accounts the Fords have and always have had a very happy marriage. It has been a traditional marriage: Jerry established himself in politics and Betty raised the children. Betty admitted to being resentful of her husband's unending travel, but this did not seem to diminish her love and support of him.[79] She trusted him implicitly and she told an interviewer, "I have perfect faith in my husband."[80] A longtime aide to Gerald Ford writes that Mrs. Ford's trust was well placed, and comments that Ford "was as devoted to his wife as he was career oriented."[81]

The Fords respected each other's opinions. Betty Ford had always spoken her mind; her candor in the White House did not startle Gerald Ford. To his credit, Gerald Ford never attempted to muzzle his wife, even when her views caused him political problems.[82]

Mrs. Ford was not afraid to tell her husband what she thought, but tried to temper her remarks with consideration and love. She told a reporter, "I don't hesitate to tell him when I disagree with something he's done or said."[83] One of Gerald Ford's associates felt that Betty was one of the few people who could tell the President when he was not making sense.[84]

Access to Presidential Decision Making

Betty Ford influenced her husband's thinking on a variety of issues and topics during his administration. Mrs. Ford said that she and her husband had always discussed the pros and cons of various issues, "and occasionally I did step in and say, 'You know, I don't believe it'll work that way.' "[85] She went on to say that when Gerald Ford was President, the couple would have extended dialogues and exchange ideas on a given topic: "Once he went back to the Oval Office and went into a cabinet meeting for a discussion and a decision, how much of what I said was carried back, I'll never know, but I think probably more than I suspect."[86]

Mrs. Ford used "pillow talk" to advance her ideas.[87] When the President came home to the White House residential quarters, the First Lady might gently—or not too gently—air her opinions. She found this to be a useful method in influencing the President. Gerald Ford admitted to a 1975 news conference: "She [Betty] does propagandize me on a number of matters. She obviously has a great deal of influence."[88]

Mrs. Ford influenced the most crucial decision of Gerald Ford's political life, the Nixon pardon. Mr. Ford told his wife that he was considering a full pardon for the former President and listed his reasons. Mrs. Ford concurred with her husband's decision, though her position was based on personal considerations. "She thought that Nixon had suffered enough and she felt enormous sympathy for the family. 'I'll support whatever you decide,' " she told the President.[89]

Gerald Ford consulted a number of advisors and found them divided on the idea or the timing of the pardon.[90] Still Ford persisted in his course of action. Helen Thomas writes, "I was told that the First Lady's opinion was a crucial factor in the President's final decisions."[91]

On September 8, 1974, Gerald Ford granted Richard Nixon a "full, free and absolute pardon."[92] Despite warnings, the furor, controversy, and bitterness that resulted from this action surprised both the Fords. Later Mrs. Ford wrote that she felt the pardon, more than anything else, had cost Gerald Ford the 1976 presidential election.[93]

Mrs. Ford had probably always influenced her husband's thinking. As First Lady she continued to have access to Gerald Ford's decision making, and presented her views on appointments and domestic and political issues.

The President's and First Lady's Perceptions of Women

Just before signing Executive Order 11832 establishing a National Commission to Observe International Women's Year, President Ford asked his wife if she wished to make a statement. Mrs. Ford responded: "I just want to congratulate you, Mr. President. I am glad to see you have come a long, long way."[94]

In her autobiography Mrs. Ford comments that she had "worked hard" on educating her husband about women.[95] Apparently that education was successful. Mrs. Ford said that her husband had the highest respect for women and that they had input into the decisions of his administration.[96]

Like his wife, Gerald Ford had supported the Equal Rights Amendment, voting in its favor as a member of the House of Representatives. As President, he signed a proclamation personally backing the measure.[97] He hoped that ERA would be passed in 1975, but when the measure failed to win approval, the President looked ahead. "Before America completes its Bicentennial celebration, I hope the Equal Rights Amendment will be part of the United States Constitution," he said.[98]

Gerald Ford aided women in other respects. In a memorandum on equal opportunity in federal employment, the President encouraged opening more employment opportunities for women.[99] To eliminate discrimination within the federal government, "the President directed the Attorney General to review the entire United States Code to determine the need for revising sex-based provisions that are not justified in law."[100]

Mrs. Ford strongly urged her husband to appoint a woman to his cabinet; taking his wife's views into consideration, the President named Carla Hills to serve as Secretary of Housing and Urban Development.[101] The First Lady also lobbied unsuccessfully with her husband to appoint a woman to the Supreme Court.[102] Fourteen percent of Gerald Ford's appointees to high office were women. A total of sixty-six women held important positions in the Ford administration.[103]

Both the Fords were committed to the concerns of women. Mrs. Ford set a national example as an advocate who never missed an opportunity to underscore women's achievements. Gerald Ford perceived women as competent and innovative, and let them contribute to decision making in his administration.

Prior to the 1976 presidential election, Betty Ford said: "Either way the election turns out, I win. If my husband loses, I win more of his time. If he wins . . . then I have the chance to continue my own work."[104] The last part of Mrs. Ford's statement demonstrates that the First Lady perceived herself to be an advocate independent of her husband. The country perceived her this way as well. She was a public person in her own right.

Her communication efforts were responsible for this. Betty Ford told Americans that she felt strongly about ERA, cancer, the arts, and certain unpopular issues. She told them often and in many ways, using speeches, statements to the press, interviews, and television. There was never any doubt about Betty Ford's stand on an issue, and the public knew that the First Lady was representing her own views.

Perhaps her cancer operation made some of Mrs. Ford's candid persona possible. Her surgery in September 1974 was a shock to the Ford family and the country. Her courage during this difficult time and her universally respected decision to tell the public about her disease created a climate of sympathy and admiration among the American people. Betty Ford was thus permitted a certain amount of leeway because she was perceived as courageous and tough. Later, when she spoke out on abortion, marijuana, and other topics, she was again permitted some latitude; she could get away with being a bit outrageous and too liberal. In the aftermath of Watergate, Betty Ford's forthright manner was reassuring.

Despite the controversy she generated, Mrs. Ford was immensely popular. In her first Gallup Most Admired Women Poll in 1974 she ranked second behind Prime Minister Golda Meir of Israel.[105] In 1977 Gallup rated her at number one, the most admired woman in the world.[106]

Perhaps Marshall McLuhan offered the best summation of the much respected, sometimes criticized, and invariably honest Betty Ford when he wrote, "She seems to have just what it takes . . . to make people feel at home in the world again."[107]

NOTES

1. Biographical information has been culled from: Betty Ford with Chris Chase, *The Times of My Life* (New York: Harper, 1978); Gerald R. Ford, *A Time to Heal: The Autobiography of Gerald R. Ford* (New York: Harper, 1979); Jane Howard, "Forward Day by Day," *New York Times Magazine*, December 8, 1974, VI, pp. 36–94; and "Elizabeth Ford," in *Current Biography Yearbook, 1975*, Charles Moritz, ed. (New York: Wilson, 1975), pp. 133–135.

2. B. Ford and Chase, *Times*, p. 21.

3. B. Ford and Chase, *Times*, p. 8.

4. B. Ford and Chase, *Times*, p. 17.

5. B. Ford and Chase, *Times*, p. 18.

6. B. Ford and Chase, *Times*, p. 23.

7. B. Ford and Chase, *Times*, p. 24.

8. G. Ford, *Time to Heal*, p. 65.

9. B. Ford and Chase, *Times*, p. 57.

10. G. Ford, *Time to Heal*, pp. 71–72.

11. B. Ford and Chase, *Times*, p. 120.

12. Moritz, *Current Biography*, p. 134.

13. Betty Ford interviewed on "60 Minutes" television show, August 10, 1975.

14. G. Ford, *Time to Heal*, p. 99.

15. Jean Libman Block, "The Betty Ford Nobody Knows," *Good Housekeeping*, 178 (May 1974), p. 142.

16. Karen Paterson, "I Am Just Plain Betty Ford," *Ann Arbor News*, December 6, 1973, p. 8.

17. Helen Thomas, *Dateline: White House* (New York: MacMillan, 1975), p. 273.

18. B. Ford and Chase, *Times*, p. 152.

19. John Herbers, "Mrs. Ford Tells News Parley She's Busy and Happy," *New York Times*, September 5, 1974, p. 25.

20. Betty Ford "60 Minutes" interview.

21. Jane E. Brody, "Inquiries Soaring on Breast Cancer," *New York Times*, October 6, 1974, p. 21.

22. Howard, "Forward," p. 64.

23. B. Ford and Chase, *Times*, p. 194.

24. Betty Ford with Chris Chase, *Betty: A Glad Awakening* (Garden City, N.Y.: Doubleday, 1987), p. 39.

25. B. Ford and Chase, *Times*, p. 207.

26. "Notes on People," *New York Times*, August 20, 1975, p. 32.

27. "Betty Ford Ranks High in Study by Harris Poll," *New York Times*, November 11, 1975, p. 11.

28. John L. Moore (ed.), *Guide to 1976 Elections* (Washington, D.C.: Congressional Quarterly, 1977), p. 23.

29. Ron Nessen, *It Sure Looks Different from the Inside* (Chicago, Ill.: Playboy, 1978), p. 23. Sheila Weidenfeld makes numerous references to Mrs. Ford's inconsistent behavior in her book *First Lady's Lady* (New York: Putnam, 1979).

30. B. Ford and Chase, *The Times of My Life*, p. 208.

31. B. Ford and Chase, *The Times of My Life*, p. 202.

32. Mrs. Gerald R. Ford, interviewed by the author, Vail, Colorado, July 17, 1979.

33. Nessen, *Sure Looks Different*, p. 28; Sheila Rabb Weidenfeld, interviewed by the author, Washington, D.C., July 9, 1982.

34. "First Lady Supports Equality for Women," *Ann Arbor News*, September 5, 1974, p. 8.

35. "Mrs. Ford to Continue Equal Rights Lobbying," *New York Times*, February 15, 1975, p. 31.

36. "Mrs. Ford Scored on Equality Plan," *New York Times*, February 21, 1975, p. 32.

37. "Mrs. Ford Scored on Equality Plan," p. 32.

38. Betty Ford, "60 Minutes" interview.

39. Betty Ford interview with author.

40. Betty Ford interview with author.

41. "Mrs. Ford's Speech to the International Women's Year Congress, October 25, 1975, Cleveland, Ohio," Frances K. Pullen Papers, Box 3, Gerald R. Ford Library, Ann Arbor, Michigan (hereafter cited as GRF Library).

42. "Mrs. Ford's Speech to the International Women's Year Congress."

43. "Personalities," *Washington Post*, November 19, 1981, p. 12.

44. "Communicator of Hope Award, December 1, 1976," Pullen Papers, Box 4, GRF Library.

45. Weidenfeld, *First Lady's Lady*, p. 264.

46. Nessen, *Sure Looks Different*, p. 22n.

47. Betty Ford "60 Minutes" interview.

48. Frances Spatz Leighton, "The Race for First Lady," *Ann Arbor News*, Family Weekly Section, October 24, 1976, pp. 4–5.

49. Leighton, "Race for First Lady," pp. 4–5.

50. "Mrs. Ford Scores Busing," *New York Times*, May 20, 1976, p. 11.

51. Leighton, "Race for First Lady," p. 4.

52. G. Ford, *Time to Heal*, p. 15.

53. Betty Ford interview with author.

54. Weidenfeld, *First Lady's Lady*, p. 257.

55. Weidenfeld, *First Lady's Lady*, p. 257.

56. "Mrs. Ford's Remarks at the Minnesota State Convention, June 25, 1976," Pullen Papers, Box 4, GRF Library.

57. James T. Baker, "To the Former Miss Betty Bloomer of Grand Rapids," *Christian Century*, 93 (October 13, 1976), p. 865.

58. Louis Harris, "Betty Ford a Strong Asset," *Detroit Free Press*, August 9, 1976, p. 31.

59. *Time* dispatch, August 19, 1976.

60. "Ingham County Phone Bank, Lansing Michigan, September 16, 1976," Pullen Papers, Box 2, GRF Library.

61. "Rochester, Michigan Rally, October 27, 1976," Pullen Papers, Box 2, GRF Library.

62. "It Is That Last Lap in Any Race That Can Be Most Important," *U.S. News and World Report*, 81 (October 18, 1976), p. 23.

63. Weidenfeld interview.

64. Betty Ford interview with author.

65. Jewish National Fund Dinner, June 22, 1976," Pullen Papers, Box 4, GRF Library.

66. Betty Ford interview with author.

67. B. Ford and Chase, *The Times of My Life*, p. 272; Ford, *Time to Heal*, p. 475.

68. Helen Thomas, interviewed by the author, Washington, D.C., June 6, 1979.

69. Betty Ford interview with author.

70. Betty Ford interview with author.

71. Betty Ford interview with author.

72. Weidenfeld interview.

73. Betty Ford interview with author.

74. Weidenfeld interview.

75. Weidenfeld interview.

76. Thomas, *Dateline*, p. 221.

77. Nessen, *Sure Looks Different*, p. 28.

78. Betty Ford interview with author.

79. B. Ford and Chase, *The Times of My Life*, p. 123.

80. Betty Ford, "60 Minutes" interview.

81. Robert T. Hartmann, *Palace Politics: An Inside Account of the Ford Years* (New York: McGraw-Hill, 1980), pp. 190–191.

82. Thomas interview.

83. Howard, "Forward," p. 66.

84. Hartmann, *Palace Politics*, p. 208.

85. Betty Ford interview with author.

86. Betty Ford interview with author.

87. B. Ford and Chase, *The Times of My Life*, p. 201; Weidenfeld interview.

88. *Public Papers of the Presidents of the United States: Gerald R. Ford, Volume II, 1975* (Washington, D.C.: United States Government Printing Office, 1979), p. 1911.

89. G. Ford, *Time to Heal*, p. 162.

90. Hartmann, *Palace Politics*, pp. 240–271.

91. Thomas, *Dateline*, p. 276.

92. G. Ford, *Time to Heal*, p. 178.

93. B. Ford and Chase, *The Times of My Life*, p. 181.

94. *Public Papers of the Presidents of the United States: Gerald R. Ford, Volume I, 1975* (Washington, D.C.: United States Government Printing Office, 1977), p. 26.

95. B. Ford and Chase, *The Times of My Life*, p. 202.

96. Betty Ford interview with author.

97. G. Ford, *Time to Heal*, p. 140.

98. *Public Papers: Gerald Ford, Vol. I, 1975*, p. 774.

99. "Women," *President Ford '76 Factbook* (Washington, D.C.: Answer Desk, Research Division, President Ford Committee, 1976).

100. *President Ford '76 Factbook*.

101. G. Ford, *Time to Heal*, p. 240.

102. B. Ford and Chase, *The Times of My Life*, pp. 201–202; "60 Minutes" interview.

103. Karen Keesling and Suzanne Cavanagh, "Women Presidential Appointees Serving or Having Served in Full Time Positions Requiring Senate Confirmation, 1912–1977" (Congressional Research Service, March 23, 1978), pp. 9, 10, 49–55.

104. Leighton, "Race for First Lady," p. 4.

105. George Gallup, *The Gallup Poll, Volume I, 1972–1975* (Wilmington, Del.: Scholarly Resources, 1978), p. 401.

106. George Gallup, *The Gallup Poll, Volume II, 1972–1977* (Wilmington: Scholarly Resources, 1978), p. 973.

107. Howard, "Forward," p. 64.

POLITICAL SURROGATES AND INDEPENDENT ADVOCATES

Rosalynn Carter

Whenever a First Lady appears to have a sustained interest in a project or utilizes newspapers or television to discuss her ideas or opinions, she is immediately anointed as "another Eleanor Roosevelt." Usually there is no comparison, but in the case of Rosalynn Carter there are more than a few commonalities.

Mrs. Carter was involved in every phase of her husband's presidency, and she was a complete public communicator. Television, the press, speeches, interviews, and magazine articles all provided fora for the First Lady to express her views. Mrs. Carter did not consciously pattern herself after Mrs. Roosevelt, but both women had an agenda for improving the lives of Americans, and both were tireless in advancing their programs.

ROUTE TO THE WHITE HOUSE

In a 1977 article Rosalynn Carter was quoted as saying, "my philosophy is that you do what you have to do."[1] There is little doubt that the former First Lady has lived her life according to this principle.

The oldest of four children, Rosalynn Smith was born in Plains, Georgia, on August 18, 1927. Times were hard and the Smith family was poor, but Rosalynn and her siblings were unaware of their economic state and enjoyed a small-town upbringing in the rural South. Though Rosalynn had responsibilities, she also played with other children, enjoyed dolls, and read voraciously. Her reading, she said, led her to dream of "faraway places."[2]

Her father's death from leukemia in 1940 brought an end to Rosalynn's carefree days. As the oldest child, she was expected to take a major role in running the Smith household. Hard work and responsibility took a toll, and though Rosalynn continued to maintain a high academic average at school, she conceded that she had lost much of [her] childhood enthusiasm and confidence."[3] She yearned to see the world, but was forced by a lack of funds to commute to Georgia Southwestern, a junior college in nearby Americus, Georgia.

It was at this time that Rosalynn developed a serious crush on Jimmy Carter, the older brother of her best friend, Ruth Carter. Jimmy, three years Rosalynn's senior, was a midshipman at the U.S. Naval Academy. He had paid little attention to Rosalynn until the summer of 1945 when he was home on leave and his sister had arranged a date between them. After that date, Jimmy Carter announced to his mother that he intended to marry Rosalynn Smith.[4]

Rosalynn and Jimmy corresponded regularly when he returned to Annapolis. During his Christmas leave, Jimmy proposed to Rosalynn and received a prompt rejection. The eighteen-year-old girl from Plains was not ready to marry, and she certainly did not feel sophisticated or confident enough to deal with Carter.[5]

They continued to write almost daily, however, and when Rosalynn visited Annapolis a few months later, Jimmy proposed again. This time, Rosalynn accepted. They were married shortly after Carter graduated from Annapolis and was commissioned an ensign in the U.S. Navy.

During the next seven years the Carters lived in Virginia, Hawaii, and Connecticut. The family grew to include John William (Jack), born in 1947; James Earl Carter III (Chip), born in 1950, and Donnel Jeffrey (Jeff), born in 1952.

Rosalynn had always been a shy, nonassertive girl, but now she had to manage her own household and raise three sons in the absence of a husband who frequently spent four of every seven days at sea. The young Mrs. Carter rose to the challenge and enjoyed a variety of new experiences while establishing her independence. She was devastated when Jimmy announced his decision to leave the Navy and return to Plains to take over his father's peanut business upon the latter's death in 1954.

The decision, wrote Mrs. Carter, precipitated the most serious argument of their marriage. Rosalynn loved navy life, and the idea of living in the same small town with her mother and mother-in-law was discouraging.[6] Her husband was adamant, however, and the Carters returned to Plains.

The first year in Plains was the most difficult. Rosalynn was miserable and the peanut business cleared under two hundred dollars.[7] Jimmy devoted his energies to increasing profits, and slowly Rosalynn began to play a role in the business too, first answering telephones, and later keeping the books. Jimmy also became active in local civic groups.

In 1962 Jimmy Carter ran for and was elected to the Georgia State Senate. Rosalynn's part in the campaign was to take over full operation of the peanut business and to call voters and urge them to cast their ballots for her husband. Carter was reelected in 1964, and Mrs. Carter comments: "I liked being a political wife. . . . I liked the feeling that I was contributing to our life and making it possible for him to pursue a political career."[8]

Carter ran unsuccessfully for Governor in 1966. However, the family's disappointment was dispelled when Amy Lynn Carter was born in October 1967. In 1970 Carter announced another attempt to try and win the governorship. Despite misgivings, Rosalynn left baby Amy to campaign for her husband. For many months she traveled independently of Jimmy, meeting the people of Georgia at construction sites and shopping centers. This campaign also marked Rosalynn's initiation into public speaking. It made her terrified, and at times even physically ill, but she persisted.[9] At the conclusion of the gubernatorial race she was successfully making brief speeches, and Jimmy Carter was elected Governor of Georgia.

While she was campaigning Mrs. Carter learned about serious deficiencies in mental health services in her state. She became very interested in the problem, and when she became the First Lady of Georgia, she served as a volunteer at a mental health facility. Her husband appointed her to serve as a member of the Governor's Commission to Improve Service for the Mentally and Emotionally Handicapped, and she shared her experience and perspectives with fellow members. The commission compiled a report that was sharply critical of mental health services in Georgia; over the next three years, sweeping changes were implemented and Georgia's mental health programs became models for other states.[10]

Late in 1974 Jimmy Carter announced his candidacy for the 1976 Democratic presidential nomination. He faced a stiff, uphill battle, because even though he was well known throughout the South, his name did not appear in the Gallup Poll's list of the thirty-one top contenders for the presidency.[11]

Undeterred by this lack of recognition, Carter planned to enter all the state primaries and "pursue delegates in non-primary states."[12] To accomplish this task, both Carters embarked on a nonstop campaign to persuade Americans that "Jimmy Who?" would be an excellent chief executive. For many months, Rosalynn Carter traveled by herself and stayed in private homes as she conducted grass-roots persuasion. A year after he had declared his candidacy, a reporter made the pronouncement that "Jimmy Who?" had become a serious contender for the presidency.[13] At least partial credit for this success belonged to Rosalynn Carter.

Once the primaries began Mrs. Carter was even more active in meeting voters and raising funds for the campaign. The Carters were aided by the "Peanut Brigade," a large aggregation of Georgians who traveled all over the country and to all the primary states stumping for Jimmy Carter. When the final primary had been concluded, Carter had the 1,505 delegates needed for nomination, and in July 1976 the long-sought-after prize was his.[14]

The Carter campaign model that had been so successful in the primaries was employed in the presidential race. Rosalynn, Jimmy, members of the Carter family, the Peanut Brigade, and a well-organized staff campaigned continuously. A reporter asked Mrs. Carter why she campaigned five days a week and twenty hours a day. She responded: "It's a labor of love. Besides I won't have any regrets if he loses because I'm doing everything I can possibly do."[15] His wife's efforts were rewarded when Jimmy Carter was elected, defeating Gerald Ford by a vote of 40,830,763 to 39,147,793.[16]

The White House was a bittersweet experience for the Carters. Mrs. Carter received plaudits for her work in mental health, but was sharply criticized for attending cabinet meetings and engaging in statecraft during a trip to Latin America. Her husband's presidency began with a sense of optimism but trouble began when he announced efforts to achieve a comprehensive national energy plan. Problems with staff members, the SALT (Strategic Arms Limitation Talks) II negotiations, the Panama Canal, and finally the Iranian hostage crisis limited the President's effectiveness and caused his popularity to plummet.

Jimmy Carter hoped to right numerous wrongs during a second administration. The Carter team, especially Rosalynn, campaigned even more vigorously in 1980 than in 1976 but to no avail. On Election Day the voters overwhelmingly rejected Jimmy Carter in favor of Republican Ronald Reagan. Never one to suppress her feelings, Mrs. Carter admitted that she was bitter about the defeat and wrote that the repudiation of Jimmy Carter by the American people "for whom he'd worked so hard and for whom he cared so much," was very hard to bear.[17]

Rosalynn Carter remains actively involved in a number of endeavors. She is a member of the boards of the Gannett Corporation, the Menninger Foundation, and Habitat for Humanity, which builds homes for the poor. She directs an annual Rosalynn Carter Symposium on Mental Health at the Carter Presidential Center, and organized a major conference, "Women and the Constitution," which was held in Atlanta in January 1988.[18]

MAJOR COMMUNICATION ACTIVITIES OF THE FIRST LADY

Mrs. Carter told an interviewer: "I have learned that I have influence. I can look at a program and it gets some attention. . . . [I feel] I have a responsibility to do that."[19]

Rosalynn Carter was an extremely active communicator who took maximum advantage of the national podium afforded her to discuss the problems of mentally ill Americans, passage of the Equal Rights Amendment, and a host of other issues. Speeches, press conferences, interviews, articles authored by the First Lady, and continuous travel dramatized her commitment to these concerns.

In unprecedented actions the First Lady attended cabinet meetings, met with the President weekly for "working" lunches, and conducted substantive dialogues with Latin American leaders during a trip to that part of the globe. She was readily acknowledged as one of her husband's most influential advisors.[20]

Rosalynn Carter, a woman referred to by her husband as a "perfect extension of myself," was a political surrogate, an independent advocate, and a skilled and effective public communicator.[21]

Advocacy

Perhaps no First Lady came to the White House as well prepared to undertake major projects as Rosalynn Carter. She had both the framework and the goals planned before her husband's term of office commenced.

Prior to Jimmy Carter's inauguration, members of Rosalynn Carter's staff interviewed members of Betty Ford's staff to ascertain how the First Lady's East Wing operation could be improved. Two of the findings of the report suggested that there had to be more cordial and productive relations between the East and West Wings, and that the First Lady's staff had to be streamlined for maximum effectiveness.[22] The East Wing was subsequently reorganized to include five distinct divisions: projects and community liaison, press and research, schedule and advance, and social and personal.[23]

In her autobiography, Mrs. Carter notes that she made only one promise during the 1976 presidential campaign: to study the nation's mental health needs.[24] She decided that it would be her primary project in the White House, but worried that it was not a glamorous issue and might be perceived as a typical lightweight First Lady's endeavor.

Her concerns were dispelled when her husband indicated that mental health was a priority in his administration by signing an executive order creating the President's Commission on Mental Health in February 1977.[25] Dr. Thomas E. Bryant was appointed chair, and Mrs. Carter was named honorary chair.

Though her position was honorary, there was never any question that Mrs. Carter intended to be intimately involved in the work of the commission. The first step in the commission's work was to hold public hearings, which the First Lady attended. Hundreds of people were interviewed, and almost a year was spent amassing data.

In an interview on the "Today Show" in September 1977, Mrs. Carter described the fact that there had not been an indepth study of mental health since 1960, that only a small percentage of Medicare and Medicaid funds were available for mental health, and that only ½ to 1 percent of the federal budget was devoted to research in the area.[26]

In addition to commission testimony and television appearances, Mrs. Carter spoke about mental health to numerous audiences, including the Washington Press Club (September 1977) and the National Association of Retarded Citizens (November 1977).

The commission presented its report to the President on April 27, 1978. In appearances on "Good Morning America" and the "MacNeil-Lehrer Report" that day, the First Lady discussed the report's 117 recommendations. The commission had found that Americans were unserved, underserved, or inadequately served. In conclusion, the First Lady added, "We have to develop a national attitude of caring."[27]

Mrs. Carter's involvement with mental health did not end here. She continued to speak to a variety of constituencies about the topic, and stayed current on the progress of the Mental Health Systems Act, the proposed legislation that had resulted from the recommendations of her commission.

In February 1979 Mrs. Carter testified before the Senate Subcommittee on Human Resources, which was considering the Mental Health Systems Act. During her testimony the First Lady took issue with Senator Edward M. Kennedy, the subcommittee's chairman, when Kennedy asserted that funds for mental health research had increased substantially in the preceding years. Mrs. Carter responded that "mental health funds had declined sharply in the last 12 years."[28]

After almost four years of hard work, the Mental Health Systems Act was overwhelmingly approved by both the House and the Senate. It was signed into law by President Carter in October 1980.[29] The law, which might have helped revolutionize mental health care in the United States, never achieved its desired result as it fell victim to the budget slashing of new President Ronald Reagan. In a bitter postscript Mrs. Carter commented that the Mental Health Systems Act could have achieved a great deal. Instead, she writes, the legislation "is gathering dust on a government shelf and sick people and their families continue to suffer needlessly. That's a real shame."[30]

Another disappointment for the First Lady was the fate of the Equal Rights Amendment. She delivered dozens of speeches on the topic, and telephoned legislators, wrote letters, and appeared at fund-raising events, but to no avail. The deadline for ratification of the ERA expired in 1982.[31]

Mrs. Carter believed that part of ERA's problem had to do with its image. Many people believed that ratification meant unisex bathrooms, compulsory military service for women, and the removal of men as the heads of households.[32] Indeed, a White House summary of Mrs. Carter's mail indicated that many respondents linked ERA with gay rights and abortion.[33] On a more optimistic note, Mrs. Carter expressed hope for eventual passage: "An Equal Rights Amendment to the Constitution would protect women's gains and not discriminate against them. But great progress comes slowly."[34]

Her commitment to the elderly and involvement in the "Rosalynn Plan," a plan to encourage volunteerism and "stimulate business and foundation support to revitalize neighborhoods" rounded out Mrs. Carter's activities in the White House.[35]

Politics and Campaigning

Rosalynn Carter was truly her husband's political surrogate. She helped to formulate strategy and maintained her own busy schedule during the 1976 presidential campaign.[36] Unlike First Lady Betty Ford, who focused on her husband's qualifications for office, Mrs. Carter was not afraid to tackle substantive issues or engage in partisan politics. She criticized President Ford "for not holding more press conferences and for refusing to make public his complete income tax statement."[37] She also harangued the President, saying, "Mr. Ford has been in Washington 28 years; look at what a mess the government is in."[38] When asked in an interview what issue was most on people's minds, Mrs. Carter responded: "Distrust of government. People are so completely turned off by government. They don't think it cares for them. People do not feel secure."[39]

During her husband's White House tenure, Mrs. Carter spoke in support of Democratic office-seekers. She was an effective fund-raiser and was considered a Democratic heavyweight. For example, a West Wing staff member requested that the First Lady attend a ceremony honoring retiring Congressman Paul Rogers of Florida. It was the staff member's belief that Mrs. Carter's visit would aid the President politically and would provide support for Dan Mica, a Democrat running for Rogers's seat.[40]

As a campaigner, Mrs. Carter was superb. Her press secretary Mary Hoyt offered the opinion that Mrs. Carter was one of the best campaigners she had ever seen: "She has great instincts. She understands people, she likes people. She gets rejuvenated from being out there."[41] Edith (Kit) Dobelle, who later served as Mrs. Carter's Chief of Staff and accompanied the First Lady during the 1976 campaign, offered this assessment: "She speaks of her family and experiences and her hopes in a way that is totally natural and . . . is very effective."[42]

Nineteen-eighty was decidedly different from 1976. In his first presidential campaign, Jimmy Carter was the major attraction in drawing huge crowds. In 1980 much of the campaigning was left to Mrs. Carter as the President was preoccupied with the Iranian hostage situation and other White House duties. Speaking to campaign audiences, Mrs. Carter would recite a list of her husband's achievements,[43] but she would also tell voters that she, Rosalynn Carter, had worked hard for the country and deserved to be returned to the White House.[44]

Mrs. Carter's stature as a political surrogate and her husband's political alter ego was further enhanced by her selection by the President to represent him in talks with Latin American leaders in 1977.

The First Lady was thoroughly briefed on the nations she would be visiting and their specific problems. There were many delicate issues, especially human rights and the export of drugs to the United States. Those who briefed the First Lady were impressed with "her insatiable curiosity, quickness and also her toughness."[45] Some Latin American diplomats had misgivings about Mrs. Carter's visit: She was a woman, and the attitude toward women in Latin American countries was clearly chauvinistic. Undeterred, Mrs. Carter continued to prepare, and wrote, "I was determined to be taken seriously."[46]

The trip included stops in Jamaica, Costa Rica, Ecuador, Peru, Brazil, Columbia, and Venezuela, and the talk was indeed substantive.[47] In Quito, Ecuador, Mrs. Carter spoke to the ruling military government about a military buildup in the Andes; in Brasilia, Brasil, she discussed nuclear power and human rights; and in Venezuela the major topic of conversation was trade preference. Before returning to the United States, Mrs. Carter told reporters: "I don't think there's anything that I haven't discussed with them that Jimmy would have discussed with them. . . . I think in the future we're going to see some developments that were probably not expected to come from my visit."[48]

When she returned home, she was asked what gave her the right to conduct foreign policy. The First Lady responded: "I thought I could develop some personal relationships between the heads of state that I visited. . . . I thought I could convey to them the goals and policies of the Carter administration."[49] A public opinion survey found that 70 percent of the respondents rated Mrs. Carter's performance as a representative of the United States as either good or excellent.[50]

Mrs. Carter was a witness to and a well-informed observer of the Camp David summit between President Carter, Israel's Menachem Begin, and Egypt's Anwar Sadat.[51] When the Panama Canal treaties seemed to be facing certain defeat in the Senate, Mrs. Carter "summoned hundreds of influential Americans to the White House for a Presidential pep talk."[52] She visited refugee camps in Thailand and submitted a full report to the President.[53]

Rosalynn Carter once remarked, "I have always been more political than he [Jimmy] is."[54] This statement may be true, for as a strategist, campaigner, surrogate, and practical politician she seemed to have few equals.

Ceremonial Activities

Though she had little interest in the social side of the White House, Mrs. Carter was a gracious hostess who dispensed Southern hospitality at hundreds of luncheons, teas, and dinners. The Chief of Protocol gave her high marks on organizing state dinners and entertaining visiting heads of state. She commented, "Mrs. Carter . . . is very interested in the details of the [State] visit and . . . she makes the visitors as comfortable as possible."[55]

Socially prominent Washingtonians and others criticized the Carters for being too informal and thus diminishing the prestige of the presidency. The Carters carried their own bags, Mrs. Carter wore the same evening gown to her husband's inauguration that she had worn to his inauguration as Governor of Georgia, and the President would not permit the playing of "Hail to the Chief" on certain ceremonial occasions. All of these transgressions were viewed as detracting from the dignity of the country's highest office.

Both Carters were serenely indifferent to this criticism, and while she understood the importance of the ceremonial aspect of the First Lady's position, it was never a priority for Rosalynn Carter.

APPROACHES TO COMMUNICATION

Preparation for Speaking

Mrs. Carter admitted, "I do pray before I stand up in front of a group. I say 'I need your help Lord.' "[56] Early in her public career Rosalynn Carter was so terrified by the prospect of facing an audience that it made her physically ill.[57] Jimmy Carter suggested that she jot down a few key words that would remind her of what she wanted to say and then "just get up and talk about them."[58] This formula was especially successful for Mrs. Carter and she became a competent speaker.

Preparation of Texts

Mary Hoyt was Mrs. Carter's principal speech-writer, but the First Lady was also assisted by various members of her staff. Sometimes entire speeches were drafted for Mrs. Carter, and she merely made a few changes. This, however, was the exception. More often speeches were a combination of Mrs. Carter's ideas and phrasing, background material on the topic that had been prepared for her, and contributions from speechwriters. Hoyt complimented the First Lady: "She has very good instincts. . . . She has a great ability to simplify and to speak in a way that she is comfortable with and does seek to reach her audience."[59] At times Mrs. Carter would show her speech to the President for comment, but generally she served as her own editor.

Communication Style and Delivery

The First Lady probably delivered five hundred speeches during her time in the White House.[60] Hoyt points out that many presentations were remarks, short discourses that were ceremonial in nature. Remarks were more numerous than speeches because the First Lady always spoke to groups and organizations visiting the White House; frequently she would see seven or eight groups in a day.[61]

Rosalynn Carter was a competent communicator. She spoke clearly and deliberately, her voice soft and her accent Southern.[62] (One critic uncharitably characterized Mrs. Carter's delivery as girlish and giggly.)[63] She spoke more effectively when her remarks were extemporaneous, and she was especially adept at this when she spoke about her husband, his goals as President, and her own projects.

The First Lady's speeches lacked humor, quotes, and anecdotes. She presented facts or opinions in a plain style, without embellishment. One observer noted, "It is not her style to loosen up an audience." He characterized her presentation as "icy."[64]

Press Relations

Mary Finch Hoyt, Rosalynn Carter's press secretary, said that the role of the First Lady's press secretary "should be to try . . . to translate as accurately as possible the kind of person that person [the First Lady] is."[65] Ms. Hoyt attempted to do this for Mrs. Carter, but she achieved mixed results.

The First Lady was continuously frustrated by the fact that "her" stories did not merit front-page consideration and were either not covered at all or were relegated to the society pages. She told an interviewer that controversial topics were covered extensively by the media but that it was difficult to get headlines about mental health, the elderly, or the poor.[66] (UPI Correspondent Helen Thomas later responded to this charge by saying that the First Lady would have to *do* something that deserved to be featured on page one.)[67]

Like other First Ladies, Mrs. Carter was bothered by the media's occasional inaccuracies and misperceptions.[68] She read and reacted to her press notices and those of the President. On one occasion she wrote to Presidential Press Secretary Jody Powell: "I think we should demand equal time with *New York Times* op. ed. articles. . . . I don't see how they can refuse."[69]

Mrs. Carter did not hold press conferences. Hoyt said that the First Lady saw the press virtually every day and "there just didn't seem to be any call for it."[70] Mrs. Carter did meet periodically with out-of-town editors to answer questions and discuss her interests.[71] On trips she always made herself available to the local press for comment and interviews.

As stories of her power grew, Mrs. Carter found herself to be a frequent target of press criticism. The criticism grew so vociferous that at one juncture Jody Powell, reacting to a particularly critical story about Mrs. Carter, wrote to one reporter: "You can . . . say anything you wish about the President, but cheap shots at the First Lady are out of bounds. You ought to be ashamed of yourself."[72]

Rosalynn Carter's press relations were uneven. Some reporters felt that the First Lady's press office was at fault;[73] two persistent gripes were that Mary Hoyt "seemed oblivious to the needs or time constraints of news reporters" and that the press office had not sufficiently spread the word of the First Lady's substantive activities.[74] Mrs. Carter seemed to tolerate the press, but she did not give the impression that she liked reporters. There was an uneasy relationship between the two that appears to have been reflected in the inconsistent quality of the First Lady's relations with the fourth estate.

FACTORS THAT INFLUENCED THE FIRST LADY'S PERFORMANCE AS PUBLIC COMMENTATOR

Relationship with Her Husband

The Carters had and continue to have a loving, mutually supportive marriage. Jimmy Carter told a reporter that Rosalynn was his best friend,[75] and Mrs. Carter told an interviewer: "We do have a good relationship. . . . We have a mutual respect for each other and what the other is doing."[76]

Theirs was a symbiotic relationship, but Rosalynn Carter pointed out that her life had never been submerged in Jimmy's.[77] Instead they enjoyed a genuine partnership, and Mrs. Carter said, "I've always been able to do the things that are important to me and always helped Jimmy with the things that are important to him."[78]

The Carters also seemed to be unabashedly affectionate. As he was greeting reporters, President Carter blurted out, "Hi, I miss my wife." (She had been away campaigning for two days.)[79] One writer commented that the Carters were an extremely close couple who often demonstrated "spontaneous displays of affection."[80]

Their strong, symbiotic relationship was responsible for Rosalynn's activism in the White House. The President implicitly trusted his wife; he encouraged her and expected her to play a major role in his administration. The result was what some reporters labeled "the mom and pop presidency." Jimmy Carter was not threatened by Rosalynn's power; he used it as efficiently as possible. Both parties and many people in the United States benefitted from the arrangement.

Access to Presidential Decision Making

Veteran Washington observers Hugh Sidey of *Time* and Tom Wicker of the *New York Times* attested to Rosalynn Carter's influence in separate but similar articles. Sidey wrote: "The second most powerful person in the United States is Rosalynn Carter. There is virtually no dispute about that." Sidey goes on to quote a veteran White House staffer who said that Rosalynn had more impact on policy than any other President's wife in this generation.[81] Wicker adds his endorsement: "Among the most influential voices in its [the Carter administration's] policy councils is Rosalynn Carter. She may be the most powerful First Lady since Edith Bolling Wilson virtually took over for a stricken President."[82] Finally, in his memoirs, President Carter wrote, "She and I . . . discuss(ed) a full range of important issues and, aside from a few highly secret and sensitive matters, she knew all that was going on."[83]

The Carters had always functioned as a team in business and in politics, and they continued this partnership in Washington. In a speech in 1979, Mrs. Carter said: "The President of the United States cares what I think. . . . I have influence. And I know it."[84] Mrs. Carter attended cabinet meetings,[85] although she never participated in discussions and only took notes.[86] The President and First Lady met every Tuesday, when possible, for regularly scheduled working lunches. These were not frivolous get-togethers but rather serious problem-solving sessions.

Mrs. Carter did not formulate policy. She counseled her husband on appointments,[87] and functioned as his speech critic and sounding board.[88] The First Lady was delegated to represent the United States in substantive talks with Latin American leaders and conducted an inspection tour of Cambodian refugee facilities. Many times she spoke as an official representative of the Carter administration.

The woman Jimmy Carter called "a very equal partner,"[89] was "the most powerful unelected public figure in the country."[90] Indeed, no First Lady has

had greater access to presidential decision making in the twentieth century than
Rosalynn Carter.

The President's and First Lady's Perception of Women

Jimmy Carter had always respected and utilized the abilities of women. Rosalynn Carter also had positive perceptions of women, and in the White House
she constantly prevailed on her husband to appoint qualified women to government positions. In one speech Mrs. Carter assured an audience that she used
her influence on behalf of women. She said, "I have been known to mention
that he [the President] needs more women on the White House staff, more
women in departmental jobs."[91]

Twenty-two percent of all President Carter's appointments went to women.
"The previous best record was in the Ford administration when 12.9 percent of
the appointments were held by women."[92] During the Carter administration, three
cabinet secretaries, and nine general counsels to federal departments were female.[93]

The President directed all department and agency heads to enforce the executive order originally signed by President Lyndon Johnson to prohibit sex
discrimination in federal employment.[94] He supported flextime schedules and
more effective ways of handling sexual harassment complaints.[95] In addition,
the Small Business Administration offered entrepreneurial training workshops
and increased loans to women. The Department of Housing and Urban Development (HUD) held seminars to teach women about financing homes and
obtaining mortgage credit.[96] Women also realized gains in family- and childcare-
related concerns during Jimmy Carter's White House tenure.[97]

Both Carters were genuinely committed to women as could be seen through
their support of ERA, the President's appointments, and his other policies.
Interestingly, it has been Southern Presidents, Johnson and Carter (who might
have been thought to be historically and traditionally less supportive of women)
who in reality have significantly advanced and improved the position of American women in this century.

In a 1981 article, former Carter speech-writer James Fallows refers to Jimmy
Carter's White House tenure as "the passionless presidency."[98] Fallows praises
Carter for strong ethical beliefs and commitment to a course of action to improve
the quality of life in the United States. Unfortunately, writes Fallows, Carter
was never able to inspire passion and he was unable to persuade his followers
to view his White House programs as part of a holy mission. The President was
a decent man, but an unexciting leader and personnel manager.

Perhaps the same criticism could be leveled at Rosalynn Carter. She had the
best of intentions and was sincerely committed to her projects, but she was not
able to inspire and was not especially well-liked. She seemed to lack the qualities
that might have endeared her to the American people.

If she was not liked, she was nonetheless respected. Rosalynn Carter achieved a great deal as First Lady by embracing a variety of projects and dealing with substantive issues. A trusted advisor to the President, she had input into decisions that were certainly not within the traditionally defined purview of the First Lady.

Like Eleanor Roosevelt, Mrs. Carter had an agenda for twentieth-century America. Like Mrs. Roosevelt, she utilized all available communication outlets to achieve her goals. Hopefully, as with Mrs. Roosevelt, history will applaud the achievements of the woman from Plains, Georgia, who deserves admiration for having been an active, caring First Lady.

NOTES

1. Kandy Stroud, "Rosalynn's Agenda in the White House," *New York Times Magazine*, March 20, 1977, p. 58.

2. Rosalynn Carter, *First Lady from Plains* (Boston: Houghton-Mifflin, 1984), p. 12.

3. R. Carter, *First Lady*, p. 19.

4. Bruce Mazlish and Edwin Diamond, *Jimmy Carter: A Character Portrait* (New York: Simon, 1979), p. 105.

5. R. Carter, *First Lady*, p. 25.

6. R. Carter, *First Lady*, p. 36.

7. "Rosalynn Carter," in Charles Moritz, ed., *Current Biography Yearbook 1978* (New York: H. W. Wilson Co., 1978), p. 17.

8. R. Carter, *First Lady*, p. 53.

9. Mary Finch Hoyt, interviewed by the author, Washington, D.C., August 2, 1979.

10. "Rosalynn Carter," *Current Biography*, p. 17.

11. Wayne King, "Georgia's Governor Carter Enters Democratic Race for President," *New York Times*, December 13, 1974, p. 1.

12. King, "Georgia's Governor Carter, p. 1.

13. P. Anderson, "Peanut Farmer for President," *New York Times Magazine*, December 14, 1975, p. 80.

14. R. W. Apple, Jr., "Carter Wins the Democratic Nomination: Reveals Vice-Presidential Choice Today," *New York Times*, July 15, 1976, p. 1.

15. Kandy Stroud, *How Jimmy Won* (New York: Morrow, 1977), p. 17.

16. John L. Moore (ed.), *Guide to U.S. Elections* (Washington, D.C.: Congressional Quarterly, 1985), p. 364.

17. R. Carter, *First Lady*, p. 343. See also, Jimmy Carter, *Keeping Faith: Memoirs of a President* (New York: Bantam, 1982), p. 571.

18. Rosalynn Carter Still Breaking Barriers as a Former First Lady," *Atlanta Journal and Constitution*, July 12, 1987, p. 11A.

19. Rosalynn Carter, interviewed on "Over Easy," February 15, 1980; Audiovisual Archives, Jimmy Carter Library, Atlanta, Georgia (hereafter referred to as JC Library).

20. "Who Runs America? Seventh Annual Survey," *U.S. News and World Report*, April 14, 1980, p. 39.

21. B. Drummond Ayres, Jr., "The Importance of Being Rosalynn," *New York Times Magazine*, June 3, 1979, p. 39.

22. "Rationale for Reorganization of the Office of First Lady," January 6, 1977, ADP/ First Lady's Staff, JC Library.

23. Memo, Mary Hoyt to White House Staff, November 1, 1978, PP5, September 16, 1978-December 31, 1978, JC Library.

24. R. Carter, *First Lady*, p. 272.

25. President's Commission on Mental Health," February 17, 1977, in *Public Papers of the Presidents: Jimmy Carter, Book I*, January 20-June 24, 1977 (Washington, D.C.: U.S. Government Printing Office, 1977), pp. 185–188. Federal laws forbid Mrs. Carter to serve as the official chairman of the commission: Memo, John M. Harmon to Douglas B. Huron, February 18, 1977. PP5-1, January 20, 1977-May 15, 1977, JC Library.

26. Rosalynn Carter and Dr. Thomas Bryant, interviewed on "Today" television show, September 19, 1977, Audiovisual Archives, JC Library.

27. Rosalynn Carter, interviewed on the "MacNeil-Lehrer Report" television show, April 27, 1978, Audiovisual Archives, JC Library.

28. Marjorie Hunter, "Mrs. Carter Supports Health Aid in Senate Debut," *New York Times*, February 8, 1979, p. B9. Mrs. Carter was the first First Lady to testify before a Senate Committee since Eleanor Roosevelt did so in the 1940s.

29. "The Mental Health Systems Act," October 7, 1980, *Public Papers of the Presidents: Jimmy Carter, Book III, 1980–1981* (Washington, D.C.: U.S. Government Printing Office), pp. 2098–2104.

30. R. Carter, *First Lady*, p. 281.

31. R. Carter, *First Lady*, p. 286.

32. R. Carter, *First Lady*, p. 286–287.

33. Weekly Mail Report, February 24, 1978, First Lady's Correspondence, December, 1977-December, 1978, Hugh Carter's files, JC Library.

34. R. Carter, *First Lady*, p. 288.

35. Neal R. Pierce, "People, Neighborhoods and the Rosalynn Plan," Staff Files/ Holcombe, Box 2, Undated. JC Library.

36. Hoyt interview; Ayres, "Importance;" p. 46.

37. Wayne King, "Rosalynn Carter, A Tough, Tireless Campaigner, Displays Same Driving Quality as Her Husband," *New York Times*, October 18, 1976, p. 34.

38. King, "Rosalynn Carter," p. 34.

39. "We've Worked Hard—I've Done All I Could Do," *U.S. News and World Report*, October 18, 1976, p. 25.

40. Memo, Dick Pettigrew to Rosalynn Carter, September 28, 1978, pp. 5–1, June 1, 1978–September 15, 1978, Box PP-3, JC Library.

41. Hoyt interview.

42. Ambassador Edith (Kit) Dobelle, interviewed by the author, Washington, D.C., May 10, 1979.

43. Jay Billington, "On the Road: The Litany's a Bit Longer," *Washington Star*, October 21, 1979, pp. D1, D5.

44. Christopher Bonner, "Unlike in 1976, Mrs. Carter Now Carries the Show," *Philadelphia Inquirer*, April 6, 1980, p. 3C.

45. *Time* dispatch, May 27, 1977.

46. R. Carter, *First Lady*, p. 188.

47. A full discussion of the Latin American trip may be found in Carter, *First Lady*, pp. 185–214.

48. "First Lady on the Go," June 13, 1977, Audiovisual Archives, JC Library.

49. Rosalynn Carter, interviewed by Judy Woodruff on "Today" television show, June 14, 1977, Audiovisual Archives, JC Library.

Rosalynn Carter   161

50. Memo from Patrick Caddell to Rosalynn Carter, July 30, 1977, "Memorandum: First Lady's Staff," February 2, 1978–October 2, 1978, Jody Powell's Files, JC Library.

51. A complete discussion of Mrs. Carter and the Camp David Summit may be found in Carter, *First Lady*, pp. 235–269.

52. Ayres, "Importance," p. 42.

53. "Report of Mrs. Rosalynn Carter on Cambodian Relief," PP5/1, November 1, 1979–February 29, 1980. JC Library.

54. "Selling True Grit—and by God She's Good At It!" *Time*, August 6, 1979, p. 13.

55. Dobelle interview.

56. "First Lady on the Go."

57. Hoyt interview.

58. R. Carter, *First Lady*, p. 105.

59. Hoyt interview.

60. This estimate is based on two reports prepared by White House Staff: "First Lady Rosalynn Carter, Summary of Activities, 1979," and "First Lady Rosalynn Carter, Summary of Activities, January 1, 1979–January 31, 1980," respectively: Personnel—First Lady's Staff, Staff Files/Malachuk, Box 1, JC Library.

61. Hoyt interview.

62. Bonner, "Unlike in 1976," p. 3C.

63. Alice Leone Moats, "Rosalynn's Pitch is More Mush," *Philadelphia Inquirer*, October 16, 1980, p. 11.

64. Bonner, "Unlike in 1976," p. 3C.

65. Hoyt interview.

66. Rosalynn Carter, interviewed on the "Phil Donahue Show," May 30, 1979.

67. Helen Thomas, interviewed by the author in Washington, D.C., June 6, 1979.

68. R. Carter, *First Lady*, p. 174.

69. Note from Rosalynn Carter to Jody Powell, August 5, 1979, WHCF, PP5–1, May 1, 1979–October 31, 1979, Box PP–3, JC Library.

70. Hoyt interview.

71. Hoyt interview.

72. Letter, Jody Powell to Sarah McClendon, October 7, 1978, WHCF, PP5–1, September 16, 1978–December 31, 1978, Box PP–3, JC Library.

73. Thomas interview. Thomas said that frequently, the press office did not return reporters' telephone calls.

74. Nancy Lewis, "Rosalynn Carter's Story Just Isn't Getting Across," *Atlanta Constitution*, August 1, 1978, p. 6A, First Lady's Office, 1978, JC Library.

75. King, "Rosalynn Carter," p. 34.

76. Rosalynn Carter, "Over Easy" interview.

77. "We've Worked Hard—I've Done All I Could," p. 25.

78. Linda Charlton, "Mrs. Carter Balancing 2 Poles: Influential Person and Stand-In," *New York Times*, November 6, 1977, p. 21.

79. Gail Sheehy, "Hers," *New York Times*, December 13, 1979, p. C2.

80. Jill Gerston, "Rosalynn Carter Sticks to the Task at Hand," *Philadelphia Inquirer*, October 14, 1980, p. D3.

81. Hugh Sidey, "Second Most Powerful Person," *Time*, May 7, 1979, p. 22.

82. Tom Wicker, "Speaking for Carter," *New York Times*, July 24, 1979, p. A15.

83. J. Carter, *Keeping Faith*, p. 32.

84. Ayres, "Importance," p. 39.

85. Memo from H. Donaldson to Tim Smith and Fran Voorde, April 27, 1977, WHCF, PP5–1, January 20, 1977–May 5, 1977, JC Library.

86. R. Carter, *First Lady*, pp. 175–176.

87. See for example Martin Schram, "Carter's Dismissal of Bella Abzug: Basically, It Was for Being Herself," *Philadelphia Inquirer*, January 21, 1979, p. 3K; Ayres, "Importance," p. 42.

88. *Time* dispatch, April 21, 1977.

89. Ayres, "Importance," p. 39.

90. Ayres, "Importance," p. 39.

91. "Women and America," April 26, 1979, Publications File, Sarah Weddington's Files, Office of Women's Affairs, Box 44, JC Library.

92. "Fact Sheet: Women Appointed To Top Governmental Posts by President Carter," undated, Publications File, Sarah Weddington's Files, Office of Women's Affairs, Box 44, JC Library.

93. "Fact Sheet."

94. "Rosalynn Carter's Remarks at the National Women's Conference," Houston, Texas, November 19, 1977.

95. Rosalynn Carter's Remarks at the National Women's Conference."

96. R. Carter, *First Lady*, p. 291.

97. "Honoring a Commitment: The Record of President Carter on Women's Issues," Publications File, Sarah Weddington's Files, Office of Women's Affairs, Box 44, JC Library.

98. James Fallows, "The Passionless Presidency," *Atlantic*, May 1979, pp. 33–47, and June 1979, pp. 75–81.

8

A FIRST LADY IN TRANSITION

Nancy Reagan

Few First Ladies have attracted as much media attention as Nancy Reagan, and no presidential wife has had to tolerate as much criticism as the forty-second First Lady. Negative news stories preceded Mrs. Reagan into the White House, and she soon learned that she could not be a social hostess and ceremonial presence. She initiated an impressive transformation by utilizing various communications media. Slowly she emerged as a strong, independent woman who, if not wholly comfortable, was certainly a competent public communicator.

ROUTE TO THE WHITE HOUSE

Even though her critics charged that she occasionally behaved as if "to the manor born," this was not the case. The forty-second First Lady began life in fairly humble circumstances.

She was born Anne Francis Robbins on July 6, 1923, in New York. (Smith College records indicate that she was born in 1921.) Her parents, actress Edith Luckett and Kenneth Robbins, a car salesman, separated shortly after her birth. When she was two years old, Nancy, as she was always called, was sent to live with relatives in Maryland. Her early years were lonely and she only saw Edith when the latter was performing in New York. "Her early childhood was very unhappy, insecure and lonely," says a childhood friend.[1]

Just before Nancy's seventh birthday, her life changed drastically when her mother married Chicago neurosurgeon Loyal Davis. An eminent and successful physician, Davis was able to provide Nancy with an affluent upbringing. She attended private school, summered with the Walter Huston family at fashionable resorts, and was presented to society in a debut at the Casino Club.

Davis was also able to furnish much-needed emotional support for Nancy. She found him to be a man of strength and integrity, and while he was strict, he was also fair. "He was, I feel, the way a father should be," wrote Mrs. Reagan.[2] The two developed a strong, loving relationship; when she was fourteen, Davis legally adopted Nancy.

Nancy majored in drama at Smith College and spent her summers working in stock productions. After graduation in 1943, her mother's friend Zasu Pitts gave the young actress her first break and offered Nancy a small part in her play, *Ramshackle Inn*. After roles in a few Broadway plays, Nancy went to Hollywood for a screen test and signed a contract with Metro-Goldwyn-Mayer. She appeared in some generally forgettable movies including *Donovan's Brain*, *It's a Big Country*, and *Shadow in the Sky*.

In 1951 Nancy became distressed when her name turned up on a list of Communist sympathizers. This was, of course, the McCarthy era, and such an association could sound the death knell for an acting career. Nancy conveyed her apprehensiveness to Mervyn LeRoy, her director on the film *East Side, West Side*. LeRoy told Nancy that he would consult his friend Ronald Reagan the President of the Screen Actor's Guild. A few days later LeRoy reported that Reagan had indeed looked into the matter. There were at least four Nancy Davises, and Nancy Davis of Chicago had been mistaken for someone else. Nancy was assured that she need not be concerned about further Communist allegations.

After some matchmaking by LeRoy, Reagan called Nancy for a date. In her autobiography she wrote, "I don't know if it was love at first sight, but it was something close to it."[3] Her goals were simple, and she stated, "I've often said my life really began with Ronnie and I think to a great extent it did. What I really wanted out of life was to be a wife to the man I loved and mother to our children."[4] The couple dated for a year, and Nancy got to know Reagan's children Maureen and Michael (by his first wife, actress Jane Wyman). Nancy and Ron were married on March 4, 1952.

The Reagans made one film together, *Hellcats of the Navy*, and then Nancy officially ended her movie career. (Years later she would remark, "I was never really a career girl".)[5] A family followed: Patricia Ann was born in 1952 and Ronald Prescott was born in 1958.

Ronald Reagan had been acting in "B" movies since 1937. He had had a moderately successful career and was actively involved in the Screen Actors Guild, serving as president six times. By the 1950s Reagan realized that his movie options were limited. He appeared in Las Vegas in a nightclub act and then became the host and corporate representative of "General Electric Theatre."

Reagan had grown up a Democrat, but by 1960 he was campaigning for the Republican national ticket. He became a Republican officially in 1962, and served as California state co-chairman for Barry Goldwater in 1964. It seemed only a short jump to candidate in his own right; Reagan was elected Governor of California in 1966 by a huge margin.

A reporter writes that when Reagan arrived in Sacramento he had no idea what was expected of him as Governor.[6] The same might have been said of Nancy Reagan and her new position as First Lady of California. She arrived at the capitol with the reputation of being a member of the country club set, she preferred her rich friends to less affluent people, and she could not accept criticism. Moreover, reporters and other observers made fun of what they called "the gaze." This "indiscriminate soulfulness" was Mrs. Reagan's way of showing her love for her husband,[7] but one writer likened it to "looking at her husband like he's a hot fudge sundae and she hasn't eaten all day."[8]

Gradually Mrs. Reagan began to play a role in her husband's administration. She became involved with the National League of Families of American Prisoners of War and Missing in Action, visited hospitals, and began a long association with the Foster Grandparent Program. She also endorsed antidrug programs. These activities carried over to her husband's second term as Governor.

Ronald Reagan sought the Republican presidential nomination in 1976 but lost to Gerald Ford. Four years later he was successful, and in November 1980 he defeated Jimmy Carter, carrying forty-four of the fifty states and 489 of 533 electoral votes.[9]

Nancy Reagan's years as First Lady were difficult, and she went through a series of transitions to try and meet the challenges posed by the White House. At times she seemed to be a woman of the 1950s trapped in the 1980s. As conservative as her husband, she steadfastly opposed abortion,[10] the Equal Rights Amendment,[11] and gun control.[12] She also became closely identified with a well-publicized antidrug campaign "Say No to Drugs," and the Foster Grandparent Program.

When her husband completed his term in 1989, the Reagans retired to California.

THE FIRST LADY AS PUBLIC COMMUNICATOR

Unlike the other eleven First Ladies analyzed in this book, Nancy Reagan defies pigeonholing. She has not been wholly a ceremonial presence, an emerging spokeswoman, or a political surrogate and independent advocate. Instead she has shuttled between these classifications as her role has evolved during the Reagan administration.

In many ways she is one of the more interesting subjects of this book because she has been truly a First Lady in transition. A fascinating question concerns the reasons why Nancy Reagan in fact moved from category to category.

Because she cannot be definitely classified as belonging to one of the three communication classifications, the parameters used to analyze Mrs. Reagan's predecessors will not be used here. Another reason for not employing the schema is that much of the information that contributes to a thorough communication analysis is simply not available at this time. Materials of the incumbent or most recent First Lady are not easily accessible, and when a presidential family leaves the White House, researchers must wait two to three years before the papers of that administration are organized and opened to scholars. Even then the First Lady's papers rarely have a high priority, and the wait may be longer than originally anticipated.

THE FIRST LADY AS SOCIAL HOSTESS AND CEREMONIAL PRESENCE

Even before Mrs. Reagan entered the White House, there were two minor flaps that generated negative publicity. It was reported that the First Lady-elect had suggested that the Carters move out of the executive mansion early so that she could begin redecorating; Mrs. Reagan denied that she ever made the comment.[13] Later Mrs. Reagan told interviewers that she kept "a 'tiny little gun' in a drawer near her bed in her California home for protection."[14] Both comments prompted scores of unfavorable news stories.

It seemed that initially Mrs. Reagan planned to be a social hostess and ceremonial presence. Most news stories written after the election discussed the new and exciting style that Nancy Reagan would bring to Washington. Near the end of these stories one could always find an obligatory paragraph devoted to the incoming First Lady's probable project. Typical of stories at this time was one that appeared in the New York Times a few days after Ronald Reagan's electoral victory. The article analyzed Mrs. Reagan's anticipated effect on fashion, and said that she represented "a return to the things we know best. . . . [She is] a woman who knows how to entertain, protect her husband and raise a family and who never errs, when she dresses, on the side of excess or the socially inappropriate."[15] Time referred to Mrs. Reagan as "hostess-elect."[16]

After Ronald Reagan's inauguration, things seemed to degenerate further. The First Lady was criticized for her twenty-five-thousand-dollar inaugural wardrobe and for spending exorbitant amounts of money on her regular wardrobe.[17] She was taken to task for associating with wealthy, socialite friends and entertaining lavishly at a time of economic uncertainty. In an instance of incredibly poor timing, the White House announced that it was spending $209,000 on new china (with funding provided by a private source) on the same day that the Department of Agriculture decided that catsup would be considered sufficient as a vegetable in school lunches.[18] Conspicuous consumption seemed to be running amok when it was revealed that friends of the Reagans had contributed eight hundred thousand dollars to renovate the White House living quarters.[19]

Former Reagan advisor and close personal friend Michael Deaver believes that Mrs. Reagan began to change on March 30, 1981.[20] It was on this day that John Hinckley tried to assassinate the President as he emerged from a speech at a Washington hotel. Nancy Reagan was devastated, and later explained, "When you go through something like that, things that were important to you before, things that upset you before, they don't upset you so much."[21]

Changes were not immediately forthcoming, but there were some indications of things to come. A postcard of Mrs. Reagan dressed as a queen in crown and ermine cape appeared in card stores, but rather than becoming angry or sulking, the First Lady used humor to defuse the problems of her negative image. She told an audience: "Now that's silly. I would never wear a crown—it messes up your hair."[22] She went on to announce her new pet cause, "The Nancy Reagan Home for Wayward China."[23] In November 1981 Mrs. Reagan kicked off her real project, an antidrug campaign, but her efforts received little coverage. Later Mrs. Reagan would reveal to reporters that she had been discouraged from pursuing the antidrug campaign as her White House project. She said: "Nobody was very keen on my taking this up. . . . I knew I wanted to do it, but everybody thought that it was a downer, and too depressing."[24]

The American public did not respond immediately to Mrs. Reagan's attempts to become more likable or independent. A December 1981 *Newsweek* poll reported that 26 percent of those surveyed disapproved of the way in which Mrs. Reagan performed her duties. More damning was the 62 percent of the public who believed the First Lady "put too much emphasis on style and elegance."[25] It was not surprising that Mrs. Reagan looked back at 1981 as a lost year. "It was not exactly the happiest year of my life," she told reporters.[26]

Yet another setback occurred in early 1982, when it was reported that Mrs. Reagan was accepting designer clothing on loan. This raised troubling questions of ethics.[27] White House aides met to discuss the First Lady's problems: " 'They worked out a scenario of how to turn her image around,' said a senior White House official."[28] Charged with selling the new image was James Rosebush, who became Mrs. Reagan's new Chief of Staff.

Perhaps the campaign to remake Nancy Reagan flourished, or perhaps Mrs. Reagan began to relax and let her personality shine through, but by mid–1982 the First Lady was becoming a more independent person, traveling to anti-drug-abuse program locations, speaking out about the Foster Grandparent Program, and tolerating criticism with greater equanimity. She was no longer the adoring presidential wife without goals or a program. She appeared poised to become an emerging spokeswoman—focused, more aware of her potential, and ready to communicate her concerns to the American people.

THE FIRST LADY AS EMERGING SPOKESWOMAN

From late 1982 through mid–1984 Nancy Reagan functioned as an emerging spokeswoman. She still seemed unsure about the podium afforded her, but she began to seek exposure and took greater advantage of the available communication outlets. During this period, she hoped to define her antidrug program and to rehabilitate her image.

To achieve the first goal, she made a number of trips to publicize her cause.

The main thrust of her campaign, however, was aimed at television. In March 1983 she appeared on the situation comedy "Diff'rent Strokes" as herself. She narrated a two-hour Public Broadcasting System special, "The Chemical People." By late 1985 she had appeared on twenty-three television shows to discuss drugs.[29] She also endorsed a comic book about drug abuse aimed at elementary school students. The comic book, "The New Teen Titans," contained a letter from Mrs. Reagan and a certificate of heroism for "saying no to drugs."[30]

The second goal was more elusive, for it required altering public opinion and presenting Mrs. Reagan as a warmer, more concerned First Lady. Television appearances were helpful, and once again, Mrs. Reagan used self-deprecating humor to win over the unconvinced. In a much ballyhooed appearance before the 1984 Gridiron Dinner, Mrs. Reagan startled the audience when she arrived on stage dressed as a bag lady and sang a parody of the song "Second Hand Rose," now called "Second Hand Clothes." The audience loved her.

The publication of Mrs. Reagan's book *To Love a Child*, a discussion of the Foster Grandparents program, also helped depict the First Lady as caring and sensitive.

THE FIRST LADY AS POLITICAL SURROGATE AND INDEPENDENT ADVOCATE

By mid–1984 Nancy Reagan had established herself as a political surrogate and independent advocate. She had become cognizant of the power of the White House and was using all available communication outlets to support projects or positions. Her press relations had improved considerably, and in 1985 she was the subject of an extremely complimentary news documentary. Friends and critics acknowledged that she had a significant impact upon presidential decision making.

"Say no to drugs" became synonymous with Mrs. Reagan, and she traveled constantly to treatment facilities and schools and spoke to scores of organizations about the seriousness of drug abuse in the United States. Nineteen-eighty-five was an especially memorable year for the First Lady, as she hosted eighteen foreign First Ladies at the First Ladies Conference on Drug Abuse at the White House, spoke about drug abuse in Europe, and hosted another international First Ladies Conference on Drug Abuse at the United Nations.

When materials become available, the extent of Nancy Reagan's commitment to her project will be accurately documented; however, I estimate that the First Lady gave hundreds of speeches on this topic. Mrs. Reagan told an audience that as of May 1987 she had traveled to sixty cities in thirty states and seven foreign countries to make people aware of the enormity of the drug problem. "I've tried to get the message across through hundreds of interviews, tapings, speeches, events and visits," she said.[31]

The President paid tribute to his wife's efforts during the 1988 State of the Union message when he said: "She [Nancy] has helped so many of our young people say "no" to drugs. Nancy, much credit belongs to you, and I want to express to you your husband's pride and your country's thanks."[32]

Mrs. Reagan continued to perform the tasks of hostess, and estimated that in her first six years she had attended hundreds of dinners, lunches, teas, and receptions.[33] She also performed political tasks and entertained or campaigned for Republican candidates, usually with her husband. She maintained her own busy schedule during the 1984 presidential campaign. Finally, Mrs. Reagan became the first First Lady since Eleanor Roosevelt (and the first Republican First Lady) to be accorded the honor of addressing a national nominating convention when she spoke to the 1988 Republican National Convention.

Actor Jimmy Stewart once remarked: "If Ronnie had married Nancy at the time he married Jane Wyman, he would have won an Oscar. She would have *made* him do it."[34] This observation seems to underscore the role that Nancy Reagan has played in her husband's life.

Michael Deaver points out that Mrs. Reagan has always influenced her husband deeply, but that she does not do his thinking for him.[35] She did urge him to run for Governor of California in 1964, she pressed him to fire aides whose usefulness she felt was questionable, and she opposed his running for the Senate in 1974.[36]

As First Lady, Mrs. Reagan was said to have broad access to presidential decision making. The President acknowledged his wife's influence, but was careful to qualify it. He commented: "You can't have been together for almost 30 years without being an influence on each other. She does not inject herself and say, 'You ought to sign this or do this.' She never has."[37]

Other observers have not been so gentle. Though it cannot be confirmed, many believe that Mrs. Reagan engineered the firing of Reagan Campaign Manager John Sears, that she urged the removal of certain staff members from their posts, and that she excoriated aides for having poorly prepared the President for his 1984 debate with Walter Mondale. In a well-publicized incident, Mrs. Reagan cued the President when he seemed to be at a loss for words during the 1984 presidential campaign.[38]

Mrs. Reagan believed that her primary mission was to protect the President, and she did this literally and figuratively. In a speech she said: "I think it's an important, legitimate role for a First Lady to look after a President's health and well being. And if that interferes with other plans, then so be it."[39]

Frequently the staff would over-schedule the Chief Executive, and Mrs. Reagan was quick to respond. On one occasion she telephoned Michael Deaver and said angrily: "I just received this week's schedule and I want to know what you think you are doing. . . . You are going to kill him."[40] Another view is presented by a White House staff member who said that he had been told that if his name appeared in the press criticizing the President or First Lady, "the next time I would see my name in the paper . . . it would say I was looking for work and I would know that Mrs. Reagan caused that to happen."[41] Even an admirer, former White House Chief of Staff Howard Baker, acknowledged that when Mrs. Reagan "gets her hackles up, she can be a dragon."[42]

At the height of the controversy over her power, Mrs. Reagan poked fun at what she felt were exaggerated stories of her influence. She told an audience:

I was afraid I might have to cancel. You know how busy I am—between staffing the White House and overseeing the arms talks. In fact, this morning I had planned to clear up U.S.-Soviet differences on . . . nuclear missiles. But I decided to clean out Ronnie's sock drawer instead.[43]

Mrs. Reagan's most well-known altercation was with White House Chief of Staff Donald Regan, whom the First Lady wanted her husband to replace. Mrs. Reagan purportedly blamed Regan for letting the President become embroiled in the Iran-Contra affair. When the Tower Report (the official inquiry) was released, Regan was implicated. He resigned shortly after.

In May 1988 Regan exacted his revenge and embarrassed the presidential couple when he disclosed in his published memoirs that the First Lady consulted a friend who was an astrologer about the timing of her husband's decisions.[44] Press and popular reaction was immediate and predictable: derision, scorn, and laughter. Both Reagans became the target of political cartoons, editorials, and news articles. Even Democratic presidential nominee Jesse Jackson referred to the episode in his speech to the Democratic National Convention in July 1988.

Two events of her husband's second term of office deserve mention. In October 1987 Mrs. Reagan underwent surgery for removal of a cancerous left breast. Nine days after surgery, Edith Davis, Mrs. Reagan's elderly mother, passed away. The two incidents created great sympathy for Mrs. Reagan, and she enjoyed a complimentary press until Regan's book appeared.

In the waning months of her husband's presidency, another disclosure rocked the Reagan administration when Elaine Crispin, Mrs. Reagan's press secretary, admitted that the First Lady had continued to borrow designer clothes despite possible legal and ethical problems. Crispin told the press, "She set her own little rule and she broke her own little rule. . . . I'm admitting for her that she basically broke her own promise."[45] Mrs. Reagan had borrowed, and in some cases failed to return, thousands of dollars of clothes furnished to her by the designers Galanos, Adolfo, and Bill Blass.[46] The First Lady was contrite according to Crispin, who said, "Mrs. Reagan regrets that she failed to heed counsel's advice" (referring to the White House Counsel's original ruling about Mrs. Reagan's borrowed clothing).[47]

Once again Nancy Reagan found herself to be the target of criticism, and her good works were obscured by a practice she had probably rationalized as acceptable but that was in fact ethically inappropriate. Mrs. Reagan's last days in the White House were as controversial as her first weeks as First Lady. Perhaps Nancy Reagan should have just said "no."

Helen Thomas notes that Nancy Reagan's tenure as First Lady has been composed of highs and lows.[48] This is an accurate assessment, as Mrs. Reagan found her actions alternately condemned and applauded. The day that the story about her continued borrowing of the clothes became public and was prompting a negative response, she was invited to address the United Nations General Assembly on the drug problem, an unprecedented honor for a President's wife. There was indeed an unevenness about Mrs. Reagan's White House tenure.

Nancy Reagan did not determine public policy, attend cabinet meetings, or promote her own agenda.[49] While critics have charged that she has been the most influential presidential wife in history, this view ascribes too much power to the former actress. She did nothing that previous First Ladies had not done: She merely spoke to her husband about the issues of the day. Perhaps her observations and evaluations of staff carried more weight than those of other First Ladies, but this would seem to be the single area in which she wielded influence.

Mrs. Reagan began her White House tenure as a ceremonial presence, probably hoping that she would be accepted as the Jacqueline Kennedy of the 1980s. However, it became abundantly clear to both Mrs. Reagan and White House advisors that this stance was unacceptable. The forty-second First Lady emerged slowly as a spokeswoman for drug abuse prevention, and gradually employed various communications media, most notably television, to carry her cause to the people and to improve her image. After almost four years at 1600 Pennsylvania Avenue, Mrs. Reagan seemed to have accomplished a complete turnaround; she was now a political surrogate and independent advocate, taking advantage of every opportunity, speech, interview, and conference to support her project.

Nancy Reagan has demonstrated that it is possible for a First Lady to redefine her image and mission by employing the various communications media. However she had to surmount criticism and ride an emotional roller coaster that saw her soar to the peaks and land, slightly battered, in the valleys.

It is a testament to Mrs. Reagan that she was able to tell delegates to the 1988 Republican National Convention, "You really gave me the chance to be more than I thought I could be and brought something out in me that I didn't know was there and you helped me, and I thank you a great deal for that."[50]

NOTES

1. Lou Cannon, *Reagan* (New York: Putnam, 1982), p. 141.
2. Nancy Reagan with Bill Libby, *Nancy* (London: Robertson, 1981), p. 25.
3. Reagan, *Nancy*, p. 111.
4. Reagan, *Nancy*, p. 122.
5. Anne Edwards, *Early Reagan: The Rise to Power* (New York: Morrow, 1987), p. 379.
6. Cannon, *Reagan*, p. 139.
7. Garry Wills, *Reagan's America: Innocents at Home* (New York: Doubleday, 1987), p. 188.

8. Jill Gerston, "The Stargazer," *Philadelphia Inquirer*, October 13, 1980, p. D1.

9. John L. Moore (ed.), *Guide to U.S. Elections* (Washington, D.C.: Congressional Quarterly, 1985), p. 312.

10. Ronnie Dugger, *On Reagan: The Man and His Presidency* (New York: McGraw-Hill, 1983), p. 232.

11. Gary Clifford, "The New First Lady is a Former Debutante, But Watch Out: 'She's a Fighter,' " *People*, November 17, 1980, p. 44.

12. Andrew Feinberg, "Why Do They Pick on Nancy Reagan?" *Cosmopolitan*, May 1982, p. 262.

13. "White House Decides on Yuletide Political Cease Fire," *New York Times*, December 16, 1980, II, p. 10.

14. "Mrs. Reagan Says She Has Gun," *New York Times*, December 11, 1980, p. 23.

15. "Notes on Fashion," *New York Times*, November 11, 1980, II, p. 10.

16. "A First Lady of Priorities and Proprieties," *Time*, January 5, 1981, p. 25.

17. Leslie Bennett, "With a New First Lady, a New Style," *New York Times*, January 21, 1981, II, p. 6.

18. Fred Barnes, "Nancy's Total Makeover," *New Republic*, September 16/23, 1985, p. 19.

19. Barnes, "Nancy's Total Makeover," p. 16.

20. Michael K. Deaver, *Behind the Scenes* (New York: Morrow, 1987), p. 105.

21. Deaver, *Behind the Scenes*, p. 105.

22. "The World of Nancy Reagan," *Newsweek*, December 21, 1981, p. 25.

23. "The World of Nancy Reagan," p. 22.

24. Johanna Neuman, "First Lady Tells of Fight to Start Battle on Drugs," *Camden Courier Post*, April 29, 1985, p. 7A.

25. "The World of Nancy Reagan," p. 25.

26. Maureen Santini, "Mrs. Reagan is Trying to Shelve the China," *Philadelphia Inquirer*, February 21, 1982, p. 8F.

27. "For Mrs. Reagan, Gifts Mean High Fashion at No Cost," *New York Times*, January 16, 1982, p. 15.

28. Barnes, "Nancy's Total Makeover," p. 16.

29. Barnes, "Nancy's Total Makeover," p. 20.

30. Donnie Radcliffe, "Nancy Reagan in a Comic-Book War on Drugs," *Philadelphia Inquirer*, May 1, 1983, p. 1H.

31. "Mrs. Reagan's Remarks to the Associated Press Publisher's Luncheon," New York, May 4, 1987.

32. "Transcript of Reagan's State of the Union Message," *New York Times*, January 26, 1988, p. 16.

33. "Mrs. Reagan's Remarks."

34. Wills, *Reagan's America*, p. 333.

35. Deaver, *Behind the Scenes*, p. 103.

36. Cannon, *Reagan*, p. 102.

37. "As Reagan Sees Her," *Newsweek*, December 21, 1981, p. 27.

38. Wills, *Reagan's America*, p. 191.

39. "Mrs. Reagan's Remarks."

40. Deaver, *Behind the Scenes*, p. 110.

41. Joyce Gemperlein, "Nancy Reagan, Protector, Steps to the Fore in a Crisis," *Philadelphia Inquirer*, July 21, 1985, p. 20A.

42. Owen Ullman, "Remarks Dog Baker on First Lady," *Philadelphia Inquirer*, March 3, 1987, p. 12A.

43. "Mrs. Reagan's Remarks."

44. Donald T. Regan, *For the Record* (New York: Harcourt, 1988), pp. 73–74, 367–370.

45. Donnie Radcliffe and Bill McAllister, "Nancy Reagan Reportedly Broke Promise on Borrowed Clothing," *Philadelphia Inquirer*, October 18, 1988, p. C1.

46. "Why Mrs. Reagan Still Looks Like a Million," *Time*, October 24, 1988, pp. 29–30.

47. Radcliffe and McAllister, "Nancy Reagan Broke Promise," p. C1.

48. Helen Thomas, "Clothes Can Hide Good Work of the Woman in Them," *Philadelphia Inquirer*, October 23, 1988, p. 2E.

49. Deaver, *Behind the Scenes*, p. 113.

50. Nancy Reagan's speech to the Republican National Convention, August 15, 1988, author's transcription from videotape.

9
CONCLUSIONS

There have been sweeping but not continuous changes in the role of the First Lady as public communicator from 1921 to 1989. A number of conclusions support this finding.

Since 1921, First Ladies have assumed one of three distinct stances as public communicators: social hostesses and ceremonial presences, emerging spokeswomen, or political surrogates and independent advocates. Relative to the three distinct communication stances has been the development, consciously or unconsciously, of three separate communication philosophies. The social hostesses and ceremonial presences devoted little if any thought to the idea of communicating with the public. The emerging spokeswomen were more aware of the need to share their ideas or projects with a national audience, and made limited use of the press and other media. The political surrogates and independent advocates utilized all available means of persuasion to dramatize their commitment to certain endeavors.

Patterns regarding both communication stance and philosophy are discernable. Social hostesses and ceremonial presences received little or no support from their husbands and generally had little input into presidential decision making. The First Ladies in this category received no encouragement to be involved public communicators, and they were publicly silent presences. The emerging spokeswomen received at least tepid endorsements from their husbands. Most of the husbands of emerging spokeswomen had favorable perceptions of women, and would allow their wives some access to decision making if they desired. The political surrogates and independent activists received unqualified support from their husbands. Moreover, their husbands had positive perceptions of women, appointed women to high-level positions within their administrations, and permitted their wives broad access to presidential decision making.

Three of the most active communicators, Eleanor Roosevelt, Lady Bird Johnson, and Betty Ford, came to the White House at times of national crises. While only Mrs. Roosevelt addressed the problems of the Depression, it would seem that crisis demands or encourages some response from the First Lady. It might be argued further that crisis creates a sympathetic environment in which the First Lady may deliver her remarks.

Expectations have changed over the years, and Americans seem to want an involved First Lady, ideally one with a record of concern for a given cause, who comes to the White House and proclaims her support for that cause or other projects. At the same time, the First Lady treads a narrow line. She may advocate feminine concerns or issues with little fear of condemnation. However, if she chooses to become involved in the more substantive issues of her husband's administration, or if she presents views on public policy that differ from those of her husband, she risks criticism that might ultimately hurt her husband's career. She might also damage her own credibility and personal popularity by taking publicly unpopular stands.

The changes in the First Lady's role as public communicator have not reflected changes in the status of women or shown corresponding growth. The First Lady has not historically reflected the time in which she inhabits the White House. Most women are middle-aged when they reach the executive mansion, and are not likely to embrace or endorse current trends in social history or thought (especially in the changing status of women). Most First Ladies reflect the social customs and habits of their upbringing.

Age, state of health, family obligations, the president's attitude toward the degree of his wife's participation in his administration, and the social and historical context of the time are all determinants of how active a woman will be as a public communicator in the White House. The working relationship between the President and First Lady is also a critical factor in determining how active a woman will be as a public communicator.

The press plays a critical role in transmitting both the image and the substance of a First Lady. In 1971, Norma Foreman found that a double standard existed between male and female reporters covering the White House. The men were covering the President and producing "hard news" while many newspapers relegated female reporters' coverage of the First Lady's efforts to the society or women's page. Female reporters were still striving to legitimize their coverage of the First Lady and their presence in the White House press office. Foreman concluded that "a First Lady who generates substantive news about public issues and provides newswomen open access is likely to receive a bonus of gratitude from the newswomen for what they view as an opportunity to increase their prestige."[1]

Parity between male and female White House reporters has changed since 1971, but inequality still exists. The implication of this finding is that First Ladies who generate news and are active public communicators are almost guaranteed more favorable press treatment than their less active counterparts.

In addition, national interest in the First Family and a more energetic and curious media have made it virtually impossible for a First Lady to remain incommunicado in the White House.

James David Barber has suggested that presidential performance can be predicted by analyzing a man's character, worldview (consisting of "his primary, politically relevant beliefs, particularly his conceptions of social causality, human nature and the central moral conflicts of the time"),[2] style ("the president's habitual ways of performing his three political roles: rhetoric, personal relations and homework"),[3] the power situation, and a climate of expectations (the President must alternately reassure, project a sense of action, and lend legitimacy to the presidency).[4] While the differences between the presidency and the role of First Lady brook almost no comparison, three of Barber's five elements provide a schema for predicting how a First Lady might function as a communicator in the White House.

One of the findings of this study supported the belief that age, state of health, relationship with husband, and similar factors were important in determining how active a woman might be as a communicator. These factors are subsets of character. What is a woman likely to do in the White House based on her overall behavior? Is she enthusiastic, reticent, or aggressive? If we can identify these traits, can we argue that they will surface in behavior in the White House? Few women—indeed, few people—change their behavior or major character traits when they arrive at 1600 Pennsylvania Avenue.

Recent history suggests that the wife of a President will have already been a political wife for many years. This woman will have a developed worldview, especially primary, relevant political beliefs and opinions about the central moral dilemmas of the time. She may well have political beliefs as strongly held and supported as those of her husband, and could come to the White House identified as an enthusiastic Republican or simply a woman who embraces her husband's beliefs. By analyzing this pre–White House activity, we might derive some sense of how much political communication might emanate from the First Lady. Furthermore, what does the First Lady identify as the central moral dilemmas of the time, and will she enter the fray?

The First Lady will have developed an observable style prior to residence in the White House. She will have performed the visible and expected tasks of hostess and public relations person for her husband, and she may have been a political presence or surrogate for him. Her preference for one or both of these roles may suggest whether the First Lady will view her White House role in ceremonial terms or become a well-defined person in her own right.

There is no absolutely accurate method for predicting how a First Lady will function as a communicator in the White House, but by assessing character, worldview, and style we might begin to see a pattern of potential activity or nonactivity emerging.

Future First Ladies will feel greater media and public pressure to assume a more visible and committed communication presence. Those who choose to be political surrogates and independent advocates (within the accepted parameters of feminine issues) probably will be accorded more favorable press attention and public support and admiration than those who remain inactive.

The First Lady has one of the most influential podiums in the world at her disposal. No First Lady has ever used that podium for personal gain or to questionable ends. Some have chosen to ignore it or make limited use of it. The political surrogates or independent advocates have taught us that the podium provides a magnificent instrument for educating, persuading, and ultimately improving the lot of "all the people."

NOTES

1. Norma Ruth Holly Foreman, "The First Lady as a Leader of Public Opinion: A Study of the Role and Press Relations of Lady Bird Johnson," (unpublished doctoral dissertation, University of Texas at Austin 1971).

2. James David Barber, *The Presidential Character* (Englewood Cliffs, N.J.: Prentice-Hall, 1977), p. 9.

3. Barber, *The Presidential Character*, p. 9.

4. Barber, *The Presidential Character*, pp. 8–9.

BIBLIOGRAPHIC NOTES

There is a substantial body of information about the First Lady and, as one might expect, the quality of primary and secondary materials varies considerably. The following discussion is not exhaustive, but does point out the most useful sources and their availability.

Florence Harding's papers and letters are included with Warren Harding's papers, which are on deposit with the Ohio Historical Society, Columbus, Ohio.

Two secondary sources are worthy of note. Francis Russell's *The Shadow of Blooming Grove: Warren G. Harding in His Times* (New York: McGraw-Hill, 1968) is outstanding. It is well documented and incisive in its analysis of the public and private Warren and Florence Harding. Andrew Sinclair's *The Available Man: The Life behind the Mask of Warren Gamaliel Harding* (New York: Macmillan, 1965) is a solid account of Harding's political career, especially his White House tenure. Mrs. Harding receives critical yet fair treatment in this study as well.

There are no separate Grace Coolidge papers, but there are some references to Mrs. Coolidge in Calvin Coolidge's public papers on deposit with the Library of Congress. Additional interesting information, especially information that relates to Mrs. Coolidge as White House hostess, may be obtained by consulting the scrapbooks and general papers of President and Mrs. Coolidge on deposit with the Forbes Library, Northampton, Massachusetts.

Grace Coolidge's own reflections on the joys and disappointments of being First Lady are described in a series of magazine articles that she wrote for *Good Housekeeping* from April through June 1935, entitled "When I Became the First Lady." Views of Mrs. Coolidge as wife and mother are presented in Calvin Coolidge's *The Autobiography of Calvin Coolidge* (New York: Cosmopolitan, 1929).

Interesting perspectives on Mrs. Coolidge as First Lady and as the First Lady she might have been if permitted a more edifying role in her husband's administration can be found in *Presidents and First Ladies* (New York: D. Appleton-Century, 1936) by Mrs. Coolidge's social secretary Mary Randolph.

Two other volumes have useful observations to offer about Grace Coolidge as First Lady: Claude M. Feuss, *Calvin Coolidge: The Man from Vermont* (Boston: Brown, 1940), and William Allen White, *A Puritan in Babylon: The Story of Calvin Coolidge* (New York: Macmillan, 1939).

The Lou Hoover papers are open to researchers and are on deposit with the Herbert Hoover Library, West Branch, Iowa. Other materials including the Hoover White House social files, speeches, and magazine and newspaper articles written by Mrs. Hoover are available for perusal.

Herbert Hoover's *The Memoirs of Herbert Hoover* (three volumes, New York: Macmillan, 1951) deal with Mrs. Hoover in cursory fashion, but these glimpses may be helpful. Helen Pryor's *Lou Henry Hoover: Gallant First Lady* (New York: Dodd, 1969) is the only biographical work currently available on Lou Hoover.

The best secondary source consulted in regard to Mrs. Hoover was Joan Hoff-Wilson's *Herbert Hoover: Forgotten Progressive* (Boston: Little, Brown, 1975). Not only does Hoff-Wilson provide an excellent analysis of the Hoover presidency, but she also assesses Lou Hoover's contribution to that enterprise.

Eleanor Roosevelt has received more attention from scholars and biographers than any other First Lady. The Eleanor Roosevelt papers, an enormous body of material rich in detail and information for the researcher, are on deposit with the Franklin D. Roosevelt Library, Hyde Park, New York.

Mrs. Roosevelt wrote three autobiographies, and these are invaluable to the researcher or student of Mrs. Roosevelt's life and career. *This Is My Story* (New York: Harper, 1937) chronicles Eleanor and Franklin Roosevelt's courtship, marriage, and early years in politics, and concludes during President Roosevelt's first term in office. *This I Remember* (New York: Harper, 1949) is the most useful of the triumvirate, as it provides detail on Mrs. Roosevelt's many projects and discusses her feelings about communication. *The Autobiography of Eleanor Roosevelt* (New York: Harper, 1961) was published a year before Mrs. Roosevelt's death; it is a compilation of the first two books plus some thoughts on post–World War II America.

Many friends and associates of Eleanor and Franklin Roosevelt wrote books about the famous couple, and a number of these volumes deserve mention. The most valuable of all the books in this category is Joseph P. Lash's *Eleanor and Franklin* (New York: Norton, 1971). Lash's biography is scholarly, thorough, and insightful. It is perhaps the definitive work on Mrs. Roosevelt, and helps the reader to understand the actions of past and future First Ladies. Two companion pieces to the aforementioned work are Lash's *Eleanor: The Years Alone (New York: Norton, 1972), and Love, Eleanor* (New York: Doubleday, 1982) a compilation of Mrs. Roosevelt's correspondence.

Interesting evaluations of Mrs. Roosevelt as First Lady are presented by Frances

Perkins (former Secretary of Labor) in *The Roosevelt I Knew* (New York: Viking, 1946), and Grace Tully (former secretary to the President) in *F.D.R. My Boss* (New York: Scribner's, 1949). Mrs. Roosevelt's close relationship with reporters is evidenced by two biographies written by newswomen who covered her activities: Ruby Black's *Eleanor Roosevelt: A Biography* (New York: Duell, 1940) and Lorena Hickok's *Reluctant First Lady* (New York: Dodd, 1962). Bess Furman also presents enlightening material in *Washington Bi-Line: The Personal History of a Newspaper Woman* (New York: Knopf, 1949).

Other secondary sources look at Mrs. Roosevelt as wife, mother, relative, friend, and First Lady. The best studies in this group include: Maurine Beasley (ed.), *The White House Press Conferences of Eleanor Roosevelt* (New York: Garland, 1983); Doris Faber, *The Life of Lorena Hickok: E. R.'s Friend* (New York: Morrow, 1980); Carol Felsenthal, *Alice Roosevelt Longworth* (New York: Putnam, 1988); Tamara K. Hareven, *Eleanor Roosevelt: An American Conscience* (Chicago: Quadrangle, 1968); James R. Kearney, *Anna Eleanor Roosevelt: The Evolution of a Reformer* (Boston: Houghton Mifflin, 1968); Joan Hoff-Wilson and Marjorie Lightman, eds., *Without Precedent: The Life and Career of Eleanor Roosevelt* (Bloomington: Indiana University Press, 1984). In addition, at least seven doctoral dissertations have been devoted to various aspects of Mrs. Roosevelt's public career.

There are no separate Bess Truman papers, but the Truman Library retains numerous files relative to Mrs. Truman's tenure as First Lady. Of greatest importance is the 1,300-letter correspondence between Harry and Bess Truman, which spans forty years and provides fascinating background about the historical period and the Trumans' relationship. The papers of Reathel Odum, Mrs. Truman's secretary, and Mary Paxton Keeley, her lifelong friend, are also useful.

Bess Truman's husband and daughter have provided glimpses of the former First Lady that she herself would not have been willing to share: Harry S Truman, *Memoirs* (two volumes, New York: Doubleday, 1956), and Margaret Truman, *Harry S Truman* (New York: Pocket, 1974) and *Bess W. Truman* (New York: Macmillan, 1986).

A number of secondary sources are worthy of note. Robert Ferrell's *Dear Bess: The Letters from Harry to Bess Truman 1910–1959* (New York: Norton, 1983) is a well-edited compilation of the aforementioned Truman correspondence. Merle Miller's *Plain Speaking: An Oral Biography of Harry S Truman* (New York: Putnam's, 1973) is an exceptionally well-written oral history of the Truman period. Finally, Edith Helm, Mrs. Truman's social secretary, provides excellent insights into Mrs. Truman's efforts to avoid communicating with the public in her book, *The Captains and the Kings* (New York: Putnam's, 1954).

The Mamie Doud Eisenhower papers are on deposit with the Dwight D. Eisenhower Library, Abilene, Kansas. The papers, which are divided into the Columbia University, SHAPE, and White House series provide excellent documentation of Mrs. Eisenhower's public career.

Insights into Mrs. Eisenhower's role as wife and mother and, to a lesser degree, mistress of the executive mansion, are furnished by Dwight D. Eisenhower in *Mandate for Change, 1953–1956* (New York: Doubleday, 1963) and *At Ease: Stories I Tell to Friends* (New York: Doubleday, 1967). A more valuable view of Mrs. Eisenhower as First Lady is provided by her son John Eisenhower in *Strictly Personal* (New York: Doubleday, 1974).

The best secondary sources on the Eisenhowers are Steve Neal's *The Eisenhowers: Reluctant Dynasty* (New York: Doubleday, 1978) and Piers Brendon's *Ike: His Life and Times* (New York: Doubleday, 1986). Both books present critical analyses of Mamie Eisenhower as First Lady.

The White House social files for the Kennedy administration come closest to serving as Jacqueline Kennedy's papers, but much of the material found in these files is routine: correspondence, memoranda, and notes. The first one hundred of fourteen hundred boxes are now available to researchers at the John F. Kennedy Library, Boston, Massachusetts. Archivists at the Kennedy Library estimate that the entire White House social files collection will not be available to researchers before 1997. Even then, researchers may question the value of the papers.

There are occasional references to Mrs. Kennedy in the papers of Pierre Salinger. Some excellent information about the First Lady can be gleaned by reading the oral history interviews of former Kennedy administration employees, friends, and reporters.

Secondary sources range from enlightening and incisive to sensational and tawdry. In the former category are three works: Letitia Baldridge (former social secretary to Mrs. Kennedy), *Of Diamonds and Diplomats* (Boston: Houghton Mifflin, 1968); Theodore Sorenson (Former Special Counsel to the President), *Kennedy* (New York: Bantam, 1966); and Mary Van Rensselaer Thayer, *Jacqueline Kennedy: The White House Years* (Boston: Little, Brown, 1967).

Primary and secondary material relative to Lady Bird Johnson is excellent. Mrs. Johnson's papers are open to research and are on deposit with the Lyndon B. Johnson Library, Austin, Texas. Mrs. Johnson's book *A White House Diary* (New York: Holt, 1970) proved to be an invaluable source as it chronicled the First Lady's tenure as mistress of the executive mansion in almost day-by-day installments from 1963 through 1969.

Lyndon Johnson's memoir, *The Vantage Point: Perspectives on the Presidency 1963–1969* (New York: Holt, 1971), contains relatively few references to his wife as First Lady, but those provided are worthwhile.

The files of Liz Carpenter (former staff director and press secretary to Mrs. Johnson) and Bess Abell (former White House social secretary) reveal that a great deal of thought and planning went into communicating with the public about Mrs. Johnson's concerns. Oral history interviews with Carpenter and Sharon Frances (an assistant to Mrs. Johnson in the beautification program) are especially enlightening.

Among secondary sources, Merle Miller's *Lyndon: An Oral Biography* (New York: Putnam's, 1980) offers former friends' and enemies' recollections of both

President and Mrs. Johnson. Lewis L. Gould's *Lady Bird Johnson and the Environment: A First Lady's Commitment* (Lawrence: University of Kansas Press, 1988) is an exhaustive, scholarly study of the beautification program. Also useful in assessing Mrs. Johnson as a communicator are Liz Carpenter's *Ruffles and Flourishes* (New York: Pocket, 1971) and Eric Goldman's *The Tragedy of Lyndon Johnson* (New York: Knopf, 1969).

Archivists at the Nixon Presidential Materials Projects in Washington, D.C., have begun processing the files of Mrs. Nixon's appointments and social and press secretaries. This material will be opened piecemeal and is now available to researchers in the fall of 1988. The Nixon White House social files will not be available until a future date. Mrs. Nixon's personal papers could be deposited with the Nixon Presidential Materials Project or with the Richard M. Nixon Library, San Clemente, California, which is currently under construction.

The best source about Pat Nixon is Julie Nixon Eisenhower's *Pat Nixon: The Untold Story* (New York: Simon and Schuster, 1986). It is rich in detail and presents information not available from any other source, as Mrs. Eisenhower was given access to her mother's private correspondence and notes.

Richard Nixon mentions his wife numerous times and speaks of her contributions to his political career and his presidency in two books: *Six Crises* (New York: Doubleday, 1962) and *RN: The Memoirs of Richard Nixon* (two volumes, New York: Warner, 1978).

Lester David has written a sympathetic yet critical account of Mrs. Nixon as a political wife and First Lady: *The Lonely Lady of San Clemente: The Story of Pat Nixon* (New York: Crowell, 1978). Additional details on Mrs. Nixon's White House tenure may be gleaned from Madeline Edmondson and Alder Duer Cohen's *The Women of Watergate* (New York: Stein, 1975), and an excellent article by Judith Viorst, "Pat Nixon Is the Ultimate Good Sport," *New York Times Magazine*, September 1970, pp. 25–147.

Primary materials relating to Betty Ford's White House tenure are plentiful and generally of high quality. Portions of the Betty Ford papers on deposit with the Gerald R. Ford Library, Ann Arbor, Michigan, have been opened to researchers. Information currently available includes files on Mrs. Ford's speeches, the Francis Kaye Pullen Papers (former speech-writer for the First Lady), the Sheila Weidenfeld Files (former press secretary to Mrs. Ford), and files of the correspondence and appointment offices. Additional material will become available as it is processed.

Mrs. Ford's autobiography, *The Times of My Life* (New York: Harper, 1978), follows her from girlhood through the White House with special attention to the White House years. Gerald Ford's autobiography, *A Time to Heal* (New York: Harper, 1979) mentions his wife numerous times but offers little in the way of an evaluation of Betty Ford as First Lady. Sheila Weidenfeld's book, *First Lady's Lady* (New York: Putnam, 1979) analyzes the public relations and, to a lesser extent, communication activities of Mrs. Ford's tenure as First Lady.

Portions of Rosalynn Carter's papers are open and on deposit with the Jimmy

Carter Library, Atlanta, Georgia. Materials relative to mental health, the elderly, ERA, and the First Lady's speeches are available. Mrs. Carter's autobiography, *First Lady from Plains* (Boston: Houghton Mifflin, 1984) is excellent, and furnishes unique perspectives on both advocacy and communication. Jimmy Carter's autobiography, *Keeping Faith: The Memoirs of a President* (New York: Bantam, 1982) mentions Mrs. Carter frequently and discusses the First Lady's impact on decision making.

The best secondary source accounts of Mrs. Carter have been written by journalists: Kandy Stroud, "Rosalynn's Agenda in the White House," *New York Times Magazine*, March 20, 1977, and B. Drummond Ayres, Jr., "The Importance of Being Rosalynn," *New York Times Magazine*, June 3, 1979.

At present, Nancy Reagan's papers are not available to researchers. It may be assumed that they will eventually be deposited with the Ronald Reagan Library. Even before leaving the White House, secondary sources were providing perspectives on Mrs. Reagan as First Lady. These studies vary in quality and include Michael K. Deaver's *Behind the Scenes* (New York: Morrow, 1987) and Donald T. Regan's *For the Record* (New York: Harcourt, 1988).

Some of the books most valuable to this study were written by reporters. Helen Thomas's *Dateline: White House* (New York: Macmillan, 1975) and Winzola McLendon and Scottie Smith's *Don't Quote Me! Washington Newswomen and the Power Society* (New York: Dutton, 1970) are first-rate sources and describe the difficulties of covering the First Lady. An examination of earlier First Ladies and the press (and equally first-rate) is Bess Furman's *White House Profile* (Indianapolis: Bobbs, Merrill, 1951). Ruth Montgomery's *Hail to the Chiefs* (New York: McCann, 1970) is worthwhile but is more clearly partisan about the reporter's favorites.

A number of books have been written about all or a group of First Ladies, and these volumes offer general biographical material and analysis. The best books in this group are Sol Barzman's *The First Ladies* (New York: Cowles, 1970), which focuses on the public career of the First Lady and Betty Boyd Caroli's *First Ladies* (New York: Oxford, 1987), a scholarly study of the office of First Lady with an especially good chapter about the press.

Other general background books, which vary in usefulness, are Margaret Bassett, *American Presidents and their Wives* (Freeport, Maine: Wheelwright, Bond, 1969); Margaret Brown Klapthor, *The First Ladies* (Washington, D.C.: White House Historical Association, 1975); Marianne Means, *The Woman in the White House* (New York: Random, 1963); and J. B. West, *Upstairs at the White House* (New York: Warner, 1974).

The summer 1987 edition of *Prologue* was devoted to an examination of twentieth-century First Ladies' papers and provides a comprehensive examination of both primary and secondary source material.

INDEX

Douglas, Helen Gahagan, 63
Douglas, William O., 22

EEOC (Equal Employment Opportunity
   Commission), 123
Eisenhower, Doud Dwight (Icky), 28
Eisenhower, Dwight D., 33, 68; appointed Supreme Commander of the
   Allied Powers in Europe, 29; appointment of women to high office, 32; assessment of wife as First Lady, 29;
   campaigns for presidency, 29, 30; children of, 28; Columbia University, 29;
   consulted wife on budget and personnel, 31; death of son, 28; declares candidacy for presidency, 29; divorce
   letter, 29; heart attack, 30; marriage,
   28; meets Mamie Doud, 28; named
   Supreme Commander of the Allied
   Expeditionary Forces, 28; perception of
   women, 31; refutes rumors of wife's alcoholism, 29; relationship with wife,
   31; retires, 30; seeks re-election, 30;
   states priorities, 28; wins nomination,
   29
Eisenhower, John, 28, 31
Eisenhower, Julie Nixon, 65, 69, 70
Eisenhower, Mamie, 2, 7, 27–32, 33–34;
   access to presidential decision-making,
   31; adores grandeur of White House,
   27; birth, childhood and education,
   27; birth of children, 28; campaigns
   with husband, 29, 30; ceremonial activities, 30; death, 30; death of son,
   28; Gallup poll rank, 33; husband's
   priorities, 28; marriage, 28; meets Eisenhower, 28; opposes presidential
   race, 29; perception of women, 32;
   played minor role in husband's official
   life, 31; press relations, 30; relationship with husband, 31; resurrects social
   season, 30; retires, 30; rumors of alcoholism and husband's infidelity, 29;
   unprepared for domestic life, 28; war
   years, 28–29
Elsey, George, 25
Emerging spokeswomen, 3, 41–72, 167–
   68, 175

En-lai, Premier Chou, 67
Equal Employment Opportunity Commission (EEOC), 123

Fallows, James, 158
Federal Emergency Relief Administration, 88, 101
Ferrell, Robert, 26
Fields, Alonzo, 50
First Family, 33, 61
First Lady: changes as a result of the 19th
   Amendment, 4; changes in expectations regarding the First Lady, 176;
   conclusions, 175–78; development of
   communication philosophies, 175; factors that determine degree of activity
   in the White House, 32; First Ladies
   Conference on Drug Abuse, 168; The
   First Lady of the Land (play), 2; first
   mentioned in Congressional Directory,
   2; importance of age, state of health,
   family obligations in determining activity, 176; model for predicting activity, 177; 1960 as a turning point in
   the evolution of the First Lady's role,
   71; origin of term, 2; press relations,
   11, 18, 24, 30–31, 49–50, 58–59, 67–
   68, 98–99, 120, 139, 155–56; problems with methodology, 2; responsibilities, 2; role of crisis, 176; role of the
   press, 176
Food Administration Girl's Club, 44
Forbes, Charles, 12, 13
Ford, Betty, 3, 26, 54, 124, 129–42,
   151, 152, 176; access to presidential
   decision-making, 141–42; activities in
   the 1976 primary campaign and general election, 136, 137; birth, childhood and education, 129–30; birth of
   children, 130; declares intention to be
   an active First Lady, 131; delivers husband's concession statement, 138; delivers impromptu prayer for Dr.
   Maurice Sage, 137; divorce, 130;
   ERA, 134–35; expresses her opinions,
   140–41; founds Betty Ford Center,
   133; husband becomes President, 131;
   interest in women's concerns, 133–34;

Harding, Warren, 32, 44, 84; appointment of women to high office, 13; attitude toward suffrage, 13; dies suddenly, 11; elected to U. S. Senate, 9; increasing stain of the presidency, 10; keynotes 1916 Republican National Convention, 9; marriage interest in politics, 9; meets Florence Kling DeWolfe, 8; mentioned as potential presidential candidate in 1920, 9; nominated for President, 9; popularity with Senate colleagues, 9; promises to women during presidential campaign, 13; purportedly fathers a child, 12; reaction to wife's desire to be a part of his administration, 12; rumors of Negro ancestry, 10; sexual affairs, 12; Teapot Dome Scandal, 10; trip to Alaska, 10; unhappiness of, 12; wife's illness causes him to become more serious, 10

Hayes, Lucy Webb, 2

Helm, Edith, 24

Henry, Charles Delano, 42

Henry, Florence, 42

Henry, Jean, 42

Hickok, Lorena, 85, 96, 98

Highway Beautification Act (Lady Bird Bill), 114–15

Hills, Carla, 142

Hinckley, John, 166

Hodgson, James, 70

Hoover, Allen Henry, 43

Hoover, Herbert, 85, 93; appointment of women to high office, 51; becomes informally engaged to Lou Henry, 42; career as mining engineer, 42–43; Commission for Relief in Belguim, 44; death, 45; elected President, 45; marriage, 43; meets Lou Henry, 42; perception of women, 50–51; relationship with wife, 50; role in protecting foreign settlement during Boxer Rebellion, 43; Secretary of Commerce, 44; sets up credit agency to help Americans obtain funds to go home at outbreak of World War I, 43; signs legislation favorable to women, 51;

stock market crash, 45; supports wife during DePriest incident, 48–49; U.S. Food Administration, 44; wife's reaction to criticism, 50

Hoover, Herbert Clark, Jr., 43

Hoover, Lou, 3, 4, 41, 42–51, 60, 71, 72, 81, 86; abandons carding, 47; access to presidential decision-making, 50; advocacy, 46–47; arranges grants for destitute people during the Depression, 47; becomes informally engaged to Herbert Hoover, 42; becomes involved with Girl Scouts, 44, 46; birth of children, 43; birth, childhood and education, 42; bitter about Hoover's defeat, 45; calls conference on law enforcement, 44; campaigns with husband, 45; changes in social protocol, 48; concern for women and the Depression, 46; criticizes journalists, 49; death, 45; DePriest incident, 48–49; designs Camp Rapidan, 47; disappointed with White House furnishings, 47; early feminist, 51; elected Vice President of the National Amateur Athletic Federation, 44; evaluation as First Lady, 51; hires Dare McMullin to write a book about White House furnishings, 47; as hostess of the White House, 47; life in China, 43; marriage, 43; nurses wounded during Boxer Rebellion, 43; opposes competitive professional athletics for women, 44; organizes and manages American Women's Hospital at Paignton, England, 44; organizes effort to clothe, house and entertain Americans stranded in London at the outbreak of World War I, 44; organizes market for Belgian lace, 44; perception of women, 50–51; post-White House activities, 45; press relations, 49–50; pre-White House public speaking, 49; protective of the President, 50; relationship with husband, 50; role in U.S. Food Administration, 44; style of speeches, 49; translates *De Re Mettallica*, 43; use of radio, 43, 49

Nixon, Pat, 3, 41, 61–71, 172, 129, 139; access to presidential decision-making, 69; advises husband to fight impeachment, 65; birth, childhood and education, 62; in California gubernatorial race, 64; changing attitude about reporters, 68; courtship, 62; death of parents, 62; decorated by Peruvian government, 67; fund scandal, 63–64; indifferent public communicator, 70; interest in correspondence, 67; lack of impact as a public communicator, 65; loss of enthusiasm for politics, 64; marriage, 62; meets Richard Nixon, 62; Nixon's loss to John F. Kennedy, 64; perception of women, 70; political campaigns, 63; press relations, 67–68; press secretaries, 68; price analyst at the Office of Price Administration, 63; reaction to Nixon's decision to run for Congress, 63; relationship with husband, 68–69; suffers a stroke, 65; trips, 67; vice presidential years, 64; volunteerism, 61, 64, 65–66, 70; as White House hostess, 67; White House restoration, 66; wives expressing opinions, opinion of, 66; worked to earn college tuition, 62

Nixon, Patricia (Tricia) (daughter), 63

Nixon, Richard M., 53, 131, 141; accepts position with the Office of Price Administration, 62; appointment of women to high office, 70; Checker's speech, 63; courtship, 62; election campaigns, 63, 64; enlists in U. S. Navy, 62; fund scandal, 63–64; legislation favorable to women, 70; marriage, 62; meets Pat Ryan, 62; perception of women, 70; preferred the company of male friends, 69; relationship with wife, 68–69; resigns the presidency, 65; selected as Eisenhower's running mate, 63; wife influence in presidential decision-making, 69

NYA (National Youth Administration), 88, 100

OCD (Office of Civilian Defense), 90–91, 96

Odum, Reathel, 24

Onassis, Aristotle, 55

Operation Headstart, 115–16

Patillo, Effie, 110

Peanut brigade, 149

Pearce, Lorraine, 56

Pearl Harbor, 91, 111

Pendergast, Tom, 21

Pitts, Zasu, 164

Perkins, Frances, 101

Political surrogates and independent advocates, 3, 72, 81–103, 109–24, 129–42, 147–59, 168–69, 175

Polk, Sarah, 4

Potsdam Conference, 26

Poverty program, 115, 123

Powell, Jody, 156

Powers, David, 59

President Ford Committee, 136, 137

Presidential election returns 1920, 10; 1928, 45; 1932, 85; 1936, 94; 1948, 23; 1952, 30; 1964, 112; 1968, 64; 1976, 132, 150

President's appointment of women to high office, 13, 16, 19, 26, 32, 51, 60, 70, 101–2, 123, 142, 158

President's Commission on Mental Health, 151

Price, Byron, 98

Project Headstart, 115–16, 123

Pullen, Frances (Kay), 139

Radio, 3

Rapidan, Camp, 45, 47

Reader's Digest, 3

Reagan, Maureen, 164

Reagan, Michael, 164

Reagan, Nancy, 3, 135, 163–71; access to presidential decision-making, 169; acting career, 164; assassination attempt, 166; assessment as First Lady, 171; attempts to improve image, 167; birth, childhood and education, 163–64; ceremonial activities, 169; concern over Communist allegations, 164; controversy over borrowed designer clothing, 170; dependence on astrology,

ABOUT THE AUTHOR

MYRA G. GUTIN is an Associate Professor in the Department of Communications at Rider College in Lawrenceville, New Jersey.